THE LIVING TAPESTRY

Understanding the Most Powerful Messages of the Gospel Through the Meanings of Bible Names

By

Paul Strausbaugh

The Living Tapestry
Copyright © 2001 by Paul Strausbaugh
ALL RIGHTS RESERVED

Unless otherwise indicated, all Scripture references are from the New American Standard Bible, copyright © 1960, 1962, 1963, 1968, 1971, 1972, 1973, 1975, 1977 by The Lockman Foundation, La Habra, California. References marked AMP are from The Amplified Bible, copyright © 1987 by The Zondervan Corporation, Grand Rapids, Michigan, and the Lockman Foundation, La Habra, California. References marked NIV are from the New International Version of the Bible, copyright © 1973, 1978, 1984 by International Bible Society, Colorado Springs, Colorado. References marked KJV are from the Authorized King James Version of the Bible.

Fairmont Books is a ministry of The McDougal Foundation, Inc., a Maryland nonprofit corporation dedicated to spreading the Gospel of the Lord Jesus Christ to as many people as possible in the shortest time possible.

Published by:

Fairmont Books
P.O. Box 3595
Hagerstown, MD 21742-3595
www.mcdougal.org

ISBN 1-58158-033-9

Printed in the United States of America
For Worldwide Distribution

DEDICATION

To the One whose NAME is above every other name.

Acknowledgments

I must acknowledge the work of several dedicated women who were helpful in improving the manuscript. Madge Dufour, Laura Shaver and Miriam Boyd offered valuable suggestions in its early stages. I am especially grateful for the time and effort spent by Deana Persinger on the first-draft revision. And special thanks to my wife Joan for her patience during the writing process and her help with editing. I am also deeply indebted to Derek Prince for his teachings on the Tabernacle.

Contents

Preface 7
Introduction 9

1. Paul 11
2. The Names of God 23
3. Name Changes 59
4. The Irony of Malchus 95
5. The Gospel in Genesis 5 99
6. Babylon the Great 107
7. The Friendship of Ruth 137
8. The Jordan River: From Life to Death 147
9. Miriam and the Family Rebellion 163
10. Mephibosheth and the Shame of Rebellion 187
11. Hosea on America 199
12. The Children of Israel 217

Appendices:
  A. *The Order of the Contents* 233
  B. *A Brief Summary of the History of the Children of Israel* 234
  C. *The Meanings of the Names* Abel *and* Cain, *the First Two Sons of Adam and Eve* 236
  D. *Several Names Which Mean "the Gift of God" or "the Gift of Jehovah"* 237
  E. *The Names in the Book of Ruth* 237
  F. *The Names in Chapter 9: "Miriam and the Family Rebellion"* 237

Thy words were found and I ate them,
And Thy words became for me a joy and the delight of my heart;
*For I HAVE BEEN CALLED BY THY NAME, O L*ORD *God of hosts.*

Jeremiah 15:16

Preface

This is primarily a book about names and their meanings. It also deals with some of the ways the names are interrelated. Sometimes the main ideas of the narrative are simply reinforced, while at other times entirely new concepts are introduced. When there are many different names involved, lists of the names with their meanings are provided. When deemed appropriate, the lists are contained within the text. Otherwise, they are in the appendices.

At times, there may be disagreement among various scholars concerning the exact meaning of certain names. This may be due to several different factors. Most often, the names are derived from certain root words, the meaning of which is known. The precise connotation of the name itself may, however, be open to a certain amount of interpretation. This accounts for renderings that are similar but not identical.

There are a few biblical names whose meanings have been lost in antiquity, such as the original meaning of Nimrod. However, even those names have generally taken on some meaning with the passage of time.

There is also occasionally some confusion if a certain name has a "bad" connotation and someone then substitutes some aspect of the biblical person's character in place of the actual translation of the original word. This sort of thing occurs most often in modern culture when gift items, such as plaques or coffee cups, are made with printed names and meanings on them. The real meaning of the word is felt to be unacceptable in those circumstances, and a more palatable substitution is provided.

Since this book is a discussion of names and their meanings, it necessarily comes to deal with symbolism as well. The original meanings of the people's names has a great deal to add to the scriptural message. By its very nature, a consideration of symbolism is interpretive and may, at times, appear to be somewhat abstract. However, a sincere attempt has been made to restrict the discussion to straightforward types of symbolism and not obscure ideas that are open to multiple interpretations. These things should serve to enhance and expound upon basic principles contained in the text rather than open up strange and divergent ideas. They are certainly not intended to form some new doctrine within Christendom.

The organization of the book also follows the path of symbolism, and this is explained more fully in the appendices. The arrangement and number of the chapters reflects this concept.

The fact that much symbolism is present is in no way meant to detract from the historical veracity of the biblical account. All of those involved were real people living in real-life situations; they were not mythical or mystical figures who were invented for the purpose of illustration.

Introduction

In the modern world, there is generally no connection between a person's name and its meaning. This has not always been the case. Many names in common usage today, such as Smith or Cooper, were originally given because of a man's line of work. They would then be passed down through the generations as the family name, with the original logic and purpose being obscured by the passage of time.

First names are usually given to children today without any real meaning intended. However, during biblical times, especially in the Old Testament period, most names were given with a specific meaning in mind. These names have frequently been studied, and entire books have been written simply to catalogue their meanings.

Some of these names are quite familiar, being more frequently quoted in books and sermons, while others are rarely encountered. The original significance of most of them can be found in a good Bible dictionary or other reference work.

What may be new — that which I hope to convey — is a sense of purpose and connection behind these names. Although the parents who gave the names were cognizant of real reasons for choosing names for their children, God was divinely directing them. The names begin to weave individual stories and concepts (otherwise seemingly unrelated) into something beautiful and intricate, *The Living Tapestry*. Even though the people involved had immediate, logical thoughts resulting in the choices they made, God was overseeing the unfolding of events and personalities with such detailed and meticulous planning that the names have become part of the story. Without a knowledge of what these names indicate, an important part of the message may be missed.

When it comes to God, it soon becomes obvious that the names ascribed to Him actually reveal His character and the ways He desires to relate to His people. Human beings, on the other hand, may be given names for a wide variety of reasons. In some instances, the child might be named for some noble or godly trait that the parents hope to see develop. At other times the name could refer to something as simple as the circumstances surrounding the baby's birth. What becomes most amazing is the manner in which these names take on greater significance as the biblical account unfolds. The meanings begin to weave together across time and become a part of the narrative of the true message, adding immeasurably to the depth of understanding when properly integrated into the entire scheme of things.

In no way does this book purport to be an exhaustive study of this subject, but hopefully it will serve as a useful introduction. I do not expect, in my lifetime, to completely plumb the depths of the meaning of the Scriptures, even in this one limited area. I have, at times, believed that I understood a passage and the underlying meanings quite well ... only to have God open my eyes to deep and wonderful truths that would excite my soul and make me wonder what I was missing in other passages.

Much of my knowledge of Bible names and their meanings is not original and has been gleaned from many excellent Bible teachers. There are portions of the material that come directly from my own study and listening to the Lord. It is my earnest hope that all of this will bring blessing upon the people of God as they learn ever more from His Word — for He has words of eternal life.

Paul Strausbaugh
Clifton Forge, Virginia

Chapter One

Paul

We've been married for three years, so I guess it's about time for us to have a baby. I'm not real sure how we will pay our bills, though, with Stan about to get out of the Air Force and then wanting to go to school. Now I will have to miss work a good bit, too. We talked about it last night, and he said not to worry about it, that it won't cost that much extra for one more. I don't know how he can say that. Why, just the hospital bill would be over sixty dollars — if he weren't in the military! Then, more food, baby clothes, and I don't know what all else! I don't know how we'll pay the rent while he's in school.

We do want to have children, though, and it will be a long time before he completely finishes school. Neither of us wants to wait that long before starting our family. At least I can be thankful that the pregnancy is going well, and I haven't been sick much. So far, I have been able to work and get along well. Three more months to go, and I'm starting to get a little uncomfortable at times. But feeling the baby move is exciting!

Last night, we agreed that we are going to name the baby after my father. Too bad he is no longer living to see his namesake. Stan's father is still alive to enjoy such a thing, but he already has one man named for him, so it seemed best to both of us to name this one after my father. If it is a boy, we will call him Paul, and if it happens to be a girl, then we can call her Paula. Either way, the same name will work.

It's rather strange having my first baby. It may not be a new thing in the earth, but it's new to me! I wonder whether the baby will be a boy or a girl, what he will look like, and what kind of person my child will grow up to be. I don't necessarily expect greatness (although any mother can dream) like a president or a great military general. If she is a girl, she doesn't have to be a great poet or author, or a world-famous woman explorer! I do hope that he or she is happy and successful, though. And I hope he doesn't have to live through any terrible war or depression or famine! Oh, no, I've gone from wondering to worrying! Anyway, I hope the child grows up well and has a good life.

I wonder what the name Paul means. Does it have a meaning? If it does, it must be something great, since it was such a prominent name in the Bible. Oh, my, I've lost track of the time! I must get going, or I'll be late for work. Three more months, and we get to meet little Paul or Paula!

— Paul —

As I was growing up, I distinctly remember disliking my name, "Paul." I'm not sure what was objectionable about it, but I knew that there were many other names I would have preferred. Perhaps it was the way my mother and several others would, at times, pronounce both my first and middle names at once. This was done, more often, when they were perturbed with me, and then I would hear "Paul Lee!"

Actually, it seemed to me that what was really wrong with my name was just the sound of it. "Paul" just didn't sound quite right. "Paullee" (which was the way I heard it in those inopportune moments) was even worse. I never actually settled upon the name that would have been correct for me, but I definitely had an aversion to the one I had been given.

During those growing-up years, the *meaning* of my name was never part of the issue. It was simply a matter of how the words struck my ear. I had no knowledge of the meaning of the name, nor was I interested.

As a new Christian studying the Bible, I gradually began to see the importance of the meanings of names. As the importance of other names unfolded little by little in my understanding, I became interested in the meaning of my own name. What did *Paul* mean?

The first time or two that I saw the meaning of my name written, I dismissed what I saw as surely being an error. The name *Paul*, I read, simply meant "little" or "small." This only served to make matters worse, as far as my opinion of the name was concerned. If my name was to have any meaning in my personal life at all (which is generally not the case nowadays), then I certainly would have picked something different, perhaps something suggesting greatness — never smallness.

With the passing of the years, I came to realize that I had been given to the habit of thinking more highly of myself than I ought to think, and that, no doubt, was the reason I found the meaning of my name

The Living Tapestry

distasteful. I gradually learned, however, that this meaning was quite appropriate. *Paul* suits me. Perhaps most people in this present era are not given names that have real meaning in their lives, but I believe that I was. It is as though God, knowing that I would develop an interest in the subject of names and their meanings, saw to it that I was given a name that had significance for my life.

It is rather strange how long the realization of my own "smallness" took to reach me. It was a gradual process in my own mind. One would think that I would have only had to look at the greatness of the expanse of the heavens, then either look in a mirror or inwardly at my own soul to be convinced of my own smallness. Alas, it was not so!

I had a miraculous and life-changing conversion, heard from God in many ways and developed a good understanding of the Bible (above many of those around me), and this led me to feel that I was somehow either already great or headed for greatness.

It was only the repeated failures in several areas of my life, coupled with what could only be seen as a lack of Christian fruitfulness on my part, that gradually brought me face to face with the reality of my own smallness. It was not only a smallness when compared to the cosmos, but it was a smallness in God's Kingdom.

Today, I can thank God for my weaknesses! They caused me to have a much more realistic view of myself, and they also magnified my understanding of God's love. If He would pay such a great price and give so much to one as small as I, His love was vast.

As peculiar as it may seem, I was sure that I was quite humble during those years. Those who knew me would have described me that way too (most of the time), because I was never one to brag or toot my own horn (I might, however, have been guilty of interjecting a subtle suggestion from time to time). But just as *"the unfolding of [God's] words gives light"* (Psalm 119:130), the unfolding of my life, coupled with the gentle prompting of various passages in the Scriptures, gradually brought about enlightenment in this area.

One verse in particular was instructive in this regard. It is contained in a description of the New Covenant: *"...THEY SHALL NOT TEACH EVERYONE HIS FELLOW CITIZEN, AND EVERYONE HIS BROTHER, SAYING, 'KNOW THE LORD,' FOR ALL SHALL KNOW*

Paul

ME, FROM THE LEAST TO THE GREATEST OF THEM" (Hebrews 8:11). This, of course, is made possible because of God's forgiveness of our sins. On several occasions, as I read this verse, I somehow felt bothered by it. Just why was rather vague and ill-defined at the time, but I gradually became aware that the reason for my uncomfortable feeling was that I somehow felt it unfair for someone who was "the least" to know God as well as someone like me. This seemed to somehow encroach upon the uniqueness, or the special nature, of the relationship that was developing between myself and God.

When I thought of *"the least,"* I suppose that I unconsciously conjured up a mental picture of a nominal Christian whose life was a complete failure and who seemed not to care much about God at all. This mental picture contrasted with the picture I had of myself as one who loved God and studied His Word.

The first few times this feeling occurred, and I began to sense the underlying motive, I simply dismissed the whole thing as being a passing thought and not a true part of myself. It was some time before, with the realization of my own smallness, I was able to accept the appropriateness of my name. I rejoice now because even the least of us can know God, and to know Him is eternal life (see John 17:3)

"God is opposed to the proud, but gives grace to the humble" (James 4:6), but what has been truly amazing to me has been God's tenderness and patience in revealing my pride and developing the much-needed humility. His grace is wonderful.

Now, humility is not the same as self-deprecation. On the contrary, a closer look into God's greatness leads logically to a clearer revelation of our smallness. Even Isaiah, the great prophet of God, felt worthless and lost when he was in God's presence and saw His majesty and His holiness. He cried out *"Woe is me, for I am ruined!"* (Isaiah 6:5). But God did not leave Isaiah in his hopeless state. An angel touched his mouth with a burning coal from the altar, and declared: *"Your iniquity is taken away, and your sin is forgiven"* (Isaiah 6:7). After that, God sent Isaiah to the people as His own mouthpiece.

To settle the matter of self-worth for all of us, the great God Himself declared it by paying an undeniably dear price for our redemption. As we see our own weakness and smallness, we may at times feel that

The Living Tapestry

God paid too high a price for us. However, He did not consider even His Son Jesus too high a price, and so we see our true value.

Still, when the time comes for seating at His table, I intend to choose a seat near the bottom (see Luke 14:10). This would be an appropriate choice for one whose name is "Small." Actually, the truly humble response would be to choose the absolute last seat.

As a further testimony of God's grace in my life, He gave me a wonderful wife and daughter. As the Scriptures say, *"He who finds a wife finds a good thing, and obtains favor from the LORD"* (Proverbs 18:22). As it turns out, the names of both my wife and my daughter are very significant.

My wife's first name is Joan, the feminine of John, meaning "the gift of Jehovah." Her middle name is Ruth, which means "friendship." She has certainly been both my closest friend and a gracious gift from God, two facts that I have not always properly appreciated, but have, nevertheless, remained true to the meaning of her name.

Our daughter, whose name is Christina Joy, has also lived up to her name in many amazing ways. Christina is similar to Christian and means "little Christ." Of course, that is what each believer is meant to be, and it has been a marvelous experience to see Christ growing in Christina and being expressed in her life. She has, of course, been a constant joy to us, and also tends to bring joy into the lives of people wherever she goes.

A QUEST FOR UNDERSTANDING

Then He [Jesus] opened their minds to understand the Scriptures.
Luke 24:45

Many years ago, I began to see the concept of understanding in the Bible. There are three words — wisdom, knowledge and understanding — that are repeatedly emphasized in the book of Proverbs as being very important. Knowledge is a matter of the mind, whereas wisdom more directly involves the heart. Much has been written about the difference between the two.

But what about understanding? Does it deserve separate attention,

Paul

or is it simply a minor variation of the other two? I believe that it not only serves to bridge the gap between wisdom and knowledge, but also seeks to employ them in daily life to the best advantage. Real understanding comes through the marriage of wisdom and knowledge and their application over time.

It seems that we humans have the inexplicable ability to "know" something, possibly even possessing wisdom regarding the proper application of that knowledge, and yet fail to fully understand the ramifications of not acting accordingly. Perhaps an illustration would be useful.

The life of Solomon can help us to see much about the interrelationships between wisdom, knowledge and understanding. When he was beginning the daunting task of ruling as king in place of his father David, he asked God specifically for wisdom and knowledge. The Bible says that God was pleased with such a request, and He, therefore, granted it (see 2 Chronicles 1:11-12).

Most of the Proverbs were written by Solomon, and to this day, there is a saying in common use that refers to him. If we desire to describe someone as being very wise, we might say that he "has the wisdom of Solomon."

We can also say, with a fair degree of certainty, that Solomon amassed a great deal of knowledge. His accomplishments in building, commerce and government attest to this fact. But did Solomon fully understand the significance of his place in history? Did he understand the degree to which his proliferation of foreign wives would wreak havoc on his relationship with God? Did he understand that wisdom and knowledge alone, apart from ongoing obedience and dedication to God, would result in emptiness? If he had, he might not have had so much to say about the vanity of life. Toward the end of his life, Solomon wrote:

I said to myself, "Behold, I have magnified and increased wisdom more than all who were over Jerusalem before me; and my mind has observed a wealth of wisdom and knowledge." And I set my mind to know wisdom and to know madness and folly; I realized that this also

The Living Tapestry

is striving after wind. Because in much wisdom there is much grief, and increasing knowledge results in increasing pain.
Ecclesiastes 1:16-18

So I hated life, for the work which had been done under the sun was grievous to me; because everything is futility and striving after wind.
Ecclesiastes 2:17

It is apparent that even great wisdom and knowledge, as wonderful as they may be, do not guarantee a fulfilled life. There is a missing ingredient that only an ongoing relationship with the Almighty can supply. It was for this reason that I prayed that the Lord would *"give me understanding that I may live"* (Psalm 119:144). The kind of life that only God can give is full and rewarding. In some way, understanding allows us to properly incorporate wisdom and knowledge into our lives. It helps us in the practical application. If we have a better understanding of God's Word and His ways, then we are more likely to remain steadfast through life's trials and long waiting periods.

As time went by, I began to understand God's Word more fully, as anyone should who studies the Scriptures with an open mind and heart. In my particular case, however, I began to see a great deal of truth wrapped up and frequently hidden in the meanings of the various biblical names. Not only have I found that a study of names enhances the understanding of various portions of the Bible, but also I have found it to be a great faith-builder.

The reader might ask, "Why should such facts build my faith?" Certainly the bedrock of faith is not built on a compilation of facts, but rather on the Word of God and the work of the Holy Spirit. Nevertheless, we build upon that foundation and strengthen our faith as our understanding of God's ways increases.

I will not go so far as to say that a person must know the meaning of Bible names in order to have faith in God, but it has helped me to further build my trust in a sovereign Master Planner who is intimately involved in the lives of His people. The intricate and masterful work of God becomes apparent as these names are studied. It could be no acci-

Paul

dent that all of the people of the Bible were named in such a way that the meaning of their names was being woven into the very fabric of history, forming a huge and intricate tapestry. Only a sovereign God could perform such a thing.

Of course, God's handiwork is quite evident in all of creation, but the deeper we dig, the more we find of His direct and loving involvement in the details of life. A look at another passage from the Psalms will help us to understand (there's that word again) this concept a little better. There is a progression hidden in the following passage:

> *O how I love Thy law!*
> *It is my meditation all the day.*
> *Thy commandments make me wiser than my enemies,*
> *For they are ever mine.*
> *I have more insight than all my teachers,*
> *For Thy testimonies are my meditation.*
> *I understand more than the aged,*
> *Because I have observed Thy precepts.*   Psalm 119:97-100

The first thing that is evident in this passage is that simply receiving God's commandments gives us greater wisdom than His enemies, who do not accept them. Then, meditating upon the things God says leads to a great amount of insight — often to more than is possessed by those who are over us as teachers.

Real understanding, however, comes through a process of *doing* the things the Lord commands. As time goes by, the one who is obedient to God gains understanding, and this understanding surpasses even that of those of greater years who have not been so obedient. This eventually leads to the rather enviable position of actually understanding and knowing God.

Note that in the following key passage, understanding is mentioned first:

> *Thus says the* Lord, *"Let not a wise man boast of his wisdom, and let not the mighty man boast of his might, let not a rich man boast of his riches; but let him who boasts boast of this, that he understands and*

The Living Tapestry

> *knows Me, that I am the LORD who exercises lovingkindness, justice, and righteousness on earth; for I delight in these things," declares the LORD.*   Jeremiah 9:23-24

It seems that nearly all those who know anything at all about God feel that they do understand and know Him. In fact, some of the most immoral and degenerate people that I have known somehow believe that they have some sort of an "understanding" with God. I would submit, however, that in this world of confusion and imperfection, an accurate understanding of the Almighty is not automatic. This must be learned, and can only be done by listening to the revelation God Himself has given, while obeying to the best of our ability. The more attention we give to God, and the more completely we give ourselves to obeying those things which He shows us, the better understanding we will have.

At this point, some might ask, "What has all of this to do with knowing the meanings of a lot of ancient names?" I can only say that I felt I had a pretty good understanding of the Bible before I began to learn the meaning of names. After praying that God would *"give me understanding that I may live,"* however, many more truths unfolded before me. The connections between people across the ages and the sovereign hand of God in connecting them were clarified. Both the character and the work of God were constantly displayed.

Seeing the emphasis on these names helped solidify the importance of God's names as a descriptor of Himself to us. After realizing the fact that God is overseeing all of this, carefully assuring that the meanings of so many names are fulfilled in life, it became obvious that He will even more carefully assure that the meanings of His names are also fulfilled in His relationship with us.

Subsequent chapters will deal first with the names of God (Chapter Two), next with the changes that His work causes in our lives (Chapter Three), and then with the irony of our sometimes inappropriate response (Chapter Four). That will be followed by a return to some foundational issues —Chapter Five from Genesis, Chapter 6 about the domain of darkness, Chapter Seven concerning the centrality of relationships, and Chapter Eight about the symbolism of rivers in the

Paul

Bible. Chapters Nine through Eleven deal with the consequences of rebellion against God. Finally, Chapter Twelve speaks of God's overarching plan, to redeem *"a people for His own possession"* (Titus 2:14).

It is my sincere hope that these teachings will help the reader to increase his or her understanding of the Almighty, as they have done for me. In that way, we can avoid the error that Jesus said resulted from *"not understanding the Scriptures, or the power of God"* (Matthew 22:29). We can also attain to:

> *... all the wealth that comes from the full assurance of UNDERSTANDING* [emphasis added], *resulting in a true knowledge of God's mystery, that is, Christ Himself, in whom are hidden all the treasures of wisdom and knowledge.* Colossians 2:2-3

Chapter Two

The Lord

Let them praise the name of the Lord,
For His name alone is exalted;
His glory is above earth and heaven. Psalm 148:13

Therefore also God highly exalted Him, and bestowed on Him the name which is above every name, that at the name of Jesus every knee should bow, of those who are in heaven, and on earth, and under the earth, and that every tongue should confess that Jesus Christ is Lord, to the glory of God the Father. Philippians 2:9-11

The name of the Lord is a strong tower;
The righteous runs into it and is safe. Proverbs 18:10

Thy words were found and I ate them,
And Thy words became for me a joy and the delight of my heart;
For I have been called by Thy name,
O Lord God of hosts. Jeremiah 15:16

And God, furthermore, said to Moses, "Thus you shall say to the sons of Israel, 'The Lord [YHWH], the God of your fathers, the God of Abraham, the God of Isaac, and the God of Jacob, has sent me to you.' This is My name forever, and this is My memorial-name to all generations." Exodus 3:15

— The Names of God —

A discussion of the names of God is necessarily somewhat academic. Since there is so much material to cover, it requires an organized and detailed approach. It must be realized, however, that such an approach is paradoxical. God has revealed Himself as the One who, as the Source of life, is *full* of life to the point of bursting. His names are living and, because of that, He has always revealed His name to mankind through real-life experiences.

The name of the Almighty Creator of the universe hardly admits of academic treatment. The sterile pages of a book cannot, by themselves, adequately relate this subject in the fashion that it deserves. Any such consideration of this subject — the name of the King of the Ages — must admit to such a shortcoming. Nevertheless, it is an eminently worthy subject, and one that deserves serious study and apprehension.

Once studied, these truths must be assimilated. Once understood, they must be cherished. It is, after all, by name that God introduces Himself. It is through knowing Him that eternal life is available to men.

The Old Testament Revelation

The Old Testament book of Isaiah begins with a lament about the sinful condition of God's people in the nation of Israel, even comparing them with Sodom and Gomorrah. Because of the evil that was rampant in the land, there was destruction and suffering; God's help was not to be found. Throughout the entire book of Isaiah, there are alternating words of destruction and restoration, of judgment and hope.

At the beginning of chapter 52 of Isaiah, there is a particularly important passage containing not only a description of the oppressed condition of God's people, but also the solution to their problem. This passage speaks of Jerusalem and the *"daughter of Zion"* as captives, and describes how God's people first went down into Egypt and then were under the oppressive thumb of the Assyrians. Those were actual events in their history, and are also types of something more generally applicable to all of the people of God throughout the ages. [1]

After the problem is stated and the deplorable state of affairs among God's people is lamented, the solution is succinctly presented in one verse: *"Therefore My people shall know My name; therefore in that day I am the one who is speaking, 'Here I am' "* (Isaiah 52:6). On the surface, this may sound like a rather simplistic answer to such severe and deep-seated problems, especially problems that had persisted and grown for hundreds of years. However, the answer was found to lie in knowing God, who He is and what He will do, because He is the One who *is* the answer to all of the problems of mankind.

By the time of Isaiah, God had spent hundreds of years patiently revealing Himself to His people. This was done step by step, teaching by example. Each time a crucial point was reached, He revealed Himself through a particular situation, introducing one of His names that applied to a particular type of human need.

The names of God were mostly revealed in the Old Testament, as the Lord dealt with Abraham and his descendants, the children of Israel. The New Testament name of the Son of God, Jesus, is simply a fulfillment of those names that had already been revealed in the Old Testament.

A basic knowledge of the history of the Israelites is helpful in properly understanding these names of God. Furthermore, their experiences are representative of many things that take place in the lives of all God's people throughout history — Jews and Gentiles alike. Many aspects of the history of the Israelites will appear again and again in subsequent chapters as various Old Testament names are studied. [2]

The centrality of the name of the Lord in the lives of His people is not just an Old Testament concept, although it was primarily developed during that time period. In the New Testament as well, the name of God is crucial in the deliverance of His people. In fact, the name of Jesus is nothing more or less than the culmination of all of the names of God from the Old Testament.

The Names of God

As Jesus was about to leave this earth and become the sacrificial Lamb of God, He said, *"I manifested Thy name to the men whom Thou gavest Me out of the world"* (John 17:6). The same passage also says that Jesus *"was keeping them in"* His name, and finally ends by saying that He had made God's name known to them and would continue to do so (see John 17:26).

Elsewhere in the New Testament, we are told that Jesus Christ is *"the radiance of His glory and the exact representation of His nature"* (Hebrews 1:3). Jesus Christ not only had the name that, by its meaning, was the fulfillment of the Old Testament names of God, but He actually "manifested" God's name. He gave physical expression to all aspects of the Lord's name, fulfilling the hope that every previously revealed name of God inspired in the hearts of men.

God's names are of primary importance throughout the entire Bible. His name is indeed above every other name. The names of God reveal to men His character and His purposes. That is the reason Proverbs says: *"The name of the LORD is a strong tower; the righteous runs into it and is safe"* (Proverbs 18:10).

Truly, knowing the name of God and trusting in Him ultimately guarantees deliverance and safety. He will provide and care for His people. One of the earliest names of God revealed in the Old Testament was *El-Shaddai,* generally translated into English as "God Almighty," but may also mean "The All-Sufficient God." The significance of *El-Shaddai* will become more obvious, since there is no area of human need that is not addressed by one of His names.

As repeatedly seen in the Scriptures, new needs arise, and God is found faithful, causing His people not just to learn, but to experience His name. A similar process is at work in the life of each believer, as trust in God reveals His faithfulness in each new area of life. Without a doubt, the most important names in the Bible to know are the names of God.

Since the meanings of God's names reveal His character and His purposes, these meanings become important keys to the understanding of God Himself and of His dealings with His people. As a person comes to know God, that is, *really know Him,* he (or she) simultaneously comes to know God's names. God is so vast and so great that no one name adequately describes Him. The one name that comes closest to fully describing who He is, is Jesus.

The name *Jesus* is derived from Hebrew words meaning "The Lord Our Savior" or "I AM the Lord Who Saves." That is the reason the Bible says, *"this is eternal life,"* to know God the Father, and Jesus Christ whom He has sent (John 17:3). By Him, life was created. From Him, life flows. By Him, life is defined. In Him, life is fulfilled. With Him, life is meaningful and full of blessing. Without Him, life is empty and meaningless.

Following is an outline that may serve as an overview of God's names. It is not exhaustive:

I. Elohim (plural of Eloha, Genesis 1:1) — emphasizes creative power, deity as the origin of life
   A. Compound names with El (derived from Elohim)
      1. El-Shaddai — The Almighty God (or All-Sufficient God)
      2. El-Elyon — The Most High God
      3. El-Olam — The Everlasting God
      4. El-Gibbor — The Mighty God (Isaiah 9:6)

   B. Compound name with Jehovah (YHWH)
      YHWH Elohim — The LORD God (Genesis 2:4), the first of the compound names of God

II. Adonai — Lord or Master (applied to either God or man)
    Compound name with Jehovah (YHWH) — Adonai YHWH

III. YHWH (Jehovah) — The Self-Existent One (literally "He That Is Who He is" or "The Eternal I AM"). This is God's personal or redemptive name.
    A. Compound names
       1. Jehovah-Jireh — The Lord Will Provide
       2. Jehovah-Ropheka — The Lord Your Healer
       3. Jehovah-Nissi — The Lord My Banner
       4. Jehovah-Tsidkenu — The Lord Our Righteousness
       5. Jehovah-Shalom — The Lord Our Peace

The Names of God

      6. Jehovah-Shammah — The Lord Who Is Present
      7. Jehovah-Shua — The Lord Our Savior
         (Jehoshua, Joshua and Jesus)

   B. Several other "combination" names
      1. Jehovah-Raah — The Lord Is Our Shepherd
      2. Jehovah-M'Kadesh — The Lord Is Our Sanctifier
      3. Jehovah-Sabaoth — The Lord of Hosts

IV. The many other names found throughout the Scriptures: Messiah or Christ; King of Kings; Lord of Lords; Alpha and Omega; Lamb of God; Sun of Righteousness; High Priest of Our Confession; Son of Man; Root of Jesse; Lion of the Tribe of Judah; The Root and Offspring of David; Bright Morning Star; Redeemer; Advocate; Ancient of Days; Rock of Ages; Stone That the Builders Rejected; King of Glory; Immanuel — and many others

    Upon consideration of these names, a reminder of God's greatness is in order. It is, without a doubt, impossible to *fully* understand or appreciate these things from the viewpoint of humanity in its fallen state. The Bible says that God's name is holy and awesome. The word *holy* actually means "other." God is "other"; His ways and His thoughts are higher than those of men and women (see Isaiah 55:9). His name is above every other name — no matter where it may be found (see Philippians 2:9).

    It is quite unfortunate that many words, such as *holy* and *awesome*, have been used so glibly to describe various undeserving things in modern-day culture, clouding the real meaning and stealing the proper impact when they are applied in earnest. Having the word *holy* bantered about in phrases like "holy cow" serves only to cheapen a word that should be reserved for the purpose of instilling in a person a sense of the altogether "other-ness" and utter perfection of God. Also, describing a car or a new dress as "awesome" does something to desensitize the listener to the true meaning of the word, and thereby makes it that much more difficult for a person to grasp the concept that God is not just some white-haired old man sitting in the sky wishing

The Living Tapestry

He had the power to change things. It is essential to maintain some sense of the awesome greatness of God in order to properly understand anything about Him.

ELOHIM

Elohim is a Hebrew word that is plural, and is used to refer to God. It may also refer to gods, or even, sometimes, to angels. When speaking of God, this name refers to Him as Creator of the world and the One who is in charge of all of creation. It conveys the idea of His power, and is used in Genesis 1:1.

We should all be quite thankful that *Elohim* is not the only name by which God revealed Himself, since this one, by itself, would essentially preclude a personal relationship between God and man in his fallen state. The name for deity used by the Moslems, *Allah,* is derived from this name. That religion portrays the strict legalism and basic lack of redemptive grace that name requires.

When *Elohim* is used in combinations to form other names, such as *El-Shaddai, El-Elyon and El-Gibbor,* the sense is still that of supreme power and eternality, but not necessarily of a personal, redemptive relationship.

The first of the compound names of God in the Bible is found in Genesis 2:4, combining *Elohim* and *Jehovah [YHWH Elohim],* and is translated "The Lord God" in English. Within this combination of names reside the ideas both of supreme creative power and of personal redemption and relationship with God. Deity is expressed by *Elohim,* but the hope of relationship with the Almighty is brought to light in the various names formed from *YHWH.*

ADONAI

The Hebrew word *Adonai* is used to mean "Lord" or "Master," and can be used to refer to God in this capacity, or also to man. This word, by itself, does not necessarily describe deity, but simply authority. This name also is found in compound forms, such as *Adonai YHWH,* translated most often into English as "The Lord God." The Jews have

The Names of God

historically attached such a reverence to the name *YHWH* that they refuse to pronounce the name, instead substituting *Adonai*. The name *Adonai*, therefore, carries a significance in its use by the Jews that it does not necessarily have for Christians. It must be remembered by all that *Adonai* is commonly applied to God, either alone or in combination with other names.

YHWH

The most personal, hope-inspiring name of God is *YHWH*, or in the anglicized form, *Jehovah*. This name first appears in Scripture in Genesis 2, but the first real usage by God in His dealings with man (the first time God introduces Himself to a man by using this name) is in Exodus 3:14. There, it is associated with the deliverance of God's people from Egyptian bondage.

Exactly how to pronounce this name has been the subject of some debate. Any record of it among the Jews has been lost because of their scrupulous avoidance of speaking "The Name," instead substituting another name in its place whenever reading the name *YHWH* aloud. *YHWH* is sometimes referred to as the Hebrew tetragrammaton, and a pronunciation developed in more recent times led to the name *Jehovah*.

As to the meaning of the name *YHWH*, a clue is contained in Exodus 3:14, where God said to Moses, "I AM WHO I AM." The verb *HAYAH* is "to be," and is related to the name *YHWH*. In other words, God *is*, but not because He was created; He simply *is*.

There are also scholars who believe that certain evidence suggests the name may mean not only that *God is*, but that *He causes to be* — in other words, that He creates. God is the only One who *is* without someone else's intervention, and He, in turn, causes all others to exist.

The Jews living during the time of Jesus must have had an understanding of these things, because when Jesus said *"before Abraham was born, I AM"* (John 8:59), they took up stones with the intention of stoning Him for having made that statement.

Considering the most simple and straightforward meaning of the name most commonly used for God in the Hebrew Scriptures [*YHWH*], I AM is the One who is speaking, and HE IS the One to

The Living Tapestry

whom all should listen. However, it seems that most people have a rather difficult time listening to and receiving from God as they should. Because God knows this very well, and He is the ultimate Teacher, He reveals the various aspects of His nature, one at a time, through real-life experiences.

This truth is demonstrated in the Scriptures by the way God revealed Himself and His purposes to His people. He did it one clue, one revelation, and one name at a time over many years. One of the clearest pictures of this process is seen by following the name YHWH, remembering the meaning of the name (I AM), and looking at the series of compound names revealed in various situations in the Old Testament.

YHWH-JIREH

The first of these compound names of God is found in the Old Testament book of Genesis. A man called Abraham chose to name a place of sacrifice *YHWH-Jireh,* meaning *"The Lord Will Provide,"* or *"I AM the Lord Your Provider"* (Genesis 22:14). The root word in the Hebrew language actually means "to see," and that, in itself, is a reminder of something very important when considering God's provision. He provides for the needs of His people from a place of perfect vision. In other words, He sees the needs in advance and also sees them in their entirety. From the human perspective, it may, at times, seem as though God could well provide for His people in a better or more complete way, but from the point of view of "complete" vision, He is the perfect Provider. He sees, He perceives, and He knows completely what is needed long before it becomes apparent to natural eyes.

The story surrounding the introduction of this name is quite familiar and is full of symbolism regarding the sacrifice of Jesus Christ on the cross by His heavenly Father. The story involves Abraham, whose name means "father of a multitude." He lived in Mesopotamia about four thousand years ago. God called him to leave the land of idolatry where he lived and go to a new place that He would show him.

During Abraham's travels, God appeared to him and promised to bless him and multiply him. As time passed, however, this last prom-

The Names of God

ise seemed more and more impossible, since he and his wife, Sarah, had no children. (At that point, his name was Abram, and hers was Sarai.) [3]

At one point, out of desperation, Sarah encouraged Abraham to have children with her maidservant, and he agreed. Out of that union came Ishmael, who is the father of the modern Arabic peoples.

After that, God appeared to Abraham again and told him that he would have a son by his own wife in spite of the fact that, by this time, both were quite elderly and well past the childbearing years. Finally, after many years, their son was born and he was named Isaac, whose name means "laughter" — since his mother had laughed at the prospect of becoming pregnant at such an advanced age. It was this son, Isaac, who was at center stage in the story of how God revealed Himself as *YHWH-Jireh* to Abraham.

When Isaac was about twelve years old, God appeared to Abraham and commanded him to take his son to the land of Moriah, and there to offer him as a sacrifice to the Almighty. This seems like a very strange command, especially knowing how opposed to human sacrifice God is, but He had greater things in mind in all of this. Now that Christ has come, we can see some of the greater picture, and some of the powerful symbolism God had in mind in His command to Abraham. However, at that time, Abraham was not privileged to know all of this. His response was one of simple obedience, knowing something of the greatness and power of God, but not knowing any details of how it might all fit together.

As Abraham approached the place of sacrifice with Isaac, the son asked his father, *"Where is the lamb for the burnt offering?"* To that potentially very troubling question, Abraham replied, *"God will provide for Himself the lamb for the burnt offering, my son"* (Genesis 22:8). The Bible tells us that they walked on together to the top of Mt. Moriah, where Abraham built an altar, placed wood on it, bound his son Isaac and laid him on top of the wood on the altar. As he was about to slay him with a knife, the angel of the Lord called out and stopped him. Then Abraham looked up and saw a ram with its horns caught in a thicket, and he then offered the ram on the altar in the place of his son Isaac. At that point in time, Abraham saw what God had already seen. God could see the need and the outcome in advance. He could also see the ram coming up the other side of the mountain, while Abraham was still struggling with the circumstances before him.

The impact of the story is greatly enhanced when the meanings of the various names are added. Abraham means "father of a multitude," and it soon becomes apparent that he is being made to symbolize our heavenly Father. God was looking forward to the time when He would sacrifice His only Son for the sins of the world, and Jesus Christ would become the spotless Lamb of God. The meaning of Moriah, the mountain where the sacrifice was to have taken place, is "the bitterness of Jehovah." This adds further intensity to the picture and begins to tell something of the price God chose to pay to redeem His creation.

The imagery surrounding the life of Abraham goes on and on. The Bible says that he is, in a sense, the father of every person who is "of" the faith of Abraham (see Galatians 3:7).

YHWH-Ropheka

The second of the compound names of God to be considered is *YHWH-Ropheka*, "I AM the Lord Your Healer." To find the origin of this name, one must look to the time of Moses and the deliverance of the children of Israel from Egyptian bondage. In Exodus chapter fourteen, the Egyptian pharaoh, with his army, pursued the Israelites to the Red Sea. There, the sea was divided, and the Israelites crossed over on dry ground. When the Egyptian army attempted to follow them, the sea closed in on them, and they were all destroyed. The fifteenth chapter of Exodus is mostly a song of praise to the Lord for this mighty victory.

Almost immediately after this wonderful experience, the people traveled into the desert and found no water for them to drink. How often hardships are encountered on the tail end of a victory! Through such hardship, God demonstrates who He is and how He desires to work on behalf of His people. Each time, He does it differently, always revealing that He is God Almighty.

When the Israelite people reached a place called Marah, they found water, but it was not drinkable. The water was *"bitter." Marah* means

The Names of God

"bitterness." (Compare this word with *Moriah*, "the bitterness of Jehovah.") The people, of course, were not happy about this, and they *"grumbled at Moses"* (Exodus 15:24). When Moses prayed to God on their behalf, he was shown a tree. Upon casting the tree into the water, a miraculous change occurred, and the water became good for drinking.

This tree can be seen as symbolic of the cross of Christ, coming into the life of a believer and affecting a miraculous change. In connection with these events, the name *YHWH-Ropheka* was revealed to the Israelites as one of the names of God (see Exodus 15:26). The Hebrew word used in that passage is written as *rapha* in Strong's concordance, a word that is also translated as "physician" several times in the Old Testament. The form of the word *rapha* used in Exodus 15:26 is *ropheka*, making this even more personal than would otherwise be the case. The ending *ka* signifies "you" or "your" in a personal sense. By nature, God is the Great Physician, and in this passage He is the Lord *Your* Physician.

Examining this passage a little more closely, while looking at some of the symbols used, makes the application to present-day life a little clearer. The Bible says that God formed man from the dust of the earth. It is now known that, in addition to all of the elements that might be seen as *"dust,"* the human body contains a great deal of water. What was present might, then, be spoken of as "mud"! The saying that He is the potter and we are the clay (see Isaiah 64:8) is therefore much more literally true than is commonly realized.

It has been determined by scientific measurements that the majority (over one-half) of the body weight of most humans is composed of water, although the exact composition varies from person to person. Realizing these common facts lends an added meaning to the "bitterness" of the waters in the story from Exodus, since water is such a major part of our bodies.

In the New Testament, when a demon was cast out of a person, it was said to wander about in *"waterless places"* seeking rest. Not finding any, it would seek to return to its previous dwelling. This suggests that a demon's dwelling place was a place with water. Also, when Jesus was speaking of the new birth, He said it would become a *"well of water springing up to eternal life"* (John 4:14). This, of course, has a much deeper spiritual meaning, but it also reminds us of the importance of a "flow" of water in the physical body.

If these concepts are applied to the scene in the desert of Sinai and the "bitter" waters, there appears a picture of a bodily dysfunction or a disease, as a "bitterness" of the waters in an otherwise dry body of dust. Modern medicine has shown that many diseases involve some type of imbalance in body fluids. This may involve the composition, flow, pressure or amount of fluid. In this passage, this is represented by a "bitterness" of the waters. When the cross of Christ is added, as the tree was thrown into the water by Moses, the waters can again be made "sweet," returning to their proper balance and function.

Healing can be wrought by the Great Physician. His Name tells us that it is part of His very nature to be the Healer of His people. Often, in the practice of medicine, healing is achieved by restoring some type of proper function or composition to body fluids. How much more knowledgeable and capable God is, in this regard, than men! There is an undeniable chasm between man and God where knowledge and ability is concerned. No matter how hard modern man works to deny or overcome this huge gulf, it will always remain.

What a wonderful thing it is to know that God introduces Himself and reveals His nature as the Healer, your personal Physician. His ability can come to the rescue when man's ability is inadequate. At a time of thirst, in the middle of the desert, with nothing available but bitter water, God reveals Himself as *YHWH-Ropheka*.

YHWH-Nissi

The third in the list of covenant names to be considered is *YHWH-Nissi*, translated "The Lord Is My Banner." This is described in a passage in Exodus chapter 17, in which the children of Israel were attacked without provocation by a group of people called "Amalek." The people of Amalek were apparently a warlike group of nomads descended from Esau who attacked the children of Israel at a place called "Rephidim."

The meaning of *Rephidim* is "rests." Since the Israelites found no water there when they arrived, making it a good resting place in the desert seemed an unlikely prospect. Nevertheless, God miraculously provided water for them in the desert and made Rephidim into a place of rest. Almost immediately after the provision of water, however, the Israelites were attacked by the Amalekites, prematurely spoiling their rest.

This entire passage is a very important one, with a great deal of symbolic meaning for the people of God throughout the ages, including the modern Christian. In fact, this passage is so important that for the first time God told Moses to write it down for a memorial, and gave the promise that He would utterly blot out the memory of Amalek from under Heaven (see Exodus 17:14). Then God said that He would make war against Amalek from generation to generation, indicating the ongoing nature of the struggle symbolized by the battle that day.

In order to gain some insight into the meaning contained (and to some extent hidden) in this passage, it is instructive to study the meaning of the name of each of the men involved, along with the meanings of the names of the people groups. Following is a tabulation of these meanings:

> Moses — Hebrew, *Mosheh,* meaning "drawn out." In Egyptian *ms,* meaning "a child or son"
> Aaron — Hebrew meaning uncertain. The first high priest of Israel
> Hur — "Prison" or "hole"
> Joshua — "Jehovah-Savior," or "Jehovah saves." It has the same meaning as the name *Jesus.*
> Amalek — It is difficult to be certain of the meaning. It probably means "warlike," "valley dweller" or "one who licks the dust." Descendants of Esau, an aggressive and warlike people
> Israel — "One who strives with God," representative of the true children of God [4]

After studying these names and their meanings, the insertion of them into the text while reading the story results in an entirely different perspective. Some insights into the current Christian struggle

The Living Tapestry

against spiritual forces of wickedness and the ongoing nature of that conflict begin to emerge. The promise that the *"memory of Amalek"* will be done away with then becomes a much greater promise, with a much more inclusive significance. The hope this insight brings is a much greater hope than simply ridding the earth of the memory of a single warlike group of nomads. God is actually promising to rid the earth of the memory of the warlike aggressor who continually attacks God's people and prevents them from resting in His provision. This applies to the devil and all of the fallen angels and demons under his authority. What a wonderful promise this is for the people of God!

Following is the passage with the meanings inserted alongside the actual names:

> *Then Amalek [warlike] came and fought against Israel [he who strives with God, or the people of God] at Rephidim [rests].*
> *So Moses [child, drawn out] said to Joshua [Jehovah Savior], "Choose men for us, and go out, fight against Amalek [warlike]. Tomorrow I will station myself on the top of the hill with the staff of God in my hand."*
> *And Joshua [Jehovah Savior] did as Moses [child, drawn out] told [literally means "said to"] him, and fought against Amalek [warlike]; and Moses [child, drawn out], Aaron [the high priest], and Hur [prison] went up to the top of the hill.*
> *So it came about when Moses [child, drawn out] held his hand up, that Israel [he who strives with God, or the people of God] prevailed, and when he let his hand down, Amalek [warlike] prevailed.*
> *But Moses' [child, drawn out] hands were heavy. Then they took a stone and put it under him, and he sat on it; and Aaron [the high priest] and Hur [prison] supported his hands, one on one side and one on the other. Thus his hands were steady until the sun set.*
> *So Joshua [Jehovah Savior] overwhelmed Amalek [warlike] and his people with the edge of the sword.*   Exodus 17:8-13

It becomes an amazing story when the meanings are substituted for

The Names of God

the names in the text and then applied to life today. When the warlike demonic aggressors attack the people of God, generally without provocation and often while the people are trying to rest, one child of God can intercede for the people of God. This one child, "drawn out" of the world and also "drawn out" from among his fellows to be an intercessor, can then speak to the Lord (Jehovah Savior) about the situation, and He will go forth and fight against the enemy and give the victory to the people of God.

However, as is illustrated here, the natural weakness of the flesh gets in the way. That is the reason the hands of Moses were held up by Aaron and Hur, and he was seated upon a stone. The stone is a common symbol of Christ in the Bible, and Moses was seated on the stone to give him support and some degree of rest.

Moses' hands were held up by the high priest on one side (Jesus Christ is the High Priest of the people of God) and by the prison (Hur) on the other. Since men are imprisoned in frail bodies of flesh, that weakness keeps them humble and continually urges them to seek God and depend upon Him. The believer is helped in intercession by Christ on the one hand and his own weakness on the other!

The passage ends with the statement: *"The LORD will have war against Amalek from generation to generation"* (Exodus 17:16). This is a strong hint that this story has an ongoing meaning and does not simply apply to the battle against the Amalekites of that day. There is hope to be gained, not only in the fact that God will go forth against the enemy at the bidding of the persistent intercessor, but also that, ultimately, this aggressor will be done away with. The Bible says that God *"will utterly blot out the memory of Amalek from under heaven"* (Exodus 17:14). Not only is there victory available during the present struggle, but ultimately deliverance from the enemy altogether! Indeed, *"the name of the LORD is a strong tower; the righteous runs into it and is safe"* (Proverbs 18:10).

As important as the name *YHWH-Nissi* is, it is only one of many names of the Lord! Each one adds to an understanding of who He is and what His purposes are, until the complete picture will show that He is *El-Shaddai* (God Almighty), The All-Sufficient One.

The Living Tapestry

YHWH-Tsidkenu

The fourth of the compound names of Jehovah to be considered is *YHWH-Tsidkenu*, "The Lord Is Our Righteousness." Although all of the names which God has revealed about Himself are very important, and each one is filled with special meaning as He relates to His people, this is perhaps the one name that could be considered a key to all the others. Let us consider why that may be the case.

One of the great philosophical problems in Christianity, or religion in general, for that matter, is how God can be perfectly just and yet forgive the sinner. Especially problematic in the minds of some would be the forgiveness and justification of a particularly "bad" sinner (for instance, a serial murderer, or child molester). When God made man (and woman) as His special creation, making them *"in His image,"* He then had quite a sticky problem on His hands when sin entered into the picture. How could He remain a just and righteous God and yet forgive or justify sinful men? Or would He be defeated by the enemy who tempted them and brought about their fall?

Certainly, the devil must have thought that he had God in a rather impossible position. But he underestimated God in several areas — especially in the area of self-humbling and self-sacrifice in the expression of His love for His creation. This had to have been an unexpected action on the part of the great and awesome Creator and Ruler of the entire universe! Nevertheless, the Bible declares that God is *just* and the *Justifier* of all who have faith in Jesus Christ as the payment for sin (see Romans 3:26).

This was foreseen by the prophet Jeremiah (Jeremiah 31-33), as he foretold the restoration of God's people after they had suffered judgment for their sins. Jeremiah 33:14-16 speaks of a righteous Branch of David (a reference to the Messiah, who was to come from the lineage of David), who would one day *"spring forth"* in order to execute justice and righteousness on the earth. Verse sixteen then says that when God's people are saved, they shall be called by the name *YHWH-Tsidkenu*, or "The Lord Is Our Righteousness."

It was not clear precisely how this would take place until the New Testament was written some six hundred years later, but we now

The Names of God

know that indeed the Lord *is* our righteousness. He personally paid the price to redeem His people from their sins, and it can therefore properly be said that He *is* their righteousness. No good deeds would suffice, no self-help seminar would be enough, and no one would be able to lift himself [or herself] up by his bootstraps.

After considering these things, it becomes apparent why this name, in particular, is possibly *the* key, without which none of the others could be enjoyed. Had God not personally provided the means of justification (He actually *became* the means of justification), no sinner could receive God's blessings. There would be no hope for mankind, but only the certainty of the wrath of the Almighty. Thank God that He did pay that awful price so that we can be restored to fellowship with Him and enjoy His blessings! It is appropriate, as some have said, to consider grace to be "God's riches at Christ's expense."

YHWH-Shalom

YHWH-Shalom means "I AM the Lord Your Peace." The peace this name describes is a direct result of the righteousness that was given to the people of God, as described in the discussion of *YHWH-Tsidkenu*. This concept is stated clearly in the New Testament book of Romans: *"Therefore having been justified by faith, we have peace with God through our Lord Jesus Christ"* (Romans 5:1). The concept of justification is the same as being declared righteous in God's sight, and that is what paves the way for being at peace with Him. Of course, this was made possible through the sacrificial shedding of the blood of Jesus Christ on the cross of Calvary.

In order to properly appreciate the significance of this name, one must first have an understanding of the *greatness* of God Almighty. The Bible says: *"His greatness is unsearchable"* (Psalm 145:3). There is no limit to what He can do, so the importance of making peace with Him cannot be overstated.

Perhaps it might be instructive to begin with some thought about the potential impact of *not* being at peace with God, in order to better appreciate the importance of actually *being* at peace with Him. Begin, first of all, by reflecting upon a situation involving opposition or anger

The Living Tapestry

from a boss or supervisor and the trouble which that can create. Then, consider the impact of local government officials or the police being "out to get you" for some reason. Or, if a person lived under a dictatorship or was ruled by a king, it would be a very serious thing to have the one in charge (and empowered to do something about it) as an enemy. Any of these possible scenarios would pale into complete insignificance when compared with the thought of having God Almighty as an enemy! He has all power, knows everything and has control over the fate of each man and woman who ever lived! Anyone with an ounce of sense ought to have a healthy fear of such a God as that, and be looking for a means of achieving peace with Him!

This, fortunately, is precisely what God desires. His name reveals this desire as an integral part of His nature. In fact, the Bible says that God is busy reconciling the world to Himself through the blood of Jesus Christ, and He has committed to us (the Church) the message concerning this great fact (see 2 Corinthians 5:19).

YHWH-Shalom appears in the Old Testament story involving a man named Gideon (see Judges 6:11-24). As Gideon was secretly threshing wheat inside a winepress in order to hide from the oppressive Midianites, the angel of the Lord appeared to him, instructing him to deliver Israel from her enemies.

At that point, Gideon asked the angel to remain until he could offer a sacrifice to God in the angel's presence. As soon as the sacrifice was presented, the angel reached out with the staff in his hand and touched the sacrifice, and the sacrifice was consumed by fire springing up from the rock beneath.

When Gideon realized that he had indeed seen the angel of the Lord face-to-face and had escaped from the encounter unharmed, he built an altar there and named it *YHWH-Shalom,* because his life had been spared (see Judges 6:24). The clear implication was that any meeting like that with the angel of the Lord by one who was not at peace with God would result in death. Therefore it is apparent, in the passage revealing God as our Peace, that there is a healthy appreciation of the awesome greatness of God. Indeed, these two concepts are inseparable because without being aware of the greatness and power of God, it is impossible to comprehend the importance of being at peace with Him.

The Names of God

It is also interesting to observe the meaning of the name *Gideon*, translated "he who cuts down." The first instruction from the Lord to Gideon was to go and tear down the altar of Baal and "cut down" the Asherah poles (idolatrous symbols of worship of a Canaanite goddess). After fulfilling a portion of his destiny revealed in his name's meaning, Gideon then defeated the huge Midianite army with only three hundred men. He was used by God to obtain a great victory against fantastic odds. The Israelites subsequently enjoyed relief from their enemies' oppression for forty years.

Peace is indeed a wonderful thing, and something to be sought after. Many generations could only wish for it, while living through terrible times of war and conflict. However, one must realize that there is no peace that even begins to compare in importance with having personal peace with God Almighty!

YHWH-Shammah

YHWH-Shammah means "I AM the Lord Who Is There." It is similar to the name *YHWH-Shalom* in one very important way: In both cases, an appreciation of the greatness of God is indispensable to understanding the importance of the name. It is also instructive in both to consider the ramifications of the *absence* of those things the name describes. In the previous example, the suggestion was made to consider the implications of living without peace with God, and in this case it is helpful to think about what might be the outcome of living without God's presence.

There is a philosophical theory that even though there may be a God or a Creator, He has started all of this and then left for a while, possibly intending to return later in order to see how things will come out. This may be called the "clock theory," since the idea is that He wound up the clock and has left it to run on its own. One reason that this theory is espoused is due to the fact that there is so much evil and suffering in the world, and that life frequently seems so capricious. That is to say, those who deserve bad things do not necessarily receive them, while others who seem more innocent often suffer more.

This theory, of course, ignores the concept of sin and the capriciousness of evil (with regard to those it harms), and concludes that if God is good, then He must not be directly involved. Those who promote such ideas also overlook the fact that God has a final judgment, and a great deal of time beyond what we presently perceive, to make sure that everything is worked out fairly and properly. Even though this philosophy about the "absentee God" is false, it highlights the fact that if God is not present, then we are susceptible to all kinds of problems and are helpless before all the evil in the world.

Thank God that He is present and has come to dwell with mankind! Christ has come and lived among us. He has paid the price for our sins, and He has said that He will never leave us nor forsake us (see Hebrews 13:5). In the original language of the Bible, this statement is extremely emphatic and could be more accurately translated, "I will never, never leave you; I will never, never forsake you." We should be extremely grateful that God has not left us unattended, as in the so-called clock theory. Instead, He has paid the very high price of coming to us, redeeming us and living with us in a loving way.

Immanuel (God with us) is the name given to express this reality in the Bible, and the ultimate goal of God is that He may dwell with men. This is stated clearly in the twenty-first chapter of Revelation, where the *"new heaven and new earth,"* and the *"new Jerusalem"* are described. One key feature spoken of is that *"the tabernacle of God is among men, and He shall dwell among them, and they shall be His people, and God Himself shall dwell among them"* (Revelation 21:3). In that situation, with God's presence so wonderfully realized, there will be no place for evil of any sort, and *"there shall no longer be any death; there shall no longer be any mourning, or crying, or pain ..."* (Revelation 21:4). God is good, and His presence causes everything around Him to become good as well.

The name *YHWH-Shammah* is found at the end of the book of Ezekiel (see Ezekiel 48:35). Leading up to this is a progression of events, strategically scattered throughout the book, giving added impact to the name when it finally appears. The first chapter of Ezekiel begins with a vision of God and of the cherubim. This passage describes the *"wheel within a wheel,"* and the strange beings with wings and four faces. These four faces were very significant, being symbolic of four aspects of Christ: the lion (king), the bull or ox (servant), the man (the Son of

The Names of God

Man) and the eagle (soaring high as God). The glorious throne of God was above the cherubim, bright and glowing with fire, while between the cherubim themselves there was visible a glowing fire and flashes of lightning. This scene is the most vivid description of the actual visible presence of God in the entire Bible.

As is frequently the case, however, the prophecies quickly turned to the sins of the people, and the fact that they would be defeated by the Babylonians and carried off into exile because of their rebellion and God's judgment. In the eleventh chapter of Ezekiel, there is a very significant passage, where God says that He will take away their heart of stone and give them a heart of flesh. He also says that He will cause a new spirit to dwell in them, and *"Then they will be My people, and I will be their God"* (Ezekiel 11:19-20). *"But as for those whose hearts go after their detestable things and abominations, I shall bring their conduct down on their heads"* (Ezekiel 11:21). It is no coincidence that the destruction of Jerusalem and the exile of the Jews into captivity in Babylon occurred quite soon after that prophecy (actually, many of the people, including Ezekiel himself, had already been carried off into captivity, but Jerusalem had not yet fallen).

Immediately after this passage, the text states that the cherubim lifted up their wings, with the *"glory of the God of Israel"* hovering over them, and the glory of the Lord departed from the city toward the east (see Ezekiel 11:23). This is very significant, because this is actually the presence of God Almighty departing from His people and from the Temple. Soon after that, the Chaldeans destroyed the city and the Temple, and the remainder of the Israelites (the southern kingdom of Judah) were carried off into exile as captives of the heathen king, Nebuchadnezzar.

After reading along through most of the book of Ezekiel, there is a prophecy at the end of chapter thirty-seven in which God promises to come back and make His dwelling with His people and to cause His sanctuary to be in their midst forever (see Ezekiel 37:26-28). This particular passage is made more meaningful if it is understood in the context of Ezekiel's previous vision in which the *"glory of God"* departed from the Temple and, as far as we know from the text, never came back.

The Living Tapestry

Remember that during God's "absence" the entire nation was utterly defeated and carried off into captivity to Babylon (which is even more significant, due to the symbolic meaning of Babylon in the Bible). [5] Here, we have a promise to reverse that train of events. Without God's presence, His people would face helpless exposure to the evil forces of His enemies, and the resultant destruction and ensuing state of captivity to the idolatrous world system symbolized by Babylon. Thank God for this prophecy about God dwelling with mankind!

It is also important that this prophecy occurs immediately following the well-known passage about God breathing life into the dry bones of the *"house of Israel"* (Ezekiel 37:1-14). No matter how dry and dead the Church or the nation of Israel may appear to the eye of man, God is able to breathe life into them and cause them to rise up as a living, breathing army obedient to God Almighty!

So far in the book of Ezekiel, there have been a couple of widely scattered references to this theme of the presence of God: the glory of the Lord departed from the Temple, followed by the promise of God's return. The next passage that relates to this idea is Ezekiel 43:1-7, in which the glory of the Lord returned to the Temple and God promised to *"dwell among the sons of Israel forever."* Along with the prophecy of God dwelling with them forever is the statement that they will no longer defile His Holy name by their abominations and their idolatry. Studying the names of God helps lead to an understanding of the significance of God dwelling with men. It also highlights some of the reasons why the third commandment prohibits a person from "taking the name of the Lord in vain."

In spite of following the theme of the presence of God through the book of Ezekiel (all the way up to God's promise to dwell among His people, and even onward to the vision of the actual return of the glory of the Lord to the Temple), the name for which this section is entitled, *YHWH-Shammah*, has not yet appeared. It seems quite significant that the actual name itself does not appear until the very last verse of the book of Ezekiel (Ezekiel 48:35), where the Lord tells the prophet that the Holy City will have a special name with a special significance. The name of the city will be *YHWH-Shammah*, "The Lord Is There." It is al-

The Names of God

most as though, by placing this name in the very last verse of the book, God is saying that this is the end, or goal, toward which He is moving.

Certainly this is also consistent with what is seen in the book of Revelation. The present age is wrapped up and there appear a new heaven and a new earth where righteousness dwells. At that point in time, the dwelling of God will be with man forever (see Revelation 21:1-7). Perhaps the fact that this verse is the last one in the book of Ezekiel may also serve as a clue to looking for this unifying theme among the widely scattered references through which the thread of this concept has been woven.

The meaning of the name *Ezekiel* is "the strength of God," or "God strengthens." It is quite evident that without the presence of God and the strength He provides to protect us from the enemy, disaster is inevitable. Thank God that, as revealed in His name, He desires to dwell with His people and to remain with them. Jesus' parting words to His followers in the book of Matthew were, *"Lo, I am with you always, even to the end of the age"* (Matthew 28:20).

JESUS

Jesus is perhaps best regarded as the embodiment and the fulfillment of all of the other names that have been considered. As the Bible says, *"in Him all the fulness of Deity dwells in bodily form"* (Colossians 2:9). Jesus' parents were instructed as to what His name should be. It was to be *Jesus*, since He would save His people from their sins.

The name *Jesus* is the Greek form of the Hebrew name *Joshua*. *Joshua*, in turn, is a contraction of the more complete name *Jehoshua*, which means "The Help of Jehovah" and could be translated as "I Am the Lord Your Savior." Understanding these interrelationships helps in seeing the symbolism contained in the book of Joshua and the wonderful reality of Jesus as the Captain of Our Salvation in the Promised Land.

In a sense, more should be said about this name than about any other single name of God. However, there will be less written here, since this one should be seen as containing *all* the meaning of *all* the other names combined. In that sense, there truly is more said about this name of God that about any other one.

This is the highest name in all of creation, as this passage illustrates:

> *Therefore also God highly exalted Him, and bestowed on Him the name which is above every name, that at the name of Jesus every knee should bow, of those who are in heaven, and on earth, and under the earth, and that every tongue should confess that Jesus Christ is Lord, to the glory of God the Father.* Philippians 2:9-11

YHWH-Raah

YHWH-Raah means "I AM the Lord Your shepherd." This name is revealed in Psalm 23, and there is perhaps nothing better to say about it than to refer to the Psalm itself. As one of the most beautiful psalms in the Bible, it is highly regarded as poetry even in secular literature. To the believer, these words contain ever-available comfort and encouragement during life's trials. Volumes have been written about the concept of the shepherd caring for his sheep, and then relating this concept to our relationship with God.

One aspect of this psalm that should be mentioned here, since this is a study of the names of God, is that all of the other names that have been reviewed (especially the more personal name *YHWH*) are either expressed or implied in the verses of Psalm 23.

> *The LORD [Hebrew, YHWH] is my shepherd;*
> *I shall not want [This expresses the lack of need since He is our Provider].*
> *He maketh me to lie down in green pastures:*
> *He leadeth me beside the still waters [Again there is provision here, and also peace].*
> *He restoreth my soul [The Lord is our Healer]:*
> *He leadeth me in paths of righteousness [The Lord is our Righteousness and our Sanctifier] for His name's sake [His name!].*
> *Yea, though I walk through the valley of the shadow of death,*
> *I will fear no evil [The Lord is our Banner and our Peace]:*

The Names of God

> *For Thou art with me. [The presence of the Lord.]*
> *Thy rod and thy staff they comfort me [The Lord is our Banner and our Peace].*
> *Thou preparest a table before me [The Lord is our Provider] in the presence of mine enemies [The Lord is our Banner and our Peace]:*
> *Thou anointest my head with oil [This speaks of the Holy Spirit as the agent of these blessings];*
> *My cup runneth over [Jesus (full of blessing, manifesting all the names in one)].*
> *Surely goodness and mercy shall follow me all the days of my life [Peace with God] and I will dwell in the house of the L*ORD *forever [The Lord's presence (God dwells with man)].* Psalm 23:1-6, KJV

It is also instructive that the psalmist refers to God in the third person ... until he walks through the valley of the shadow of death. Through experiences of God's provision and guidance and even restoration of the soul, God is still referred to as "He" rather than the more personal "Thou." Only after knowing the protection of the Almighty through the valley of death does the writer address the Lord directly in the second person. At that point, he begins to address God personally, saying *"Thou art with me."* The relationship has somehow become more intimate through trial and danger. As people experience life with its valleys and pitfalls, they can then begin to know God more personally. During such times, He reveals Himself as the One who is intimately involved in the affairs of men (and especially of believers)!

There are undoubtedly many people who would dispute the veracity of such an analogy, thinking that they are far more wise and discerning than ignorant sheep. However, considering the wisdom and knowledge of God, the comparison is completely appropriate. Especially in the spiritual realm, and when dealing with things of an eternal nature, men and women can be just as ignorant as sheep. There are many invisible predators and pitfalls. Jesus saw this clearly as He ministered to the people of Israel nearly two thousand years ago:

> *And Jesus was going about all the cities and the villages, teaching in their synagogues, and proclaiming the gospel of the kingdom, and heal-*

ing every kind of disease and every kind of sickness. And seeing the multitudes, He felt compassion for them, because they were distressed and downcast like sheep without a shepherd.   Matthew 9:35-36

The Good Shepherd could clearly see the results of generations of people not following the Lord as their Shepherd and suffering the consequences. This passage (Matthew 9:35-36) is sandwiched between two others that deal with demons. Those demons, or *"unclean spirits,"* might be viewed as invisible predators, preying upon God's sheep. Immediately preceding these verses in Matthew is the story of a man who was rendered unable to speak by a demon, but then spoke fluently when Jesus cast out the evil spirit. The very next thing Jesus did after this was to commission His disciples to go and cast out *"unclean spirits,"* and to bring healing to the people.

A look at the actual Greek words used by Jesus to describe the condition of the people makes it even more clear that there was a predator involved. The word for "distressed" can also be translated "harassed," and "downcast" literally means "thrown down." When considered in those terms, it becomes apparent that there is an external force causing the sheep to be afflicted. The rod and staff of the Good Shepherd are more necessary for the people's protection than is immediately apparent. Dangers that are obvious to the shepherd may not be so to the sheep, but if they will follow the shepherd and trust him, he will see to their welfare. So it is with God and His people, for the Lord will shepherd His flock, and those who are wise will rely on the Good Shepherd and trust in Him in every circumstance.

YHWH-M'Kadesh

This discussion of the names of God began with a consideration of the meaning of the word *holy*, and the concept that God's name is holy. In fact, the rendering of Isaiah 57:15 in the New American Standard Version of the Bible begins in this way:

For thus says the high and exalted One
Who lives forever, whose name is Holy,

The Names of God

"I dwell on a high and holy place,
And also with the contrite and lowly of spirit ... ."   Isaiah 57:15

The concept of something being "holy" involves the concept of sacredness, or being set apart for sacred purposes. As I have said, *holy* means "other." God is unlike any other. His name is above all other names and is separate. His name is to be treated differently from others, and that is the reason the "Lord's Prayer" begins with the phrase *"hallowed be Thy name,"* which means that God's name should always be held in the highest esteem and mentioned with the utmost respect.

This name, *YHWH-M'Kadesh,* basically means "I AM the Lord Who Sanctifies You." Just as God is holy, He desires for His people to be holy. Therefore the Scriptures say, *"You shall be holy, for I am holy"* (1 Peter 1:16 and Leviticus 19:2). The root words in both Hebrew and Greek translated as *"holy"* are also translated as *"sanctified."* Holiness and sanctification are synonymous, and several words in the English language that look quite different are actually all derived from the same root and retain the same meaning. Words such as *holy, holiness, sanctification, saint* and *sanctify* are all closely related terms. Therefore, a "saint" is a "holy one."

The name *YHWH-M'Kadesh* (I AM the Lord Who Sanctifies You) is to be found in Exodus 31:13, in the midst of a long passage recording God's words to Moses while he was on Mount Sinai to receive the stone tablets containing the Ten Commandments. The context in which this name of the Lord is found is very significant. A good deal of the message is hidden in a consideration of subjects leading up to the revelation of this name to Moses.

During the several chapters leading up to this point, Moses was given detailed instructions regarding the construction of the Tabernacle, its furnishings and the proper garments for the priests who would officiate in the Tabernacle service. A complete consideration of the symbolism contained in the Tabernacle would require a book of its own, and much has been written on this subject already.

A study of the Tabernacle shows that it was a structure that was literally bursting with symbolism. Practically every aspect of its construction has meaning, and that continues to apply to the lives of both Jewish and Christian believers today.

A brief overview of certain aspects of the Tabernacle symbolism is necessary in order to illustrate the connection between the detailed instructions given to Moses (regarding how it was to be constructed) and God's desire to sanctify His people. The fact that the name *YHWH-M'Kadesh* was revealed in connection with the commandment to observe the sabbath day (the fourth of the Ten Commandments) is also important. But first a discussion of the Tabernacle.

Referring to the diagram on the next page, there were three main parts to the Tabernacle, one external and two inside the tent. Each part had certain pieces of furniture, and the various parts were separated by curtains. Each part of the structure, along with each piece of furniture, was quite significant. Even the way in which the tent itself was constructed was important.

The Tabernacle was a place to worship God, to offer sacrifices and basically "to meet with God." It was, in short, a mobile dwelling of God on the earth. In this sense, the Tabernacle is representative of man, in whom God desires to dwell. He wants men's lives to be places of worship, to have their bodies offered as *"living sacrifices"* to Him (Romans 12:1) and to have them meet with Him in these "tabernacles," or "tents," on a regular basis.

Looking at several aspects of this symbolic structure reveals much about man's inner workings and also about his redemption. (This is certainly not an exhaustive study, nor is this necessarily the only type of symbolism that might be intended by God by the detail of the Tabernacle.)

The three parts of the wilderness Tabernacle represent the three parts of a man — spirit (the Holy of Holies), soul (the Holy Place) and body (the Outer Court). The first two parts are the "inner man," and hence are inside the tent, with the outer part being symbolic of the physical man.

The Outer Court had an altar made of brass for blood sacrifice and a brass laver for washing. Both blood sacrifice and washing are required before we can "meet with God" in our present sinful condition.

The Names of God

The framework of the Tabernacle was covered using four successive layers of varied materials. From inside out, the four layers were as follows: fine woven linen decorated with the faces of the cherubim, woven goat's hair, ram's skins dyed red and badger skins (the New American Standard Version of the Bible says *"porpoise skins,"* Exodus 26:14).

The inner layer of woven linen with cherubim was symbolic of the inner "beauty of holiness" that God desires to be present in His people. Remember from the discussion of the cherubim in Ezekiel that their four faces were representative of the four respective aspects of Christ (king, servant, man and God). The colors used were only three (in addition to white): red, blue and purple.

Red was the color of man, for at least two reasons: (1) He was made of the dust of the earth, which often has a red hue, and (2) his blood was red. In fact, the Hebrew words for man and for red vary by only one letter. Blue was the color of God, since His dwelling was in the heavens. Purple, of course, is the color obtained by mixing red and blue, and is therefore symbolic of the union of God and man.

All of this inner beauty was illuminated only by light from the golden lampstand with its seven oil-burning lamps. There was no

The Wilderness Tabernacle

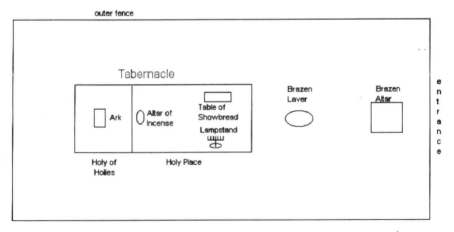

The Living Tapestry

natural light, just as these things cannot be seen with the physical eyes, but only with the illumination of the Spirit of God.

The remaining three layers each represent important aspects of the nature of man. The goat's hair "blankets" are symbolic of the "old nature," or the fallen nature of man. The ram's skins dyed red, of course, are symbolic of the sacrifice of Christ on the cross, and it is very significant that the old nature of man is "sandwiched" between the inner beauty of holiness (decorated with the four aspects of Christ and illuminated by the light of the Holy Spirit) and the atoning sacrifice of Christ on the cross. The outer layer of skin, naturally, represents the fact that man is covered over by a layer of skin on the outside that "separates" the inner man from the outside world.

Looking at the furniture inside the tent, there were three pieces in the Holy Place. Just as the Holy Place is symbolic of the soul of man, the three pieces of furniture can be seen to represent the three components of the soul: the intellect, the will and the emotions. All three pieces of furniture were made of gold (some hammered and some wrought). They were the table for the showbread, the lampstand with seven oil lamps and the altar of incense.

Upon entering, the table and the lamps (Jewish menora) were on either side, directly across from one another. In the same way, in a man, the thoughts determine the will, as a man "makes up his mind." Also, conversely, the setting of the will in a certain direction modifies the way the thoughts are arranged with regard to that particular issue, person or situation.

The altar of incense was located further into the room, near the entrance to the "Holy of Holies," and can be seen to represent the emotions. The thoughts should be arranged and the will set first, and then one can proceed to an emotional response. As the man proceeds from the soul to the spirit, the complete soul must be involved, including the intellect, the will and the emotions, and the transition from soul to spirit can be quite emotional.

The Holy of Holies was the innermost place in the Tabernacle, and it contained the Ark of the Covenant (with the Ten Commandments, a jar of manna and Aaron's rod) covered by the "Mercy Seat." There were two cherubim above this and to each side. This was the place

The Names of God

where the high priest could "meet with God" once each year, at which time he would take a blood sacrifice to sprinkle on the Mercy Seat for the sins of the people.

Now Christ has provided the sacrifice that satisfies the requirement for blood, and this opportunity to "meet with God" is available anytime because of what He has accomplished. Jesus said that *"God is spirit, and those who worship Him must worship in spirit and truth"* (John 4:24). Just as the Holy of Holies represents the spirit of man, it is there where real communion with God occurs. This communion does not bypass our intellects, our wills, our emotions or even our physical bodies, but rather occurs in the context of them all — as God has ordained.

There is much more detail that could be discussed regarding the Tabernacle and all of the meaning contained in it, but hopefully this will suffice to illustrate the importance of revealing the name *YHWH-M'Kadesh* in close association with the Tabernacle instructions. God is holy, and He is making His people to be a holy people. The Tabernacle, as an illustration of man and his relationship with God, shows many aspects of this process, especially if one considers the complex interrelationships between all of the various parts and the way in which Christ is intimately intertwined into each one. Even our inner thoughts and motives must be illuminated by His Spirit, with constant reminders of Christ and who He is, as we approach God and have fellowship with Him.

Considering all of these things, it certainly appears to be no accident that God revealed this name, *YHWH-M'Kadesh*, in connection with the Tabernacle construction.

Since this is a study of names, it is also very instructive to take a look at the names of the men whom God commissioned to do the actual construction of the tent, to make the gold and brass furniture and all of the various types of ornate work that was required. The names of these men are listed in Exodus chapter 31. The first one named was Bezalel. *Bezalel* means "in the shadow or protection of God."

> *Now the Lord spoke to Moses, saying, "See, I have called by name Bezalel, the son of Uri, the son of Hur, of the tribe of Judah. And I have*

The Living Tapestry

filled him with the Spirit of God in wisdom, in understanding, in knowledge, and in all kinds of craftsmanship, to make artistic designs for work in gold, in silver, and in bronze, and in the cutting of stones for settings and in the carving of wood, that he may work in all kinds of craftsmanship. And behold, I Myself have appointed with him Oholiab, the son of Ahisamach, of the tribe of Dan; and in the hearts of all who are skillful I have put skill, that they may make all that I have commanded you." Exodus 31:1-6

The text goes on for four more verses describing the list of things they would be making, using the skill that God would instill in them.

In order to properly see the significance of the name *Bezalel*, it is necessary to look at two other passages of scripture dealing with the protection of God in the lives of those who trust in Him:

*He who dwells in the shelter of the Most High
Will abide in the shadow of the Almighty.* Psalm 91:1

*For in the day of trouble He will conceal me in His tabernacle;
In the secret place of His tent He will hide me;
He will lift me up on a rock.* Psalm 27:5

The fact that God *"called by name Bezalel,"* and commissioned him personally *"by name,"* has great significance. Putting all of this together, along with the symbolism contained in the Tabernacle, begins to open up a great deal of meaning that might otherwise be hidden.

It is also instructive to look at other names in the passage. *Uri* means "light," and *Hur* (as was noted previously in the discussion of *YHWH-Nissi*) means "hole" or "prison." This entire progression also comes from the tribe of Judah, the tribe from which the Messiah would later appear. Just as Bezalel came forth from Uri, who in turn came forth from Hur, the position of being in the shadow of the Almighty "comes forth" from being "enlightened," and that frequently proceeds from adversity.

Just in case these things might be overlooked, God named Bezalel's helper *"Oholiab, the son of Ahisamach,"* so that the significance of the

The Names of God

names would be sure to stand out and not be missed. *Oholiab* means "the father's tent," and *Ahisamach* means "brother of strength." Oholiab was called as the "brother" to strengthen and help Bezalel in the construction of "the Father's tent." It quickly becomes apparent that all of these names were chosen purposefully by God in order to add meaning to the story and to add to our understanding of His ways and His purposes.

As if all of this were not enough, the name *YHWH-M'Kadesh* is revealed in close association with a reiteration of the commandment to observe the sabbath. Not only are all of the aforementioned things an integral part of understanding the process of being made holy, but the keeping of the sabbath is somehow closely intertwined with this concept. This may hold special meaning in today's culture, as it becomes increasingly busy and stressful, giving less and less importance to the observance of one day of the week as the Lord's Day.

The argument we hear is that, after all, Christian people today are under "grace," and not under "the Law." This is taken by many as an indication that keeping the sabbath day holy is no longer important. None of the same people, however, promote idolatry, murder or adultery (or if they do, the Bible has special things to say about them). Certainly, those who are in Christ are no longer under the Jewish Law and should not be encouraged to try keeping it! Yet, somehow, the keeping of one day each week, set apart for rest and for remembering God, is important in the process of making God's people holy. Even though not a legalistic requirement, the One who made mankind knows what works best in this process, and all of this should not be discarded offhand. The revelation of this name of God, "I AM the Lord Who Sanctifies You," in such close juxtaposition with this discussion of the sabbath day sends a very strong message.

The discussion of this name has been the longest, due mostly to the need to provide an overview of the Tabernacle symbolism. However, perhaps this is appropriate, since the process of making God's people holy sometimes seems like a rather long process. This is one of the mysteries of the Christian faith, as the Bible says of the finished work of Jesus Christ: *"For by one offering He has perfected for all time those who are sanctified"* (Hebrews 10:14). The actual meaning of this last phrase in the Greek is more accurately translated "those who are being sanctified." Therein lies the paradox: that the believer in Christ has been made perfect and is even now being perfected.

YHWH-Sabaoth

This name is generally translated as *"The Lord of Hosts"* (1 Samuel 15:2), but it actually implies not just hosts (great numbers of individuals), but armies. The root word in the Hebrew language carries the meaning of "to wage war" or "to serve." There is no way to know how many angels and people this includes, not to mention the possibility of other types of beings about which we know nothing whatsoever. At the present time, there are some who are in rebellion, [6] but that is temporary. God is simply waiting until His plan is fulfilled and all of His people are brought into His Kingdom. Then, all opposition will be eliminated.

Of the children of Abraham alone, God said that they would be as numerous as the stars of the heavens and the sand on the seashore. How much more innumerable must be all of the hosts over which He is Lord! The Scriptures are not exaggerating when they say that His greatness is *"unsearchable"*!

Endnotes:

1. This concept is developed more fully in Chapters 6, 8 and 12.
2. For a basic outline of the history of Israel, please refer to Appendix B.
3. Please refer to Chapter 3 regarding name changes.
4. Refer to Chapter 3, "Name Changes," and to Chapter 12.
5. See the chapter on Babylon.
6. See the chapter on Babylon and the meaning of the name *Nimrod*.

Chapter Three

Isaiah

I awoke this morning with an unusual sensation in my chest. It wasn't an oppressive feeling, but rather on expanding one. It felt as though I could breathe more deeply than usual, and the air seemed clearer and more crisp.

I'm not sure when it happened. It must have been gradual. But the years of hard work and busy schedules probably had a lot to do with it. Certainly there were some hard times that added their share as well. I guess the main thing that was missing was spontaneity. Everything was planned all the time, and each day was so full! Busy-ness had taken its toll. I had come to the point of believing that was all life was about. The colors had become muted and the music all too familiar.

But now, there is suddenly a new brightness around me, an invigorating sense of expectation. There is a fresh breeze blowing softly through my mind, and I can imagine a fragrance, barely perceptible, but nonetheless pleasant. Even my vision seems sharper, with more ability to see things afar off.

All this is not only unexpected, but unexplainable. I really have no good reason for it that I'm aware of. Yes, my wife is expecting our first child, but I have known about that for several months, without being affected in any way similar to this. It is as though a deep, new hope has arisen within, something enduring and far-reaching. I certainly have never felt like this before.

Last night, we discussed what name to give to our coming son. Surely it will be a son. We talked about possibly giving him the name Isaiah. Such a hopeful name! Could that have something to do with this feeling? I'm not really the type of person to have premonitions or things like that.

Some of this feeling sounds like that dream my wife had several months ago. After that dream she said to me, "Oh, Amoz, I could sense such great hope and such a wonderful future," but I am afraid that I didn't pay too much attention to her. They say that women who are with child may act strangely sometimes, and I thought no more about it. Until now ...

If this is anything like what she was trying to explain to me, then no wonder she seemed so excited about a simple dream. I wonder if these things could have anything to do with our little Isaiah.

── Name Changes ──

It should certainly be apparent by now that the meanings of the names in the Bible are very significant. Of course, the most important ones are those that apply to God Himself, since He is the Author of all of this, and it is He who is at center stage. Just as early man thought that the sun, the moon and all of the stars revolved around the earth (for so it appeared), so men throughout the ages have often thought that all of life revolved around man and all of his pursuits.

All of life actually revolves around the Creator, and the previous chapter hopefully served as a reminder of that fact. As other names are examined, and their meanings explored, it is best to remain cognizant of the fact that God's name is greater, that He is in charge of the entire scene and that it is He who oversees all of these things. That type of realization will help to keep things in perspective as various names are studied.

Even though the names of God are of paramount importance, He nevertheless imparts great significance to the names of people in the Bible. This is especially true of certain key individuals who are founders of the faith, and who, by virtue of their position, hold great importance in the establishment of patterns and figures of the manner in which God desires to relate to men.

The one individual who stands out among all others in this regard is Abraham. His entire life, along with the lives of his children for several generations, was filled with symbolism that is still relevant to the lives of all of God's people. This is what the Lord says in the book of Isaiah:

> *"Listen to me, you who pursue righteousness, who seek the Lord: Look to the rock from which you were hewn, and to the quarry from which you were dug. Look to Abraham your father, and to Sarah who gave birth to you in pain; when he was one I called him, then I blessed him and multiplied him."*   Isaiah 51:1-2

The Living Tapestry

In this chapter, I want to review several of the cases in the Scriptures when names were changed and what that meant. Since several of those name changes took place in the time of Abraham and his offspring (his name was changed, his wife's name was changed and the name of their grandson, Jacob, was changed), it is first necessary to study the symbolism present in their lives. There were several other people whose names were changed in very significant ways, including the apostles Peter and Paul, but it is important to begin with the patriarchs and then proceed from there.

ABRAM/ABRAHAM, SARAI/SARAH AND JACOB/ISRAEL

When the biblical story of Abraham began, he was living in Mesopotamia in a place called Ur of the Chaldees. The same region would later be called Babylon. It was a land of idolatry, and God called Abraham out of there to another place (apparently not telling him exactly where he was going when he left Ur).

At the time, his name was not *Abraham*, but *Abram*, meaning "exalted father." His wife's name was *Sarai*, "my princess." The two of them travelled out of Mesopotamia, making their way to the west, into the area that would become the "Promised Land" of their descendants.

Over the years, God spoke to Abraham several times. During one such encounter, the Lord promised to bless him greatly, but Abram, as he was still called, asked what God would give him, since he had no heir and was obviously getting older (see Genesis 15:2-3). God promised that Abram's heir would come from his own body, and that He would multiply his descendants as the stars in the sky (see Genesis 15:4-5). Unfortunately, Abram and Sarai grew tired of waiting, and Sarai convinced Abram to have a child by her maid Hagar. Thus Ishmael was born when Abram was eighty-six years old (see Genesis 16).

In Genesis chapter 17, when Abram was ninety-nine years old, the Lord spoke to him as "God Almighty" (El-Shaddai). He renewed His promise to multiply his seed and to make a covenant with him. During that encounter, God told Abram that he was to change his name from *Abram* ("exalted father") to *Abraham* ("father of a multitude"). Also, *Sarai* ("my princess") was to change her name to *Sarah* ("princess").

Name Changes

God made it quite clear that Sarah would bear Abraham a child, and that that child would be the one through whom God would bless Abraham's descendants. The entire idea seemed so farfetched to Abraham that he *"fell on his face and laughed"* (Genesis 17:17). Because of Abraham's response, God told him that Sarah would indeed bear his son, and that the child should be named *Isaac* ("he laughs," or "laughter").

After the birth of Isaac, the events of Abraham's life continued to contain more and more symbolism, and that symbolism became even more obvious. Abraham had become a representative symbol of the heavenly Father, so that the New Testament would call him *"the father of us all"* (Romans 4:16).

Many aspects of Abraham's life and of the lives of his offspring would take on a great deal of meaning for all people of faith down through the ages. If Abraham represented the Father, then his son Isaac could be seen to symbolize Jesus Christ in certain respects. The meaning of his name, "laughter," might at first seem out of place, since the life of Christ contained such intense suffering. When Isaiah spoke of the Christ, he called Him a *"man of sorrows"* who was *"acquainted with grief"* (Isaiah 53:3). However, it must be remembered that the period of suffering was not the final goal, but rather a step along the way. The final result is to be one of joy and great happiness, and Christ will rejoice over His people:

> *"But be glad and rejoice forever in what I create;*
> *For behold, I create Jerusalem for rejoicing,*
> *And her people for gladness.*
> *I will also rejoice in Jerusalem, and be glad in My people."*
>   Isaiah 65:18-19

When Isaac was about twelve years old, God told Abraham to go up to the land of *Moriah* ("the bitterness of Yah"), and to sacrifice his only son, Isaac (see Genesis 22:2). There God provided a ram for the sacrifice in the place of Isaac. [1] In several different ways, Abraham's role was firmly established as symbolically representing God the Father Himself. The instruction to sacrifice his only son foreshadowed the sacrifice of Jesus Christ nearly two thousand years later.

The Living Tapestry

As time passed, Abraham's life continued to consistently portray the same symbolism. Even the lives of some of those around him took on symbolic meaning, simply due to their association with him. The act of Abraham sending his servant back to Ur in order to obtain a wife for his son clearly represented the heavenly Father sending His Holy Spirit to the land of idolatry and sin to get a Bride for His Son. The young bride had to leave the place she was living in and go to live with the son in the presence of the father. So it is to be with the Church, the Bride of Christ.

The young woman who was chosen to be the bride for Isaac was named *Rebekah*, which means "a rope" or "a noose," thereby signifying an "ensnarer." Here again is a name that at first glance appears to be rather incongruous, possibly leading to the opinion that the meaning of her name held no particular significance. However, further consideration only serves to enhance the impact of her name. Hidden deep within the beautiful young bride of Isaac was a self-serving bent that was not above the use of intrigue. She was later instrumental in influencing her son Jacob to cheat his own brother out of both his birthright and his father's blessing (see Genesis 27).

Even with her innate defects, Rebekah can be seen to represent the Church (the Greek word for church, *ecclesia*, means "called-out ones") of Jesus Christ. She was called out of Ur (what would later be Babylon) to be the bride of Isaac, the one who was symbolic of Christ Himself, just as the Church is called out of the world to be the Bride of Christ. In precisely the same fashion as in Rebekah's life, the believer in Christ carries along with him (or her) some part of his lower nature, which invariably has certain untoward effects, not only upon himself, but also upon his offspring.

The changes we will shortly examine in Jacob, the son of Isaac and Rebekah, will illustrate the fact that God fully intends to deal with this unholy part of the inner nature inherited by His children when they are born into this world. In fact, God is able to change people to such an extent that the ungodly inner nature is completely done away with. There is a new life that can then be lived in fellowship with God Almighty! That is the reason the New Testament says that *"if any man is in Christ, he is a new creature; the old things passed away; behold, new things have come"* (2 Corinthians 5:17).

Name Changes

After a number of years and in spite of a problem with infertility (like Isaac's parents, but not lasting nearly as long), the marriage of Isaac and Rebekah brought forth the twins, Esau and Jacob. Esau was born first and was very hairy — hence the name *Esau*, which means "hairy." Jacob came quickly afterwards, reportedly grasping the heel of Esau, thereby obtaining the name *Jacob*, meaning "he who grasps by the heel" or "supplanter." The name not only carried the connotation of a grabber, but also of a deceiver, describing Jacob's nature quite well.

Esau was a man of the world, a hunter and the favorite of his father. Jacob, however, was the favorite of his mother, and he apparently adopted some of her less desirable characteristics. He obtained his brother's birthright by trading him a single bowl of "red stew" when he was extremely hungry (for this Esau was also called *Edom*, which means "red"). Then, upon his mother's advice, Jacob deceived his father Isaac into giving him the blessing that was reserved for the firstborn son. Jacob thus managed to take both his brother's birthright and the family blessing that would otherwise have belonged to Esau. In the process, he made Esau so angry that he intended to kill Jacob, and would have done so if his mother had not heard about it and warned Jacob to flee for his life (see Genesis 27:41-45).

These two men, Jacob and Esau, can be seen as representing two types of people born as children of the Kingdom of God on earth. Both men were of the same father, whom we have seen as representing the Lord Jesus Christ. Both were born of the same mother, the Church. They were both born under identical circumstances at practically the same moment, and yet their essential natures were different, for in Romans 9:13 the Bible says, *"Jacob I loved, but Esau I hated."* Esau represents the man of the flesh, ruled by his appetites, for whom the spiritual things have no importance. For Jacob, however, spiritual things were very important, but he nevertheless had a rather deceitful nature that caused him a lot of trouble.

After Jacob struggled with these things for many years, suffering a good deal in the process, he had an encounter with God in which he wrestled with the angel of the Lord at a stream called *Jabbok* ("emptying"). Toward the end of the encounter, the angel said to him, *"Your*

The Living Tapestry

name shall no longer be Jacob, but Israel; for you have striven with God and with men and have prevailed" (Genesis 32:28).

Israel means "he who strives with God," and Jacob limped the rest of his life because of his struggle with God at the Jabbok. When it says that he *"prevailed,"* it does not mean that he prevailed against God, but rather that he had prevailed in the struggle against his lower nature, the deceitful "Jacob" part of his nature.

Reviewing the significance of these name changes, it is important to remember that Abraham and Sarah were the first two people in the Bible to experience such a thing and the only married couple who both had their names changed by God. The fact that God changed Abram's name from "exalted father" to "father of a multitude" is quite significant in terms of what God was saying, not only about Abraham, but also about Himself!

Remember that Abraham, as the father of all believers in God, was symbolic of God the Father. God was already an exalted Father before He created man upon the earth. However, the Bible says that God is in the process of bringing many sons to glory (see Hebrews 2:10). God the Father is actually changing His own role from that of an exalted Father to being the Father of a multitude! Imagine the significance of the eternal, almighty God of all creation changing His role in some way and revealing the whole process to mankind. No wonder the Bible says that these are things into which even angels long to look (1 Peter 1:12). Certainly God already had a multitude of beings under His authority, as He is the Lord of Hosts, but only through the process of the redemption and sanctification of men will He have many sons sharing His glory!

The fact that God also told Abraham to change his wife's name further emphasizes this theme, since she was changed from simply "my princess" (*Sarai*) to "princess" (*Sarah*). She is no longer just "his princess," but rather "the Princess" in a vast line of royalty!

Keeping all of these things in mind makes the change of Jacob's name to *Israel* appear even more significant. Every child of God has to struggle with God because of the deceitful nature residing within the heart of each of us. The Bible describes the condition of mankind by

Name Changes

saying, *"The heart is more deceitful than all else and is desperately sick; who can understand it?"* (Jeremiah 17:9). The Hebrew word translated as *"deceitful"* in this well-known verse is actually very closely related to the name *Jacob*, and only serves to reinforce this entire analogy.

Unfortunately, our evil inner nature does not go away easily, and the process required for the change may result in a painful injury such as "a limp that never goes away." We cannot struggle with God and come away without some kind of lasting effect. The fact that this struggle occurred at the Jabbok is also quite significant, since an "emptying" is required when the believer comes to terms with God. We must be emptied of the selfish part that would strive with God, and we must give up the deceitful nature that insists on seeking its selfish desires by ungodly means.

The change from *Jacob* to *Israel* is therefore a general pattern that is applicable to the life of every believer. The "true Israel of God," therefore, actually includes all of His people in whom He brings this change to pass. Therefore the Bible says:

> *For they are not all Israel who are descended from Israel; neither are they all children because they are Abraham's descendants, but: "THROUGH ISAAC YOUR DESCENDANTS WILL BE NAMED." That is, it is not the children of the flesh who are children of God, but the children of the promise are regarded as descendants.*
> Romans 9:6-8

> *Therefore, be sure that it is those who are of faith who are sons of Abraham.* Galatians 3:7

Thus the name *Israel* holds great significance when understood in the context of the inner nature of man and the struggles involved in the process of being changed into God's image. When God said, *"Let Us make man in Our image"* (Genesis 1:26), there was no hint of the magnitude of the process involved. However, in the counsel of God, all of these things were understood beforehand. When the devil sought to spoil God's creation, and even when he sought to murder the Son of

The Living Tapestry

God, he was actually playing right into God's hand! Jacob would be changed into Israel, and the pattern for the making of the children of God would be established. The entire process was set in motion by the Creator of the universe and made possible by the blood of His Son, Jesus Christ.

There is another aspect of Jacob's struggle at the Jabbok which on the surface is rather shocking. As the Lord Jesus Christ is *the* pattern of faith and obedience in every particular, so even He went through this same process! In spite of the fact that He had no inner defect to be purged away, He was confronted with the same choice — whether to be a selfish grabber or to empty Himself for a higher good.

The struggle Jesus experienced in the garden of *Gethsemane* ("oil press") is well known. There He asked His Father to *"remove this cup"* from Him if there was any other way, but He then said, *"Yet not My will, but Thine be done"* (Luke 22:42). The biblical account says that He sweated great drops of blood because the struggle was so great (see verse 44).

However, there was one decision that preceded Gethsemane. It was one that required a decision not to grasp something extremely desirable ("grasping," as *Jacob's* name would suggest), but rather to undergo a great emptying (*Jabbok's* meaning) instead. This is what the Bible says regarding Jesus Christ:

> *... who, although He existed in the form of God, did not regard equality with God a thing to be grasped, but emptied Himself, taking the form of a bond-servant, and being made in the likeness of men.*
> Philippians 2:6-7

The Scriptures do not describe how great a struggle was involved in this decision, but it would not require a very great imagination to see how difficult that might have been. To give up being God to become a common Jew under the control of Rome! And yet, because of His love and obedience to the Father, Jesus did just that.

By comparison, most men's struggles should not seem so difficult, as they leave behind a deceitful and "grabbing" nature, emptying themselves so that God can fill them with His own life and love!

Name Changes

NATHANAEL

The discussion of Jesus with Nathanael is recorded only in the first chapter of the book of John. In fact, Nathanael is not even named in the other gospels. It is commonly believed that Nathanael was another name for Bartholomew, who was one of the twelve disciples listed in the other gospels. The fact that he is called Nathanael in this passage serves to emphasize and reinforce the message contained in the narrative. The name *Nathanael* means "God has given," or "gift of God," and the story describes a conversation between Jesus and Nathanael.

When Nathanael was introduced to Jesus, He immediately said of him, *"Behold, an Israelite indeed, in whom is no guile!"* (John 1:47). The story does not explain why, but Nathanael was so impressed by this statement that he then declared that Jesus was *"the Son of God"* and *"the King of Israel"* (John 1:49).

After that statement, Jesus said to Nathanael, *"You shall see greater things than these. ... you shall see the heavens opened, and the angels of God ascending and descending on the Son of Man"* (John 1:50-51). When Jesus made that statement, the reference to Jacob was made very clear, since the vision of angels ascending and descending from an opened Heaven was basically a description of Jacob's dream at Bethel (see Genesis 28:12). The reference to Nathanael as *"an Israelite indeed, in whom is no guile"* brings to mind the alteration from *Jacob* (a name that suggests "guile") to *Israel.*

All of this taken together describes the work of God in mankind, changing men from creatures of guile and deception into "true Israelites." Just as Nathanael's name would suggest, the entire process is a "gift of God." Hence we see that, even though the usage of a different name in the passage (*Nathanael* instead of *Bartholomew*) was not a name change *per se,* the appearance of the new name served several purposes. It drew attention to the passage as something set apart and special, while at the same time helping to bring to mind the name change from *Jacob* to *Israel.* Also, the meaning of the newly used name added significantly to the understanding of the entire passage, serving as yet another reminder that the entire salvation process is the "gift of God." It is also interesting that only John, among the gospel writers, used the name Nathanael, since the names of these two men have almost the same meaning. ²

Simon/Peter

Peter is the only Bible character who is routinely referred to by both his original name and his newly given name at the same time. It is not unusual to hear him spoken of as Simon Peter, and in fact, this double name is frequently used in the Scriptures when referring to him (for instance, see Matthew 16:16).

Peter is arguably the most interesting of the twelve disciples to study (for a number of reasons) and is often cited for his seemingly contrasting character traits. He seemed to have the usual human passions, but often they were accentuated to an unusual degree. Peter was generally steadfast, yet impetuous. He was bold and brave, yet he denied the Lord before a servant girl. He was full of good intentions, but he was unable to fulfill them. It is this double nature that makes Peter so interesting, and at the same time so comfortingly human. It is this very duality that stands as a reason to use both his old and new names together.

The very passage in the Bible that records the details surrounding the change of Peter's name by the Lord Jesus not only tells of a revelation given to him by God the Father in Heaven, but also says that his subsequent words were motivated by Satan. Unfortunately, we are all just like Simon Peter as we begin to relate to God and hear things from Him. We are still plagued by such contrasting motives and such limited understanding that we can hear from God at one moment and then be duped by the devil in the next. There is still hope for us, however, as we remember how much Peter changed when the Holy Spirit came upon him at Pentecost!

The circumstances surrounding the change in Simon's name to Peter and the meanings of the names themselves hold great significance not only for Peter, but for every disciple of Jesus Christ. The passage that describes this begins with a question from Jesus, *"Who do people say that the Son of Man is?"* (Matthew 16:13). The answers vary. Some say He is God, while others say He is just a good man, or at most a prophet.

Name Changes

Jesus' next question is the key not only to this passage, but to the destiny of each reader and seeker throughout the ages.

Jesus asked, *"But who do you say that I am?"* (Matthew 16:15). That question divides the potential disciple from the man who can never decide what to think. It is the question that must not be ignored, and if it is, then all is lost. It is the central "first" question of the entire Bible, where the following question is "Then how will you respond to Me?"

In Peter's response to this key question, we see the Lord changing Simon's name to Peter. *Simon* means "heard" or "hearing," and is derived from the Old Testament name *Simeon*. *Peter* means "stone" or "rock," and he is the apostle who later wrote to the Church, saying:

> *You also, as living stones, are being built up as a spiritual house for a holy priesthood, to offer up spiritual sacrifices acceptable to God through Jesus Christ.* 1 Peter 2:5

Peter had answered Jesus' question, *"Thou art the Christ, the Son of the living God"* (Matthew 16:16). To that statement, Jesus replied, *"Blessed are you, Simon Barjona, because flesh and blood did not reveal this to you, but My Father who is in heaven. And I also say to you that you are Peter [Greek, petros], and upon this rock [Greek, petra] I will build My church; and the gates of Hades shall not overpower it"* (Matthew 16:17-18). Here we see the key question, the proper response, the means of learning that led to that response and the resulting change in the person who was involved in the process. Simon had "heard" from God about who Jesus was and thereby became a "stone" to be built into the spiritual Temple of God.

Even Peter's surname *Barjona* is found to be significant. *Barjona* means "son of Jonah" or perhaps "son of John," as Jesus is later quoted as saying (see John 21:15). *Jonah* means "dove," and *John* means "Jehovah's gift." Therefore it appears that Peter's ability to hear these things proceeded forth from the Father as a gift, by the agency of the Holy Spirit, who is elsewhere referred to as a dove.

In other words, Peter's ability to hear spiritual truth was the direct "offspring" of the Father's gift from Heaven and the Holy Spirit, who brings His gifts to us. The gift of the great I AM brings forth the ability to hear the truth, resulting in a person being changed from one who hears into one who is a part of the true temple of God Almighty! *"So faith comes from hearing, and hearing by the word of Christ"* (Romans 10:17).

The first mention of the Church in the New Testament (see Matthew 16:18) is found in connection with this story, further emphasizing the significance of these things in the life of *every* believer in Christ. As Christ speaks of building His Church, He uses two different words for a rock. When He speaks of Peter, He uses the word *petros*, the basic word for a single rock. However, when Jesus says *"on this rock I will build my church,"* He uses the word *petra*, signifying a huge mass of rock, or possibly even "bedrock." When He says "on this huge mass of rock," He is saying that the Church will be built on the rock of Christ as the foundation, but the building itself will be constructed of individual rocks fitted together properly, as only God can do.

What follows almost immediately after this amazing story seems, at first, out of place, and also somewhat harsh. Jesus says to Peter, *"Get behind Me, Satan! You are a stumbling block to Me; for you are not setting your mind on God's interests, but man's"* (verse 23). This was quite a change from congratulating Peter for hearing from God the Father in Heaven! However, a closer look reveals that this is not just a strange and unusual exchange of words, but rather it expresses several typical responses of humans, and of the devil as well.

The Lord says, in the parable of the sower, that as soon as the Word of God comes, then the devil comes immediately to try to take it away (see Mark 4:15). If he is not able to take the Word of God away entirely, then he will try to trick us into applying it wrongly. This is frequently possible, since we have a rather limited understanding of the things of God and tend to interpret them in the light of our worldly point of view, especially early in our Christian experience.

The goal of Christian maturity is that eventually we will learn to discern the difference between the Word of God and anything that might be added on afterward, and not allow ourselves to be deceived. Understanding the names of God and their meanings helps immensely in understanding His nature and His purposes, and it helps to insure

Name Changes

against falling into some of these traps, since we are not so easily fooled when we know God better.

Of course, simply knowing facts *about* God is no substitute for actually *knowing God personally,* which is only achieved by walking humbly with Him. This personal knowledge of God is the only real safeguard against such errors. It is precisely this sort of personal relationship that God has been in the process of establishing in men and women throughout history.

When the children of God are completed, no devil will be able to deceive them, because they will know God's Word and will also personally know Him! They will know His name, which reveals His character and His purposes. Men and women who have heard from God will have been built into a spiritual Temple, each person an individual stone in the edifice, and it will be a holy habitation of God Almighty!

SAUL/PAUL

Saul of Tarsus was busy persecuting Christians when he was radically changed by his encounter with the risen Christ on the road to Damascus. It is generally thought that Saul's name was changed to Paul at that point in time. However, the Damascus road experience is described in Acts chapter nine, and the name Paul is not mentioned until chapter thirteen. Saul is mentioned several times in the interim, but the new name, *Paul,* is not.

It has been suggested that the change in Saul's name to Paul was because of the conversion of the proconsul of Cyprus, Sergius Paulus. Indeed, it was in the midst of that story that the name *Paul* was first mentioned. The narrative does not give the details surrounding this particular name change, but rather simply changes the name used when referring to the apostle, and from then on, it never changes back again.

Whatever we might surmise about the circumstances surrounding the changing of Saul's name to Paul would be purely conjecture. Nevertheless, there is something to be said about the meanings of the two names, and what significance that might have. The first name, *Saul,* means "desired." *Paul*, as we have already seen in chapter one, means "small." It can be no accident that this man, who said that his religious credentials had been impeccable, but who gladly relinquished them in order to serve Jesus Christ, later described himself as *"the least of the apostles"* (1 Corinthians 15:9) and even *"the least of all saints"* (Ephesians 3:8). This humility served him very well, and allowed him to serve the Lord as probably the most powerful saint and apostle of his time. The one who had been "desired" because of his outstanding performance in his religion chose to be called "small," and thereby he became great.

This same pattern applies to everyone, including Jesus Christ Himself. The Bible says that *"whoever exalts himself shall be humbled; and whoever humbles himself shall be exalted"* (Matthew 23:12). As we have seen from the discussion of Jacob and his change to Israel, even Jesus Christ "emptied Himself" and humbled Himself, and therefore *"God highly exalted Him"* (Philippians 2:9). The way to become great in the Kingdom of God is to become small.

Levi/Matthew

Matthew is the disciple who wrote the first book in the New Testament, but he was formerly named Levi. Again, we are not told the details of when and why his name was changed, but only that it occurred. The facts surrounding his former life, together with the meanings of the two names, will show that the change was quite significant. Just as in all of these instances of name changes in the Scriptures, there is a message for all believers hidden in the story.

Levi ("attached") was a tax collector and found a way to become somewhat wealthy at the expense of his countrymen. He was working for the Roman government, extracting money from his own people. Frequently, the tax collectors of that day would add a little extra to the bill and keep it for themselves. By that method, they became fairly well-to-do.

When Jesus called Levi away from that lifestyle, he threw a party and invited *"many tax-gatherers and sinners"* (Matthew 9:10), so he had apparently gained quite a few friends who were living the same way. In the books of Mark and Luke, he was called *Levi* at the time when

Name Changes

Jesus called him, and then later called *Matthew* (which means "gift of Jehovah," and is short for *Mattathias*). In the book of Matthew, the name *Levi* is not used at all. It is as though the change is so complete that the changed man no longer even recognizes the former name.

We see here a very clear picture of the man who was "attached" to the things of the world, doing whatever he had to in order to make as much money as possible. After the call of Jesus in his life, he became a true disciple, the change being the result of the "gift of Jehovah." This should be a particularly relevant example in today's world, with its emphasis on the economy and the markets. Matthew was delivered from his attachment to such things, and became a disciple of Jesus, the Messiah, eventually writing the first book of the New Testament.

Each of us must make this same type of change in our own lives in order to properly follow Jesus Christ.

HOSHEA/JOSHUA

The name *Joshua* has the same meaning as the name *Jesus* in the New Testament. Joshua was the leader of God's people during the conquest of the Promised Land, and is commonly seen as a "type" of Christ in the Old Testament. The changing of his name almost goes unnoticed, in spite of the fact that it is vitally important. It was mentioned only, almost in passing, in Numbers 13:16.

When Moses was about to send out twelve spies into the land of Canaan, the man who was mentioned as leader of the tribe of Ephraim was *Hoshea* (sometimes written *Oshea*), which means "salvation." The text then simply says, *"but Moses called Hoshea the son of Nun, Joshua."* From then on, the old name was never used again.

Joshua's name was thus changed from "salvation" to "the Lord is salvation." On the surface this change seems insignificant, but forty years later, it was this man who led the people in victory as they conquered the Promised Land. After all was said and done, and especially after the real Savior of God's people had come with the name that had the same meaning, everyone could see how very crucial had been the change that Moses had made in Hoshea's life.

How often God says or does something that seems small at the moment, but has eternal implications!

The Living Tapestry

GIDEON/JERUBBAAL

The story of Gideon took place at a time in the Israelites' history when they were being sorely oppressed by a large group of people known as Midianites (see Judges 6:1-6). The Midianites were a nomadic desert people who were descended from Abraham and his second wife, Keturah (whom he married after Sarah's death).

The name *Midian* actually means "strife." The Midianites were described as being *"like locusts"* in number (Judges 6:5). They, along with their livestock, would descend upon the Israelites soon after planting season, destroying everything in their path, and leaving the children of Israel devastated.

The children of Israel cried out to God in their distress, and He answered by sending an angel to appoint Gideon as their deliverer. Of course, Gideon, who at the time was threshing grain in a winepress hiding from the Midianites, responded by saying, in effect, "Who, me?" He did not see himself as, in any way, qualified for such an assignment. Nevertheless, after a few small tests, to be sure that it was indeed the Lord who was addressing him, he was obedient.

Gideon's first assignment was very interesting — in view of the meaning of his name (see Judges 6:25). *Gideon* means "he who cuts down." God told him to tear down the altar of Baal and to cut down the idolatrous Asherah poles. He was then to build an altar to the Lord and offer a bull on it, using the Asherah poles for firewood. The destiny contained in Gideon's name was fulfilled when he obeyed the word of God.

When the people found out what Gideon had done, they demanded that he be put to death. Gideon's father spoke in his defense by saying that if Baal were indeed a god, he should contend for himself. It was at that point that Gideon's name was changed to *Jerubbaal*, meaning "let Baal contend." The name was chosen to signify that Baal himself (rather than the people) should contend against Gideon. Baal, of course, failed to prevail.

After Gideon obeyed the Lord in this first deed, he went on to gain a great victory for Israel against the Midianites — in spite of what seemed like impossible odds.

Name Changes

There are several other truths that become apparent when the meanings of the Midianites' names are considered. The fact that *Midian* means "strife" is extremely important, and several lessons can be gleaned from this story about the causes of strife and some of its consequences. Strife is extremely damaging in interpersonal relationships and should be carefully avoided, but in spite of its dangers, every family and society has had to deal with it — to one degree or another. The human condition often seems to invite trouble.

It is pivotal in understanding this symbolism of "strife" to realize that Midian had two kings and two "lesser" leaders, each of apparently equal authority (Judges 8:3-5). When both sets of leaders were mentioned, there was no suggestion that either person was of higher rank. That was a prescription for strife, since the Lord says clearly in the New Testament that no one can serve two masters.

The Midianites' authority structure was unprecedented, there being no reference to anything similar among the many tribes and nations discussed in the Bible. It was as though the people of Midian were purposefully laying the groundwork for strife in their authority structure. Some of the results of such strife were vividly portrayed in their lifestyle and in the meanings of their leaders' names.

These leaders constantly brought affliction to the people of God, symbolic of the fact that strife always affects God's people in a similar fashion. The names of their two kings reveal a particularly dangerous consequence of strife, but only by combining the meanings of both can the significance be seen. The two kings were *Zebah* ("sacrifice") and *Zalmunna* ("shade or shelter denied"). Together they form a very strange, yet important, combination.

These men were the enemies of God. Although they offered sacrifices (*Zebah*) in an attempt to appease Him, those sacrifices would bring no benefit. Shelter or protection as a gift from God would still be denied (*Zalmunna*). They could not partake of the kind of promise given in Psalm 91:1: *"He who dwells in the shelter of the Most High will abide in the shadow of the Almighty."* The most sobering implication of this analogy is that even the people of God could find themselves in a similar position. By living lives filled with strife, bringing affliction to other people and effectively making themselves "enemies of God," even God's own people can find themselves denied the shelter of the Most High!

The Bible is full of the concept of love, even going so far as to say that *"God is love"* (1 John 4:8). There can be no doubt that the perpetrator of strife places himself in opposition to the Lord. The Bible describes such opposing actions in this way: *"Hatred stirs up strife, but love covers all transgressions"* (Proverbs 10:12).

The imagery continues in the names of the two lesser leaders, *Oreb* ("raven") and *Zeeb* ("wolf"). Both of these names describe consistently evil images in the Scriptures. A wolf is an animal that devours sheep, a common metaphor for God's people. The raven is one of the birds of the air that might devour the seed falling alongside the road in the parable of the sower. That seed is, of course, the Word of God, and the bird devouring it is symbolic of the devil (see Luke 8:11-12). These considerations make the defeat of Midian even more meaningful, showing the blessing of God that comes when strife is abolished.

After Midian was defeated, the land remained undisturbed for forty years while Gideon was alive. He lived into old age and had many sons. Those blessings that God gave through Gideon also affected the entire nation, lasting until the people began to forget how bad things had been previously.

Amazingly, the entire concept of God's help and the people's forgetfulness was implied in the names of Gideon's forefathers. His father was called Joash the Abiezrite, who was descended from Manasseh (the eldest son of Joseph). *Manasseh* means "causing to forget," and through Gideon, God allowed the people to forget their extreme oppression at the hands of the Midianites. Unfortunately, the Israelites also forgot about God's blessing at the hand of Gideon:

> *Then it came about, as soon as Gideon was dead, that the sons of Israel again played the harlot with the Baals, and made Baal-berith their god. Thus the sons of Israel did not remember the* LORD *their God, who had delivered them from the hands of all their enemies on every side; nor did they show kindness to the household of Jerubbaal (that is, Gideon), in accord with all the good that he had done to Israel.*
>
> Judges 8:33-35

Name Changes

The names of both Joash (Gideon's father) and Abiezer (one of his forefathers) fit well into the whole story of Gideon and the deliverance God provided through him. *Abiezer* means "father of help," and *Joash* means "to whom Jehovah hastens" (by implication, "to help"). Gideon brought deliverance to Israel with God's help. In fact, the Lord hastened to his aid, because the deliverance came quite rapidly.

All of this work was begun when Gideon cut down the idols (the meaning of his name), thus earning for him a change in his name. The results of this and the subsequent rapid military victories allowed the people to forget their oppression, but they soon forgot God's blessing (*Manasseh* means "causing to forget"). The meanings of Gideon's family names were wonderfully incorporated into the whole story as it was played out in history.

Pashhur/Magor-missabib

Unlike these examples, and unfortunately for the people involved, not every name change in the Bible was for the better. There are several instances of change from a name with a good meaning to one with evil connotations.

For instance, a man named *Pashhur* ("freedom") was told by the prophet Jeremiah that the Lord had changed his name to *Magor-missabib* ("terror on every side"). The reason for the change is recorded in Jeremiah chapter twenty, as the nation of Israel was about to be defeated by Babylon and the people carried off into captivity. Jeremiah had been prophesying such things for some time, as a warning to the people. However, the people would not repent and turn back to God, and all the calamity that Jeremiah had been foretelling was about to come to pass.

It is not overly difficult to imagine that Jeremiah's message might have been somewhat unpopular. In fact, he angered several prominent people with his predictions, one of whom was Pashhur the priest, the *"chief officer in the house of the* LORD*"* (Jeremiah 20:1). This is what the Bible says:

> Pashhur had Jeremiah the prophet beaten, and put him in the stocks that were at the upper Benjamin Gate, which was by the house of the

The Living Tapestry

> LORD. *Then it came about on the next day, when Pashhur released Jeremiah from the stocks, that Jeremiah said to him, "Pashhur is not the name the* LORD *has called you, but rather Magor-missabib. For thus says the* LORD, *'Behold, I am going to make you a terror to yourself and to all your friends; and while your eyes look on, they will fall by the sword of their enemies. So I shall give over all Judah to the hand of the king of Babylon, and he will carry them away as exiles to Babylon and will slay them with the sword.'"*   Jeremiah 20:2-4

In this tragic example, we see the loss of freedom and the onset of terror on every side, not only for one man, but for the whole nation. All the people were acting the same way, ignoring the warnings of God's prophet and being vindictive toward him, instead of listening to what was being said.

It is quite possible that the name of Pashhur's father is also significant. The Bible says that Pashhur was the son of *Immer*, which means "talkative." Jeremiah said that everyone was mocking him and that he had heard *"the whispering of many"* (Jeremiah 20:10). Pashhur the priest, along with the people in general, were doing a lot of talking among themselves about Jeremiah and the circumstances of the day, instead of listening to the word of God.

Here again, this name change holds meaning for the people in general as well as for the one whose name was changed. There is also a general warning against "murmuring in the ranks" instead of listening to the Lord.

LUCIFER/SATAN

Up to this point, each one of the name changes we have considered has involved a man or a woman. In this case, however, the name of Lucifer was changed to *Satan*, when he fell. It seems that everyone has heard of these names and knows that they refer to the same person — whether they perceive him to be real or fictitious. The Bible consistently portrays Satan as a real person. Never does it suggest that he was simply a "figure" which "represents" evil.

On the other hand, Satan held a central position where evil is con-

Name Changes

cerned — as both the first and the worst — so his name has frequently been used to symbolize evil. As such, the change in Lucifer's name holds meaning both for him and for anyone else who might decide to act in a similar fashion. Throughout the Scriptures, this person is referred to consistently as an evil being, with names such as *Satan* ("adversary"), *devil* ("slanderer"), *serpent*, *dragon* or simply *evil one*.

There are two passages that probably make reference to Satan before his fall, as well as making reference to some of the reasons he fell. One is in Isaiah, chapter fourteen, referring to *"the king of Babylon."* The other is in Ezekiel, chapter twenty-eight, in a discussion of *"the king of Tyre."* In both instances, a part of the narrative gives definite clues that the one referred to is not just a man, but rather it is Satan at some point in ancient history, before the creation of man.

The only appearance of the actual name *Lucifer* is in Isaiah 14:12 in the King James Version. The King James translators borrowed this name directly from the Latin Vulgate. This name *Lucifer* means "shining one" in Latin, and was used to express the Hebrew word *helel* in the Latin language. Newer translations tend to render this word in English as "star of the morning," or "morning star," but the essential meaning is still that of a "shining one."

In order to properly understand the change from *Lucifer* to *Satan*, it is best to review both the passage from Ezekiel and the one from Isaiah. Both of them refer to the "king" of a prominent ancient city, and in both instances they are preceded by a passage referring either to the "prince" or to the "leader" of that city. The "prince" or "leader" of the city is the human ruler, whereas the "king" is the one who is really ruling from above.

In Ezekiel, there is no doubt that the prophet is not talking about a man, since he describes his subject as *"the anointed cherub who covers"* (Ezekiel 28:14). In Isaiah, however, the being in question is referred to as a man at one point (verse 16), although the Hebrew word for man, *iysh*, could be translated as "person."

After considering the subject of Babylon (discussed in Chapter Six) and the fact that it consistently represents the world system of idolatry and godlessness, it becomes even more clear that *"the king of Babylon"* can be none other than Satan himself. The statements contained in the biblical text also support this conclusion:

The Living Tapestry

"Son of man, take up a lamentation over the king of Tyre, and say to him, 'Thus says the Lord God,
"You had the seal of perfection,
Full of wisdom and perfect in beauty.
You were in Eden, the garden of God;
Every precious stone was your covering:
The ruby, the topaz, and the diamond;
The beryl, the onyx, and the jasper;
The lapis lazuli, the turquoise, and the emerald;
And the gold, the workmanship of your settings and sockets,
Was in you.
On the day that you were created
They were prepared.
You were the anointed cherub who covers,
And I placed you there.
You were on the holy mountain of God;
You walked in the midst of the stones of fire.
You were blameless in your ways
From the day you were created,
Until unrighteousness was found in you.
By the abundance of your trade
You were internally filled with violence,
And you sinned;
Therefore I have cast you as profane
From the mountain of God.
And I have destroyed you, O covering cherub,
From the midst of the stones of fire.
Your heart was lifted up because of your beauty;
You corrupted your wisdom by reason of your splendor.
I cast you to the ground;
I put you before kings,
That they may see you.
By the multitude of your iniquities,
In the unrighteousness of your trade,
You profaned your sanctuaries.
Therefore I have brought fire from the midst of you;
It has consumed you,

Name Changes

And I have turned you to ashes on the earth
In the eyes of all who see you.
All who know you among the peoples
Are appalled at you;
You have become terrified,
And you will be no more." ' "   Ezekiel 28:12-19

And it will be in the day when the L<small>ORD</small> *gives you rest from your pain and turmoil and harsh service in which you have been enslaved, that you will take up this taunt against the king of Babylon, and say,*
"How the oppressor has ceased,
And how fury has ceased!
The L<small>ORD</small> *has broken the staff of the wicked,*
The scepter of rulers
Which used to strike the peoples in fury with unceasing strokes,
Which subdued the nations in anger with unrestrained persecution.
The whole earth is at rest and is quiet;
They break forth into shouts of joy.

How you have fallen from heaven,
O star of the morning, son of the dawn!
You have been cut down to the earth,
You who have weakened the nations!
But you said in your heart,
'I will ascend to heaven;
I will raise my throne above the stars of God,
And I will sit on the mount of assembly
In the recesses of the north.
I will ascend above the heights of the clouds;
I will make myself like the Most High.'
Nevertheless you will be thrust down to Sheol,
To the recesses of the pit.
Those who see you will gaze at you,
They will ponder over you, saying,
'Is this the man who made the earth tremble,
Who shook kingdoms,
Who made the world like a wilderness

The Living Tapestry

And overthrew its cities,
Who did not allow his prisoners to go home?'
All the kings of the nations lie in glory,
Each in his own tomb.
But you have been cast out of your tomb
Like a rejected branch,
Clothed with the slain who are pierced with a sword,
Who go down to the stones of the pit,
Like a trampled corpse." Isaiah 14:3-7 and 12-19

After studying these passages, it is rather difficult to envision the devil as a comical caricature dressed in red underwear and holding a pitchfork. Evidently, Lucifer enjoyed a very high place in Heaven and was an extremely bright and shining being — before he allowed pride to come into the picture. He was so great, in fact, that he did not consider it impossible to raise his throne *"above the stars of God,"* and even to make himself *"like the Most High"!*

Lucifer was also great enough to continue to cause a lot of trouble after his fall and after being expelled from Heaven. It seems that the old adage, "the bigger they are, the harder they fall," may be true after all. In the case of Lucifer, probably one of God's greatest creatures, he has fallen to being the lowest and most despised of all, the devil.

As usual, the change of names is important, not only for the one whose name is altered, but for everyone. *"For everyone who exalts himself shall be humbled, and he who humbles himself shall be exalted"* (Luke 14:11). Not only is this so, but the degree of the exaltation or humbling relates to the magnitude of the result. Lucifer tried to exalt himself to the highest place, and he fell to the lowest and most despised. Jesus Christ, on the other hand, willingly humbled Himself from the highest place to the lowest. Therefore, He was exalted to the highest place, and given *"the name which is above every name, that at the name of Jesus every knee should bow and that every tongue should confess that Jesus Christ is Lord, to the glory of God the Father"* (Philippians 2:9-11).

ZION/HEPHZIBAH

It is fascinating to look at the meaning of the word *Zion*, and then to

Name Changes

consider some of the scriptural contexts in which the name is found. The mountain called Zion is located in Jerusalem and is not a large mountain by world standards. However, it sits upon a very definite line of demarcation between land that is fairly well-watered, receiving over twenty-five inches of rainfall per year, and the Judean desert, receiving less than two inches. Therefore it sits at the junction between what might be termed productive or fertile land and very desolate-looking wilderness.

This wilderness leads abruptly down, to the lowest place on the surface of the earth, and there lies the world's saltiest body of water, where nothing can live, the Dead Sea.

Not only does this region sit at the junction of fertile land and desert, but it also sits at the "intersection" of the nations, being on the historic trade routes between Asia, Africa and Europe. The Bible states this clearly when it says: *"Thus says the Lord GOD, 'This is Jerusalem; I have set her at the center of the nations, with lands around her' "* (Ezekiel 5:5). All of this topography and geography bears symbolic significance when looking at the broader scriptural meaning of the name *Zion*.

At times, the name *Zion* has been used to refer to the entire land of Israel or to the entire people of God. This would include, of course, those Israelites who walked in faith, like Abraham, but it also includes the Church of the Lord Jesus Christ, as is suggested by the following biblical passage:

> *But you have come to Mount Zion and to the city of the living God, the heavenly Jerusalem, and to myriads of angels, to the general assembly and church of the first-born who are enrolled in heaven, and to God, the Judge of all, and to the spirits of righteous men made perfect, and to Jesus, the mediator of a new covenant, and to the sprinkled blood, which speaks better than the blood of Abel.*
>
> Hebrews 12:22-24

After stating the premise that *"Zion"* speaks not simply of a piece of real estate, but rather of *"a people for God's own possession"* (1 Peter 2:9), it then becomes quite interesting to look at the meaning of the word and God's promise to change the name to something else.

The Living Tapestry

The name *Zion* means "desert" or "wilderness," which may seem like a rather poor name for the people of God Almighty. The real significance, however, lies not only in the meaning of the name, but in the concept that God is effecting a change. Remember that Mount Zion sits on a sharply demarcated line between watered land and barren desert, representing an abrupt change at that spot. God is in the process of changing His people and changing their name as well. He has said:

> *For Zion's sake I will not keep silent,*
> *And for Jerusalem's sake I will not keep quiet,*
> *Until her righteousness goes forth like brightness,*
> *And her salvation like a torch that is burning.*
> *And the nations will see your righteousness,*
> *And all kings your glory;*
> *And you will be called by A NEW NAME,*
> *Which the mouth of the L*ORD *will designate.*
> *You will also be a crown of beauty in the hand of the L*ORD*,*
> *And a royal diadem in the hand of your God.*
> *It will no longer be said to you, "Forsaken,"*
> *Nor to your land will it any longer be said, "Desolate";*
> *But you will be called, "My delight is in her,"*
> *And your land, "Married";*
> *For the L*ORD *delights in you,*
> *And to Him your land will be married.*   Isaiah 62:1-4

The Hebrew name translated as "My delight is in her" is *Hephzibah*, and the name for "married" is *Beulah* (the source for the hymns that sing of "Beulah Land"). Herein can be seen the remarkable prophecy that foretells a change in the name of the people of God — from *Zion*, suggesting a dry and desolate condition, to *Hephzibah*. The new name is filled with righteousness, brightness and glory, one that describes the delight of God Himself in a perfected and holy people!

In order to more fully appreciate this concept and to see what God is doing with His people, it is necessary to look at the latter twenty-seven chapters of the book of Isaiah. A wonderful hint is found in chapter forty-five: *"Thus says the L*ORD*, the Holy One of Israel, and his Maker: 'Ask*

Name Changes

Me about the things to come concerning My sons, and you shall commit to Me the work of My hands' " (Isaiah 45:11). God is in the process of bringing His sons to birth and seeing them to maturity. Ultimately, He is *"bringing many sons to glory"* (Hebrews 2:10).

Before looking further at what is said by Isaiah about God's plans for His people, it is instructive to first consider a few things about the book of Isaiah itself. Isaiah's name means "the salvation of Jehovah." Isaiah prophesied during the reigns of several kings of Judah, from Uzziah to Hezekiah. This period of time extended approximately from 758 to 698 B.C.

The Bible may be viewed as the story of the salvation of man by God. Just as Isaiah's name means "the salvation of Jehovah," there are several interesting parallels between the book of Isaiah and the Bible as a whole. The book of Isaiah contains sixty-six chapters, and the Bible has sixty-six books. The Bible is divided into the Old Testament with thirty-nine books and the New Testament with twenty-seven. The book of Isaiah can be said to consist of two parts, and it is also divided between the first thirty-nine chapters and the latter twenty-seven. As if the intent was to be sure that this symbolic representation of the Old and New Testaments would not be missed, the very center chapter of the last twenty-seven is Isaiah 53, the message of which is at the core of the redemption of man. In this fifty-third chapter, the Lord's Suffering Servant was described as the one who would take the iniquity of God's people upon Himself (see Isaiah 53:11).

This division in the book of Isaiah is definite enough to have caused some "critics" in the past to say that there was a "second Isaiah" responsible for writing the final chapters. There is also another reason that this theory of "two Isaiahs" has been proposed in the past: Some people are inclined to doubt the miraculous things contained in the Scriptures.

For example, Isaiah named the Persian king, Cyrus, and told of his conquest of Babylon (see Isaiah 45:1) at least one hundred years before Cyrus was even born. That fact is taken by some as "evidence" of another man, living later in history, having written that portion of the book. However, for God, who can see *"the end from the beginning"* (Isaiah 46:10), it is no problem to name someone before he is born.

The Living Tapestry

Some of the things that were said about Cyrus sound almost messianic, in spite of the fact that he was a heathen king. He was referred to as God's *"shepherd,"* and also as His *"anointed"* (the basic meaning of the term "Messiah" or "Christ"). Those statements about Cyrus were made for very good reasons. He was the one who was to defeat Babylon, just as Jesus Christ is the one who will defeat the idolatrous empire referred to as *"Babylon the great, the mother of harlots"* in the book of Revelation.

An understanding of the meaning of the name *Babylon* and its significance throughout the Scriptures is indispensable to the proper interpretation of many prophetic passages. This theme is developed more fully in the chapter on Babylon and so will only be mentioned here.

With this view of the book of Isaiah in mind (that it was a "two-part work," not written by two different men), it is instructive to examine several passages as they relate to Zion. These are descriptions of what God is saying to or about His people. The easiest place to begin is with the first few verses of the last twenty-seven chapters of the book of Isaiah:

"Comfort, O comfort My people," says your God.
"Speak kindly to Jerusalem;
And call out to her, that her warfare has ended,
That her iniquity has been removed,
That she has received of the LORD*'s hand*
Double for all her sins."

A voice is calling,
"Clear the way for the LORD *in the wilderness;*
Make smooth in the desert a highway for our God.
Let every valley be lifted up,
And every mountain and hill be made low;
And let the rough ground become a plain,
And the rugged terrain a broad valley;
Then the glory of the LORD *will be revealed,*
And all flesh will see it together;
For the mouth of the LORD *has spoken."*   Isaiah 40:1-5

Name Changes

Remember that this is the beginning of twenty-seven chapters which are, in some ways, analogous to the New Testament itself! God begins with the promise of comfort for His people, that their iniquity will be removed.

After speaking specifically to Jerusalem, the prophet then declares that the way is to be cleared for the Lord *"in the wilderness,"* and *"in the desert."* In other words, God is about to move in His people because "wilderness" and "desert" are exactly the words describing the meaning of *"Zion,"* the people of God.

It will be a thorough work, and result in a complete change. In fact, the prophet later says that Zion will be made like the garden of Eden:

Indeed, the LORD will comfort Zion;
He will comfort all her waste places.
And her wilderness He will make like Eden,
And her desert like the garden of the Lord;
Joy and gladness will be found in her,
Thanksgiving and sound of a melody.   Isaiah 51:3

It seems, however, that this change in Zion will not come easily or without a struggle, apparently because the beginning condition of the people is so bad. Only one as great as God Himself can come to the people's aid. Consider the following passages:

"The afflicted and needy are seeking water, but there is none,
And their tongue is parched with thirst;
I, the LORD, will answer them Myself,
As the God of Israel I will not forsake them.
I will open rivers on the bare heights,
And springs in the midst of the valleys;
I will make the wilderness a pool of water,
And the dry land fountains of water.
I will put the cedar in the wilderness,
The acacia, and the myrtle, and the olive tree;
I will place the juniper in the desert,
Together with the box tree and the cypress,

The Living Tapestry

That they may see and recognize,
And consider and gain insight as well,
That the hand of the LORD *has done this,*
And the Holy One of Israel has created it."   Isaiah 41:17-20

But this is a people plundered and despoiled;
All of them are trapped in caves,
Or are hidden away in prisons;
They have become a prey with none to deliver them,
And a spoil, with none to say, "Give them back!"
Who among you will give ear to this?
Who will give heed and listen hereafter?
Who gave Jacob up for spoil, and Israel to plunderers?
Was it not the LORD*, against whom we have sinned,*
And in whose ways they were not willing to walk,
And whose law they did not obey?   Isaiah 42:22-24

But now, thus says the LORD*, your Creator, O Jacob,*
And He who formed you, O Israel,
"Do not fear, for I have redeemed you;
I have called you by name; you are Mine!"   Isaiah 43:1

"Do not fear, for I am with you;
I will bring your offspring from the east,
And gather you from the west.
I will say to the north, 'Give them up!'
And to the south, 'Do not hold them back.'
Bring My sons from afar,
And My daughters from the ends of the earth,
Everyone who is called by My name,
And whom I have created for My glory,
Whom I have formed, even whom I have made."   Isaiah 43:5-7

    Many biblical passages describe a seemingly hopeless condition of the people, due to the destructive effects of sin and idolatry. Nevertheless, God is able to turn it all around and change the people into

Name Changes

something glorious and beautiful, an object of delight. Truly the Gospel is good news, with hope available to anyone who will respond in faith to God's call. And the Lord is able to change what may at first seem like a desert into a fertile and productive garden. The day will soon come when the Lord will restore Zion, completing His work of perfection in the sight of all the nations, as it is written:

> *How lovely on the mountains*
> *Are the feet of him who brings good news,*
> *Who announces peace*
> *And brings good news of happiness,*
> *Who announces salvation,*
> *And says to Zion, "Your God reigns!"*
> *Listen! Your watchmen lift up their voices,*
> *They shout joyfully together;*
> *For they will see with their own eyes*
> *When the* LORD *restores Zion.*
> *Break forth, shout joyfully together,*
> *You waste places of Jerusalem;*
> *For the* LORD *has comforted His people,*
> *He has redeemed Jerusalem.*
> *The* LORD *has bared His holy arm*
> *In the sight of all the nations,*
> *That all the ends of the earth may see*
> *The salvation of our God.*   Isaiah 52:7-10

In addition to the fact that there is a change of name for the people of God in general, there may also be opportunity for an individual to have his or her name changed as well. In a promise given to the Church at Pergamum, the Scriptures say, *"He who has an ear, let him hear what the Spirit says to the churches. To him who overcomes, to him I will give some of the hidden manna, and I will give him a white stone, and a new name written on the stone which no one knows but he who receives it"* (Revelation 2:17).

After reviewing these name changes in the Bible and considering their significance, it becomes apparent what profound implications would be associated with acquiring a new name from God Himself. What a truly marvelous thing that would be! That name might reflect the individual's most outstanding accomplishments, or highlight his (or her) best attributes. Whatever the name might be, to have a new name, specifically and personally given by the Almighty, would have to be a wonderful experience. Not only that, but it would be an everlasting testimony — a crown of honor.

The Lord's "New Name"

During the discussion of Abraham and the change of his name from Abram, the idea was introduced that, in a symbolic way, there is a change going on with God Himself. We also discussed what a truly astounding concept this is, since He is eternal and eternally the same. Since the Word of God says that God does not change, we know that this "change" reflects the fact that He is taking on a new role or a new relationship; it cannot indicate a change in His character or in His essential nature.

The change in the role of God the Father, as we saw earlier, is revealed by the symbolism of Abraham's life and the change of his name from *Abram* ("exalted father") *to Abraham* ("father of a multitude"). We also know that Jesus Christ changed His role when He left the portals of Heaven, took on a body of flesh, and became the sacrifice for our sin.

As we have seen, the Lord has many names already, and they reveal His character and His purposes. It is not until the book of Revelation, describing the completion of His work of redemption and restoration in the lives of His people, that we are told that the Lord has a *"new name."* Every previous name revealed to men in the Bible was simply the unveiling of a name that He already had. This one, on the other hand, seems to be something entirely new, although we are not told what the name is:

> *He who overcomes, I will make him a pillar in the temple of My God, and he will not go out from it anymore; and I will write upon him the name of My God, and the name of the city of My God, the new Jerusa-*

Name Changes

lem, which comes down out of heaven from My God, and My new name.   Revelation 3:12

Any attempt to figure out what the Lord's new name might be would be purely conjecture, but there are several things that can safely be stated. The meaning of the name will undoubtedly have significance, and it will likely have something to do with the Lord's relationship with His redeemed people.

It is instructive to realize that the mention of this *"new name"* was made in the message to the Church at *Philadelphia*, which means "brotherly love." The very fact that the first and only time this is revealed in the Bible occurs in this context suggests the idea of "relationship" in connection with the *"new name"* that the Lord is to reveal. The Scriptures have already said, near the end of the book of Isaiah, that God was creating a *"new thing,"* and it seems likely that this *"new name"* goes along with that new creation:

> *"For behold, I create new heavens and a new earth;*
> *And the former things shall not be remembered or come to mind.*
> *But be glad and rejoice forever in what I create;*
> *For behold, I create Jerusalem for rejoicing,*
> *And her people for gladness.*
> *I will also rejoice in Jerusalem, and be glad in My people."*
>   Isaiah 65:17-19

The Conclusion

There is indeed a rich store of meaning hidden in these name changes, especially when the change is made by God Almighty Himself! There are several more examples of people in the Bible whose names were changed, but it was generally done by their captors. Probably the best known of them are the three Hebrew children who were captives of King Nebuchadnezzar of Babylon. We know them as *Shadrach*, *Meshach* and *Abed-nego*, but their Hebrew names were *Hananiah*, *Mishael* and *Azariah* (see Daniel 1:7).

Probably the most striking example in this group is *Abed-nego*, "servant of Nego" (or "Nebo," the Babylonian god of wisdom). The king changed Abed-nego's name from *Azariah*, "Jehovah has helped." Nebuchadnezzar believed that these captives were now servants of the gods of Babylon because the God of Israel had been unable to help them, to deliver them out of his hand!

Some years later, when the king made an image and commanded all of the people to bow down and worship it, these three Hebrew men refused to serve the gods of the Babylonians, and were therefore thrown into a very hot furnace. It was so hot that the soldiers who threw them into it were slain by the heat of the flames (see Daniel 3:22).

This story has been told many times, because God Almighty did come to their rescue, and the blazing fire had no effect on them. In spite of the fact that the king of Babylon had changed their names, God stood by the name He desired them to have. *Azariah* had been "helped by Jehovah" and had not allowed himself to be a servant of the gods of Babylon.

When men (even victorious kings) attempt to impose such name changes upon the people of God, they are not accompanied by the profound impact that is seen when God makes the changes. Only when God does such things is the result truly significant and the consequences eternal.

> *"He who has an ear, let him hear what the Spirit says to the churches. To him who overcomes, to him I will give some of the hidden manna, and I will give him a white stone, and A NEW NAME written on the stone which no one knows but he who receives it."*   Revelation 2:17

Endnotes:

1. See Chapter 2, concerning *YHWH-Jireh*.
2. Please see Appendix D for a more complete explanation.

Chapter Four

The King Named Slave
by Paul Strausbaugh

And upon the deep He gazed, and mused and sighed,
And then He spoke and said, "Let there be Light."
With no delay, nor argument, creation cried
And changed all that was dark to bright.
The sun obeyed, the moon as well,
His hand formed every planet.
Of His skill no one can tell.
Take Him not for granted.

And then He felt a great desire come rising up within,
Composed of love divine that only He could give.
A divine hand made a man from dust begin,
and Holy Breath caused the dirt to live.
The Lord provided for all his needs
And even added a lovely wife.
He wanted only godly deeds
And total lack of strife.

And hoping that the man and wife would happily obey,
The loving God then gave them good instruction.
But it wasn't long before they lost their way,
And brought about their sure destruction.
They did have help from a sly deceiver,
Who tries to spoil all God's creation.
He still troubles every believer,
Trafficking in degradation.

Upon the deep in man He gazed, and mused and sighed,
And then He spoke and again said, "Let there be Light."
But there He found resistance, and the darkness cried
Against the One who loved. O what a ghastly sight!
The One who knows again felt love arise,
Aware that no one else but He could save.
Divinity would try on flesh for size,
And the King become a slave.

— THE IRONY OF MALCHUS —

After Jesus ate the Last Supper with His disciples, celebrating the Passover in a place the gospel accounts call the Upper Room, He crossed over onto the Mount of Olives to a place called Gethsemane. The word *gethsemane* means "oil press," and it was there that He prayed, struggling with the horror of the things that He was about to endure. In that place, He was pressed until, the Scriptures say, *"His sweat became like drops of blood, falling down upon the ground"* (Luke 22:44).

While Jesus was still praying, a crowd of people, with Judas Iscariot in the lead, came to arrest Him. As those events were transpiring, Simon Peter impulsively cut off the ear of the high priest's slave with a sword. The slave's name, recorded only one place (see John 18:10), was *Malchus*, which means "king."

At times the Scriptures can be quite subtle, seemingly using understatement to such a degree that the impact of the message is easy to miss. This is one of those instances, and the key to understanding this case is (as we have frequently seen before) contained in the meaning of Malchus' name.

We see here a slave named "king" and an ear being cut off by the very one whose name means "hearing." It was Simon Peter whose name change revealed so much truth about hearing from God and becoming a "living stone" for the building of the true and eternal Temple of God. [1] This same Simon Peter was the one who, in his zeal to defend the Lord, cut off the ear of the high priest's slave.

What a bold and shocking statement is contained within this story! Throughout history, there have been countless examples of well-meaning "believers," of one persuasion or another, who have heard something of God's truth and then have used their misguided zeal to render others unable to hear the things of God. They have "cut off the ear" of the one who was a slave (whether enslaved to a man-made religious system or simply to sin).

The Living Tapestry

There would be no end to examples of this sort of thing, some very obvious and others less so. History is full of actual torture and murder of whole groups of people whose theology was not in line with those who had power over them. In addition to that, there is also a great deal of damage done on a daily basis, when condescending and judgmental attitudes are conveyed to others in the name of religion.

Stark truth alone can be destructive, when used without any grace or love. Certainly some beliefs are true and some are not, but if hate and murder are dispensed in the name of " truth," how is that supposed to win over the lost? Thank God that Jesus Christ came *"full of grace and truth,"* and that because we were so needy, the grace was mentioned first (see John 1:14).

The impact of this story about Malchus is easy to miss, but that is part of the intense irony of it all. Such a great and important message is hidden in such a small and seldom-considered incident. The slave was named *king* and the man who heard from God cut off another man's ear so that he could no longer hear.

Christ came to set the captive free, but unfortunately believers can too easily hear from God and then proceed to impair the ability of the slave to hear the liberating Gospel. While the Lord is suffering under the weight of it all, we can easily jump to some counterproductive conclusion and act accordingly.

There is undoubtedly much more that could be said about this, but in keeping with the brevity of what the Scriptures have to say about Malchus, this chapter will be the shortest one in the book. However, this is a good time to do as it says in some of the psalms, Selah. The Amplified Bible renders this word as *"pause, and think of that!"*

Endnote:

1. Refer to Chapter 3 on name changes.

Chapter Five

Seth

When Adam and I were first created, life was so simple and delightful that it now seems like it was only a dream. He named all the animals, and he named me as well. He said, "I will call you Eve, because you are the mother of all the living." I remember the first time he saw me. The look on his face was unforgettable! How I wish we could be back there and start over again!

I believed God when He told us not to eat of the tree, and I had no intention of ever touching it. Then the serpent showed me how good the fruit was and that I wouldn't really die from eating it, so I tried it. It was actually quite good, and he was right — I didn't die! So, I gave some to Adam, and he didn't die either.

I guess you might say that something died though. We had somehow lost our innocence and had begun to see things in a different way.

The next thing we knew, God was looking for us in the garden, so we tried to hide. It's not too easy to hide from God, and He had a few things to say about what we had done and what some of the consequences would be. I'm glad that the serpent didn't get off without any punishment. I think he deserved it more than we did. I just can't forget the words of God about my seed bruising the serpent's head. I can't wait.

I'm not sure I really believed God about dying. He said that on the day that we ate of the fruit we would "surely die." The serpent said we wouldn't, and I must confess that I have tended toward the opinion that maybe the serpent was right.

Life is harder, no doubt about that! It takes work getting food, and having babies is no picnic, but we're not dead. In fact, until recently, I wasn't sure what sort of thing could happen to cause us to become dead.

Now all that has changed. I knew that Cain and Abel didn't always get along as well as they should have, but I had no idea that it could come to this! Why did he do it? How could he? And could we die too? Who would kill Adam or me? It's all so horrible and so strange! Now I'm not so sure about the serpent's opinion. I just don't know what to believe.

Soon I am going to have another child, and I hope he is the one who will repay the serpent for what he has done. Perhaps then this mess will be straightened out. God said that my seed would bruise the serpent's head, and maybe this is the appointed one. I talked it over with Adam, since he is the one who usually picks the names, and he agrees that Seth would be a good name. He is also hoping that this son will be the seed who was spoken of by God. We have seen enough of hardship and death.

— The Gospel in Genesis 5 —

Genesis, the first book in the Bible, describes the creation of the world, mankind and all life on earth. The word *genesis* actually is borrowed from the Greek language and means "origin."

The first two chapters of Genesis relate the story of the creation. Chapters three and four describe the fall of man and some of the first effects of sin, including the story of Cain and Abel. Chapter five tells of the descendants of Adam leading up to the time of the flood. It is the fifth chapter that will be the focus of this chapter of the book, as the genealogy of Adam is traced through his third son, Seth.

This fifth chapter of Genesis is one of the finest examples in the entire Bible of the statement that God declares *"the end from the beginning"* (Isaiah 46:10), but it is done in a rather hidden fashion. There are ten generations from Adam to Noah, and the name of the man representing each generation had a specific meaning. When these names are lined up sequentially, they form an amazing statement of the Gospel, written several thousand years before the New Testament authors were born!

Before proceeding, credit must be given to Mr. Gary Hedrick for his excellent teaching on this subject.[1] It is from him that the basic material for this chapter is derived.

In order to see the entire message, it is necessary first to look at the individual names, and then afterward put them together to form the whole. The list begins with *Adam*, the first man, and his name simply means "man." Adam and Eve (whose name means "life") had eaten of the forbidden fruit in the garden of Eden, and God had pronounced the resultant curse on each of them, as well as upon the serpent (the devil) who had tempted Eve.

Contained in the curse upon the serpent was a statement in which God said: *"I will put enmity between you and the woman, and between your seed and her seed; He shall bruise you on the head, and you shall bruise him on the heel"* (Genesis 3:15). After Adam and Eve were expelled from the garden, Cain and Abel were born, followed by the well-known story in which Cain slew Abel. [2]

After that, Adam and Eve had another son and named him *Seth*, meaning "appointed." By that time, they had seen enough of evil and hardship to hope for the appearance of the one who would be the *"seed"* of the woman, and would bruise the head of the serpent. It was perhaps for that reason that they named their third child Seth, thinking that he could be the one appointed unto that purpose. Of course, the statement God had made to the serpent ultimately looked forward to Christ, who was to be born of a woman and who would "bruise" Satan on his head.

In order not to allow the proliferation of names and their meanings in Genesis 5 to become burdensome to the reader, a list is supplied at the end of this chapter. Here, I would like to concentrate on the family line of Seth.

The first son of Seth was *Enosh*, meaning "mortal." The next in the line leading to Noah was *Kenan*, translated as "habitation." Kenan's eldest son was named *Mahalalel*, which may be rendered as "the blessed God." The root word in Mahalalel's name, *halal*, is also used to make the word *hallelujah*. The son of Mahalalel was named *Jared*, "to descend" or "to come down."

The man who was next after Jared, who was referred to as *"the seventh generation from Adam"* in the New Testament book of Jude (verse 14), was Enoch. Concerning him, the Bible says, *"Enoch walked with God; and he was not, for God took him"* (Genesis 5:24). Apparently Enoch lived such a righteous life, in such close fellowship with God, that he was taken out of this world without passing through death on the way.

As an aside, it is worth mentioning a few things about the number "seven" at this point. It seems to be the number of completion in the Bible. There are many examples of this both in the Scriptures and in nature. In the Scriptures, there are seven days of creation in Genesis and seven Spirits of God and seven churches in the book of Revelation. There are seven years in what has come to be called "the tribulation period," as well as seven trumpets and seven seals leading up to it.

The Gospel in Genesis 5

There are seven lamps on the golden lampstand in the Tabernacle, from which the Jewish menorah is derived. The number seven also figured prominently in the scheme of the Jewish feasts in the Old Testament.

Even in nature, there are a number of these "sevens" that are very prominent. There are seven continents, seven colors in the rainbow and seven days in a week (derived from the biblical account of creation). The reason for focusing upon the number seven here is to compare the seventh generation from Adam through Cain with the same generation through Seth. It seems that this number, when applied to the generations in this fashion, resulted in a sort of "fullness," or full expression, in the basic natures of Adam's descendants.

Enoch, who was descended through Seth, was righteous and walked with God. There was a man named Lamech, descended from Cain, who boasted of his wickedness by saying that he had killed a man for wounding him, and a boy, for striking him (see Genesis 4:23). The Scriptures say that one of his sons had learned how to forge implements of bronze and iron, so he may have had a sword, a distinct advantage in battle. He seemed to be proud of his ability to mete out harsh punishment to anyone who, in his opinion, had wronged him.

In spite of the fact that Lamech was manifestly unjust in his dealings, he always had a way of justifying himself and thus was very arrogant. That is the full expression of such wickedness — the ability to justify self, willfully harm others without remorse and be proud of it at the same time. Unfortunately, the earth today seems to be filled with people who are just like Lamech! But there is also another group made up of righteous ones like Enoch, who desire to walk with God and serve Him.

There are several things about Enoch that are very interesting (such as the fact that he was a prophet). He was one of very few men in the Bible about whom it was said: *"[He] walked with God."* Enoch's fellowship with the Almighty was so close that he was transported into Heaven without dying.

The name *Enoch* means "initiated" or "dedicated," and both of these possible meanings are very significant. He was fully dedicated to God, and because of that, he initiated several things. He was the first prophet named in the Bible. He prophesied the second coming of Christ and God's judgment upon the ungodly (see Jude 14-15). Apparently, he initiated the concept! His very life and the method of his departure became a prophecy of the bodily resurrection of the one who believes in Christ as his Savior.

There is also a lesson to be learned from the name of Enoch's father, *Jared*, which means "to descend." Hidden in the relationship between father and son is the concept that humility leads to greatness (since the greatest man in the antediluvian world was the direct offspring of the one whose name holds the idea of going downward).

Even the life of Enoch's son, Methuselah, became prophetic. *Methuselah* means "his death shall bring." In the year that Methuselah died, the flood came and destroyed all of mankind (except Noah and his household). The length of Methuselah's life depicted God's patience and longsuffering, since he was the longest living human being on record (969 years — see Genesis 5:27). The judgment of God upon man's wickedness did not come to the ancient world until Methuselah's life was completed.

The people of that day must have heard Enoch's preaching about a coming judgment. In addition to that, the prophet had a son, whose name meant "his death shall bring." The message was clear, that Methuselah's death would bring the predicted events upon the earth. Still, God withheld His judgment for almost a millennium in order to give the people plenty of time to turn from their wickedness.

The next man listed in the genealogy after Methuselah was Lamech. He had the same name as the evil descendant of Cain who was discussed previously. The meaning of his name is somewhat difficult to ascertain, since the scholars are not certain of its meaning. Nevertheless, a likely meaning can be implied from the Hebrew word for king, *melech*. It seems likely that *Lamech* means the opposite of king, since the word is a reversal of the word for king. Because of this, the idea of "captive" or "slave" is the most likely meaning intended. This fits very well for the evil Lamech in the lineage of Cain, since he was obviously a slave of sin.

The son of Methuselah, on the other hand, being the grandson of Enoch, might be expected to have a better name. However, even the

The Gospel in Genesis 5

righteous are captives in a world of sin. Although they live righteous lives, trying to "walk with God," they are not without sin themselves. Therefore the name of "captive" fits in this case, as well. Man as captive to sin also forms an integral part of the declaration of the Gospel that these names form when taken together.

The final name in the list is Noah. *Noah* means "rest" or "comfort." It seems that Noah's father had this entire scheme of captivity or enslavement in mind when he named him. He had hope that they would one day be delivered from their bondage:

> *Now he called his name Noah, saying, "This one shall give us rest from our work and from the toil of our hands arising from the ground which the* LORD *has cursed."* Genesis 5:29

THE GOSPEL MESSAGE

Now that each name has been considered individually, let us look at the message contained in the sequence when they are all put together. In a few places, small words such as conjunctions may have to be added to make a complete sentence. There is also one name that must be altered slightly (to an implied meaning) in order for the sentence to make more sense:

Adam	"man"
Seth	"appointed"
Enosh	"mortal"
Kenan	"habitation"
Mahalalel	"the blessed God"
Jared	"descend" or "come down"
Enoch	"dedicate or initiate" (by implication, "to train or to teach")
Methuselah	"his death shall bring"
Lamech	"captive" or "slave"
Noah	"rest" or "comfort"

Putting all of these names together in proper sequence in a coherent fashion reveals a clear statement of the message of the Gospel, spoken

The Living Tapestry

through the lives of men thousands of years ago. Only God could do something like that, and He had to see "the end from the beginning" in order to do it. Here is the proposed sentence:

Man is appointed a mortal habitation, but the blessed God, He shall come down, teaching that His death shall bring the captive rest.

Thank God that He humbled Himself enough to come down and perform such a task for our benefit!

Endnotes:

1. "What's in a Name?" a tape by Gary Hedrick, Christian Jew Hour, 1994.
2. See Appendix C for the meanings of their names.

Chapter Six

Daniel

I know that my wife is troubled, but I do not know how to answer her in such a way as to make her feel better. She is with child, and that probably makes her more emotional, or at least I hope that is the reason.

The prophet Jeremiah has been predicting the very same things for nearly twenty years now, and nothing has happened so far. King Josiah is reportedly working on an alliance with Egypt, just to be on the safe side, and that should certainly be worth something! It is true that many Israelites from the north have been conquered and carried away into captivity to Assyria, but not the kingdom of Judah, not the house of David! Certainly God would never let that happen to David's kingdom. The old prophecies said that the throne of David would go on forever! She just worries so much!

It is true, yes, that there is much sin and idolatry in the land, just as Jeremiah says. But there are other prophets who say that we will have peace and safety and that Babylon will leave us alone. How can we know the future? I wish I could calm her fears and help her to see that things aren't as bad as that prophet says.

She wants to name the child Daniel, she is so upset by all this: "God is my Judge"! I tried to tell her that there are plenty of good names in my father's family in the past two generations, and that we should not name our son Daniel. Perhaps this one will be a girl, and then I won't have to worry about it. I can't believe this, she almost has me hoping my son will be a girl! I have never heard of anything like this! Anyway, it is the man's decision what name will be given to the child.

Yesterday, she said to me, "My dear husband, I just can't get rid of the strong feeling that the words of Jeremiah are the words of God Himself! We are about to have a child, and what if our nation is destroyed soon? What will happen to him?"

How can a man have a rational discussion in the face of such questions as that? I am glad that I am not a woman.

I had a discussion just twelve days ago with several of the most prominent men in the city. Our fortifications are good, we have plenty of food and water stored up inside the walls, and we make a good buffer between the land of the Chaldeans and the land of Egypt. The Babylonians already rule everything else, and they have no good reason to expend all the effort it would take to conquer our small nation. In the process, they would only place themselves that much closer to Egypt and thereby increase their own risk of conflict.

I hope I can help her to see things in a logical way. If God were really speaking through Jeremiah, then surely something would have happened by now. He has been saying the same thing for so many years now!

— Babylon the Great —

Although the Bible was written by many different authors over a great span of time, it is woven together into a beautiful tapestry by common names and themes. The names of God (see Chapter 2) appear throughout the Scriptures and seem to be given to men as a progressive revelation of who God is and what His purposes are. These threads describing God are the keys that tie everything together through the ages, but there are other threads in the tapestry as well.

Another common thread, representing the antithesis of God and His works, is that of the kingdom of Babylon. This may seem like a rather far-reaching concept since the Babylonian Empire has been gone for over twenty-five hundred years, and the city of Babylon itself lies in ruins. Nevertheless, the origins of Babylon can be traced far back into Genesis, and either the earthly kingdom itself or its spiritual counterpart can be followed right up to the end of the book of Revelation.

The symbolism of Babylon in the Bible is actually quite pervasive, continually reappearing, and that which is represented is invariably evil. God's purpose regarding Babylon in relation to His people is generally twofold. It first involves discipline and punishment for His people at the hands of the Babylonians. The second purpose, both for God's ancient people and for His people today, is deliverance from captivity to the idolatrous kingdom and judgment upon the kingdom of Babylon itself.

Early Events in Genesis

Before the flood, there are only hints of the concept of evil finding a homeland in the area of Babylon, and then only by inference. When Cain was exiled, the Word of God says that he went eastward and settled in the land of Nod (see Genesis 4:16). *Nod* means "wandering" or "grief" and could have been in the region that would later be called

The Living Tapestry

Babylon. Not until after the flood, however, do the evil roots that were present in that geographic area become clear.

According to the Bible, God destroyed the inhabited earth with a great flood, sparing only Noah and his family. Humanity thus was allowed to "start over" with the family of a man who was found to be righteous in his generation. That should have been a good beginning, especially since it was said that Noah *"walked with God."* However, man being the creature he is, it wasn't long until there was trouble.

Noah planted a vineyard, made some wine from the grapes and proceeded to becoming drunk on it. The precise details of what occurred next have been the subject of debate. The Bible says that Noah was uncovered inside his tent and that his son Ham *"saw the nakedness of his father"* (Genesis 9:22). He then proceeded to tell his brothers about it. This resulted in a curse upon Ham and his children, while a blessing was pronounced upon Shem and Japheth (since they cared about their father's respectableness, covering him without looking at him in that condition).

As mentioned in a previous chapter, *Noah* means "rest" or "comfort." The meanings of the names of Noah's sons are also instructive, considering the destinies of their respective offspring. *Shem* simply means "name." From him was descended Abraham and the whole nation of Israel. Hundreds of years later, it was said (speaking of Israel) that God redeemed the Israelites for Himself as a people in order to *"make a name for Himself"* (2 Samuel 7:23). Isaiah said that God *"divided the waters before them to make for Himself an everlasting name"* (Isaiah 63:12).

The name of the Lord has already been examined in some detail, especially regarding its greatness. From Shem, the one whose name meant simply "name," would come the One whose name is above every name, the Lord Jesus Christ (see Philippians 2:9)!

The next named son, Ham, was the one who incurred the curse because of his disrespect toward his father. The name *Ham* means "hot." This could be an indication of his nature, or perhaps of the final destiny in perdition of those who rebel against God, bringing a curse upon themselves.

Ham's first son was Cush, who became the father of Nimrod.

Babylon the Great

Nimrod was a key figure in the early history of Babylon and will be considered subsequently.

Another son of Ham was Canaan, who was specifically mentioned by Noah in the curse that was brought on by the actions of Ham. In fact, Ham was not personally mentioned in the curse. Only Canaan was specifically cursed, in spite of the fact that the deed was done by his father.

Canaan's descendants were famous. The Canaanites were the ones who, hundreds of years later, had so many abominable practices that God found it necessary to completely annihilate them. Ancient Canaanite altars have been discovered where they sacrificed their own children to other gods, and they had many other abhorrent practices. The Israelites were instructed to utterly destroy them from the land when God led them into the "land of Canaan," after He had delivered them from Egypt.

The third named son of Noah, Japheth, joined with Shem in covering their father's nakedness. (Even though he was named last, Japheth was not the youngest. According to Genesis 9:24, Ham was the youngest.) The name *Japheth* means "wide-spreading," and the Scriptures tell us that his offspring occupied *"the coastlands of the nations."* The King James Version of the Bible says, *"the isles of the Gentiles"* (Genesis 10:5). Again, the destiny of the man's descendants was found to be contained in his name. Only by following those descendants through history can the true significance of the name be understood.

THE STORY OF NIMROD

The book of Genesis tells the story of Nimrod, saying that *"he became a mighty one on the earth"* (Genesis 10:8). He became the first empire builder in history, and *"the beginning of his kingdom was Babel,"* along with several other cities, *"in the land of Shinar"* (Genesis 10:10). *Shinar* was the ancient name for Babylon, located in the area of ancient Mesopotamia, one of the cradles of civilization.

The meaning of the name *Shinar* is unknown, but possibly is related to the name *Sumer*, since the Sumerians lived there.

After beginning his kingdom in Babel, Nimrod expanded it to

include more of Assyria, and many times in the Scriptures the symbolism of Babylon and Assyria are pretty much inseparable.

We are told little more in scripture about Nimrod himself, except that *"he was a mighty hunter before the Lord"* (Genesis 10:9). The name *Nimrod* is still popular today in many parts of the world. In modern Iraq there are several places that carry that name. In northern Israel, there is a Crusader fortress named "Nimrod Castle." Even here in the United States, it is not unusual to see a hunting lodge with a name like "Nimrod Hall," or possibly a campground or a wildlife area carrying the name. Even though these usages display respect for the ability of the legendary character, a closer consideration will show that he was an utterly evil figure.

The fact that Nimrod founded the kingdom of Babylon in antiquity is the first clue to his evil nature, since that kingdom uniformly represents both moral and religious evil throughout the Scriptures. The biblical ideal for a king was not a mighty hunter. Christ, our greatest example, is portrayed as the Good Shepherd. The shepherd sacrifices his life for the sake of the sheep, whereas the hunter takes the life of the animal by stealth for his own advantage.

The devil is said to prowl about seeking someone he may devour, and that is the image of the hunter. This is not to say that all hunting of animals for food is evil, since God has given them as food for mankind (see Genesis 9:3). Nevertheless, an undue fixation on such activity or taking great pleasure in the act of killing cannot be a good thing, as evidenced by these scriptural images.

The ancient meaning of the name *Nimrod*, in the speech of the Hamitic people (prior to the confusion of the languages at Babel), has been lost in antiquity. In Hebrew, however, the name carries the meaning of "rebel" or "rebellion." This was undoubtedly because they understood the significance of the story from Old Testament history and knew that he was acting in rebellion to the ways of God. Thus we see that the roots of Babylon were evil and founded upon rebellion against God.

The Tower of Babel

At some point during this time period, there was an organized effort

Babylon the Great

to build a city and a tower in the land of Shinar. This tower was to be so high that its top would *"reach into heaven,"* and thereby those men hoped to make a name for themselves (Genesis 11:4). It might be worthwhile to pause and consider a few things. First, why was the building of such a tower "evil" in the sight of God? What was the real purpose of the structure? Why did God see the need to personally put a stop to the work? And finally, what has any of this to do with modern man, thousands of years later?

To begin with, it must be admitted that very little detail of that time period is recorded. However, it seems clear that the people of Babel were building the structure with more in mind than just making a pretty tower to impress their neighbors. They intended to *"reach into heaven"* and somehow, in the process, to obtain permanence or possibly even a sort of immortality. The people also hoped to attain a society which was unified around that structure, so that they would not be *"scattered abroad over the face of the whole earth"* (Genesis 11:4).

There also was a decidedly spiritual purpose in their efforts to reach upward. Perhaps they were intending to worship the sun, the moon or some other heavenly bodies. There is no way to know for sure just what their intent was in this regard, but Babylon was later noted for worship of the moon god. What is clear is that the building of a huge tower was not the proper way to reach the one true God. He cannot be reached by man's efforts, no matter how well organized.

Whatever may have been the specific intentions of the people of Babel, it seems clear that they were zealous and well organized. In fact, their unity and determination in this endeavor was such that God Himself said, *"nothing which they purpose to do will be impossible for them"* (Genesis 11:6). To avoid the spread of such a strong, unified, idolatrous empire on the earth, God confused their language, quickly putting a stop to their organized effort.

It is from this episode that the name of Babylon is derived, since *Babel* means "to confuse." It is very interesting to note that God brought confusion upon the people of Babel as a judgment, and thereby caused them to be *"scattered abroad over the face of the whole earth."* This was the very thing they had feared and worked so hard to avoid.

It is also interesting that confusion is a key tactic of the kingdom of

The Living Tapestry

Babylon throughout the ages, causing people to be confused about God, His motives and His redemptive plan for mankind. There is an unbelievable plethora of philosophical and religious beliefs in the world today, and this is due to the fact that this great spiritual evil empire called Babylon has as its *modus operandi* the promotion of confusion in the earth. It is therefore apparent that the nature of the kingdom, the name, and the first judgment against it all coincide. Confusion is the meaning of the name *Babylon* and the hallmark of its operation.

THE LIFE OF ABRAHAM

The centrality of Abraham and the importance of the events in his life as they relate to the message of the Scriptures has already been discussed. In Isaiah we read:

> *"Listen to me, you who pursue righteousness,*
> *Who seek the LORD:*
> *Look to the rock from which you were hewn,*
> *And to the quarry from which you were dug.*
> *Look to Abraham your father,*
> *And to Sarah who gave birth to you in pain;*
> *When he was one I called him,*
> *Then I blessed him and multiplied him."*   Isaiah 51:1-2

Where was Abraham when God called him? This point is crucial, since Abraham (whose name means "father of a multitude") is to be a pattern for all those who come to God throughout the ages. God called Abraham to come out of a place called Ur of the Chaldees. This was a land of idolatry, which would later be called Babylon.

Because of Abraham's faith and his obedience, God promised that He would greatly multiply his seed (or offspring) as the stars of the heavens and as the sand on the seashore, and that through him all the nations of the earth would be blessed. He became the father of the entire Judeo-Christian family of faith in the one true God, who is invisible, but no less real and involved in the lives of men. The fact that

Babylon the Great

nearly everything in Abraham's life is symbolically significant has been previously discussed, but some review is called for, as it relates to the land of Babylon.

The city of Ur was located in southern Mesopotamia, and Abraham lived there in about 2000 B.C. The fact that the Bible calls the city "Ur of the Chaldees (Chaldeans)" has seemed out of place to some, since it is believed that the Chaldeans came into that region about a thousand years later. This appellation was used to describe the region in a way that could be understood by a reader at the time when the text was written, many years after the life of Abraham.

Ancient Ur has been excavated, and a great deal has been learned about it. The city was apparently large and quite prosperous. The local god was named *Nannar*. He was the moon god, and he had a consort named *Ningal*. The remains of a ziggurat, a temple tower erected to Nannar, have been uncovered.[1] This is reminiscent of the tower of Babel and may give a clue as to that earlier tower's purpose.

It was in Ur that God appeared to Abraham, calling him to leave and travel to a place He would show him. At the time when God called him, Abraham did not know where he was going, only that he was to leave this prosperous city and follow God's directions. Abraham thus became a pattern for God's people throughout the ages, as they are "called out" of the idolatrous world system, out of "Babylon," and told to follow God to a place where He will lead them.

Remember that the Greek word for *Church* is *ecclesia*, which means "called-out ones." This concept of God calling His people out of Babylon is prominent in the book of Jeremiah (especially chapters 50 and 51), and it is summarized near the end of the Bible in Revelation 18:

> *And he cried out with a mighty voice, saying, "Fallen, fallen is Babylon the great! And she has become a dwelling place of demons and a prison of every unclean spirit, and a prison of every unclean and hateful bird. For all the nations have drunk of the wine of the passion of her immorality, and the kings of the earth have committed acts of immorality with her, and the merchants of the earth have become rich by the wealth of her sensuality."*
> *And I heard another voice from heaven, saying, "Come out of her, my*

people, that you may not participate in her sins and that you may not receive of her plagues; for her sins have piled up as high as heaven, and God has remembered her iniquities." Revelation 18:2-5

This concept of God calling His people out of Babylon also applies to the story of Abraham sending his servant back to that region in order to obtain a wife for his son Isaac. As I have said, this is symbolic of the heavenly Father sending the Holy Spirit into the land of Babylon in order to bring back a Bride for His Son. ² In a similar fashion, the entire Church is taken out of Babylon in order to be united with Christ.

This also shows how very significant it is that the Jewish nation suffered captivity in Babylon, greatly enhancing the symbolic importance of their restoration back to their homeland and the rebuilding of the Temple. This entire episode in Jewish history is a figure of the restoration of the people of God in a larger sense, and the building of the enduring Temple of God.

It soon becomes apparent that the tapestry is intricate and far-reaching, tying together Jewish history, the Church, the earthly kingdom of Babylon, the more encompassing concept of Babylon the Great, the life of Abraham and his offspring and, ultimately, all of God's people throughout the ages!

BABYLON VERSUS EGYPT

The astute reader may be wondering where the slavery of the Israelites in the land of Egypt and their subsequent deliverance fit into this scheme of things. Certainly, both the kingdom of Egypt and that of Babylon were idolatrous and full of evil symbolism, both had their origins in the sons of Ham (Egypt has even been called "the land of Ham"), and both hold an important relationship to the nation of Israel. However, there were important differences in how these two kingdoms related to the Israelites, and there are important differences in what these two areas represent scripturally.

The nation of Israel really came into existence in Egypt, whereas the Israelites were later carried off into Babylon, after they had enjoyed success as a "nation under God" for many years. In Egypt, they were

Babylon the Great

slaves, but in Babylon, they were captives who were to be integrated into the local society. The Israelites were all sequestered in one area of Egypt, but they were scattered about the empire of Babylon.

The Egyptian rulers did not willingly let the children of Israel go. The pharaoh was forced to release them by the various plagues that were visited upon his land and his people. After they were gone, the kingdom of Egypt continued to exist, and it still exists as a nation to this day.

The Babylonian empire, on the other hand, was actually destroyed to facilitate the release of God's people. This was accomplished by Cyrus, about whom Isaiah prophesied, more than one hundred years before the king's birth, that he would defeat the kingdom of Babylon.

Because of the great symbolic significance of Babylon, some unusual words were used to describe Cyrus — words such as God's *shepherd* and His *anointed* (see Isaiah 44:28-45:1). Both of these terms typically are reserved for references to Christ, but they are applied to Cyrus symbolically since he was to destroy Babylon, just as the Lord Jesus Christ is to destroy Babylon the Great.[3]

King Cyrus also decreed that the Temple in Jerusalem should be rebuilt. The significance of this temple reconstruction, as well as the names of some of the men involved, will be discussed shortly.

Many other types of comparison and contrast are possible in the study of these two kingdoms, but the goal here is to see the difference in what they represent and how that relates to the people of God (both the nation of Israel and the Church of Jesus Christ). The slavery of God's people in Egypt is symbolic of the slavery to sin that plagues us all from the beginning of our existence on this earth. The Israelites were finally set free through the events that are celebrated by the Jewish Passover, and they themselves were only saved from the *"angel of death"* by the blood of the Passover lamb. In a similar fashion, Christ, the perfect Lamb of God, shed His blood so that God's people could be delivered from a life of sin and death.

After setting them free, God then divided the Red Sea so that the Israelites could *"pass through the sea"* on their way to the Promised Land, while that same process destroyed the enemies of God. Here, the sea represents the "sea of humanity" and also relates to water baptism in the separation of the believer from his previous life of sin. Every child of God must pass through the sea of humanity on his journey to God, and the same "sea experience" that results in the deliverance of the child of God results in the destruction of those who are His enemies. Every child of God must come out of Egypt, as the Word of God says: *"Out of Egypt I called My son"* (Hosea 11:1). Even Jesus Christ Himself had to come out of Egypt, since the Bible says that He *"had to be made like His brethren in all things, that He might become a merciful and faithful high priest"* (Hebrews 2:17). Since Jesus had never sinned and was not born in sin, He had to travel to Egypt in order to come out of it (see Matthew 2:13-15).

THE CAPTIVITY OF THE PEOPLE OF GOD

The spotless Son of God never had to be called out of Babylon, because He never went there. This illustrates a very important point. The captivity in Babylon occurs due to the bad choices of God's people, and the resulting inevitable judgment upon their sins. The Israelites did not start off in Babylon, but were carried away to Babylon as captives. The people of God, including the Church, are "carried away" into captivity to the idolatrous world system because of their sin and idolatry. Deliverance can then be achieved only by a process of calling the people out of Babylon and back to the "Promised Land," the land of living in obedience to the Lord. (As discussed previously, the kingdom of Babylon must also be destroyed in this process).

The Jewish Temple, destroyed when the people were exiled to Babylon, had to be rebuilt. In a similar fashion, the spiritual Temple of the Lord has to be rebuilt when His people are brought out of Babylon, due to the destruction the enemy has wrought.

The nation of Israel was warned of a coming captivity of seventy years by the prophet Jeremiah:

> *"Yet you have not listened to Me," declares the LORD, "in order that you might provoke Me to anger with the work of your hands to your own harm. Therefore thus says the LORD of hosts, 'Because you have not obeyed My words, behold, I will send and take all the families of*

Babylon the Great

> *the north,' declares the LORD, 'and I will send to Nebuchadnezzar king of Babylon, My servant, and will bring them against this land, and against its inhabitants, and against all these nations round about; and I will utterly destroy them, and make them a horror, and a hissing, and an everlasting desolation. Moreover, I will take from them the voice of joy and the voice of gladness, the voice of the bridegroom and the voice of the bride, the sound of the millstones and the light of the lamp. And this whole land shall be a desolation and a horror, and these nations shall serve the king of Babylon seventy years.*
> *'Then it will be when seventy years are completed I will punish the king of Babylon and that nation,' declares the LORD, 'for their iniquity, and the land of the Chaldeans; and I will make it an everlasting desolation.' "* Jeremiah 25:7-12

The captivity of the Jews in Babylon, prophesied to last for seventy years, was symbolically very significant as it relates both to the Jewish people and to the Church of Jesus Christ. Because of idolatry and the formation of unholy alliances, as well as continual disobedience (in spite of repeated warnings), the nation of Israel was destroyed and taken into captivity. This is exactly what happened to the Jews again in A.D. 70, when the Temple was destroyed by the Romans, and the Jews were scattered all over the ancient world. This began a period of time the Bible called *"the times of the Gentiles"* (Luke 21:24). It will continue until its appointed time of completion during the seventieth week of Daniel (see Daniel 9:27).

An identical type of captivity has occurred in the life of the Church. God's people have been carried off into captivity to a system of confusion (*Babylon*'s meaning), due to disobedience and idolatry.

It is also apparent in the book of Revelation that Babylon includes the world economic system, that serves Mammon instead of God. Without going into specifics of Church history, there is no lack of examples of confusion, division and the serving of money rather than God. In both the case of Israel and that of the Church, restoration and the rebuilding of the Temple of God will take place along with the destruction of Babylon the Great. In fact, the beginnings of the process have been apparent for some time. The creation of the nation of Israel, after nearly nineteen hundred years without a Jewish state, has run parallel with revival and some degree of restored unity in the Church of Jesus Christ.

Completion of this process will be accomplished by God Almighty, along with the destruction of Babylon, as foretold in Revelation chapters seventeen and eighteen. The seventy-year captivity of Israel in Babylon was a comparatively brief occurrence, but it was prophetic of a much greater and longer captivity, that which the people of God would have to endure. This captivity would last for centuries and involve untold millions of people. After considering such great scope, the words of Moses take on a whole new meaning (his words were addressed to the Lord):

> *Who understands the power of Thine anger,*
> *And Thy fury, according to the fear that is due Thee?* Psalm 90:11

No wonder the Bible says that the fear of the Lord is the beginning of wisdom!

THE HOPE OF EBED-MELECH

Because of Jeremiah's continual warning that the Babylonians were going to destroy the Israelite nation, he was persecuted as a traitor and almost killed on more than one occasion. There is one particular episode that stands as a testimony to God's openness to receive anyone who will serve Him from the heart, regardless of nationality. Jeremiah was thrown into a cistern and left to die, but he was rescued by an Ethiopian named Ebed-Melech (see Jeremiah 38:6-13).

The name *Ebed-Melech* name means "servant of the king," which could have been either his name or his title. In either case, he was the one who saw that the prophet of God was going to die and worked to save his life. Because of the faithfulness of this man to serve God Almighty, effectively making him a true "servant of the King," he was told that he would be spared from destruction at the hands of the Chaldeans:

Babylon the Great

"Go and speak to Ebed-melech the Ethiopian, saying, 'Thus says the LORD of hosts, the God of Israel, "Behold, I am about to bring My words on this city for disaster and not for prosperity; and they will take place before you on that day. But I will deliver you on that day," declares the LORD, "and you shall not be given into the hand of the men whom you dread. For I will certainly rescue you, and you will not fall by the sword; but you will have your own life as booty, because you have trusted in Me," declares the LORD.' "

Jeremiah 39:16-18

The story of Ebed-Melech is significant for several reasons. The nation of Israel was about to be destroyed by Babylon, which was symbolic of the kingdom of darkness. As already mentioned, Babylon was founded by the sons of Ham, who had incurred the first curse after the earth had been cleansed of evil by the flood in the days of Noah. One of Ham's sons was Cush, from whom the Ethiopians were descended. Thus, the only man in Judah who was specifically told that he would be spared from the impending judgment was one of the sons of Ham, and that was because he was a dedicated servant of the king.

Here again, as is so frequently the case in the Scriptures, the meaning of the man's name underscores and highlights the intended meaning of the passage, helping the reader to feel the full impact God intended for the story to convey to subsequent generations. The hope of Ebed-Melech is the hope of every true servant of the King of Kings, to be spared from the judgment upon the godless and to be kept *"under the shadow of His wings."* This hope is available to anyone who purposes in his (or her) heart to serve the King of the Ages and to trust in Him — even if that person happens to be a descendant of Ham.

Satan's Kingdom

The concept of the kingdom of Babylon being representative of the greater kingdom of darkness leads to a consideration of who might be the ruler of such a kingdom. The New Testament speaks of the *"rulers ... of this darkness"* and the *"spiritual forces of wickedness in the heavenly places"* (Ephesians 6:12), as it talks of the schemes of the devil (verse 11).

The Living Tapestry

Earlier in Ephesians, the devil is referred to as the *"prince of the power of the air"* and *"the spirit that is now working in the sons of disobedience"* (Ephesians 2:2). He is never honored by being referred to as a king, except in symbolic references in connection with the kingdom of Babylon. Satan is personally viewed as being at the head of this evil empire, either expressly or by implication, throughout the Scriptures. A more complete discussion of this concept is included in Chapter Three, along with a discussion of the change of his name from Lucifer ("shining one") to *Satan* ("adversary").

NEBUCHADNEZZAR'S DREAM AND THE HEAD OF GOLD

At the time of the destruction of Jerusalem and the deportation of the Jews to Babylon, Nebuchadnezzar was the king of Babylon. Without a doubt, he was the greatest of the Babylonian kings and, as such, was a prominent figure in the Bible.

Because of Nebuchadnezzar's position in that kingdom, and because of the great symbolic significance of Babylon, he was given a prophetic dream that foretold, in a grand overview, the entire history of the great nations of the world. The dream was so vivid that he was quite upset by it and greatly desired to know its meaning. He obviously knew that it was no ordinary dream.

In order to be sure that the interpretation obtained from the wise men of Babylon was genuine, Nebuchadnezzar made a very unusual demand of them. He not only asked them for an interpretation of the dream, but commanded that they first tell him what he had dreamed. Of course, they tried to argue that no one on earth could do such a thing, but he was adamant.

Since none could fulfill this request, Nebuchadnezzar commanded that all the wise men in the land be put to death. Daniel stopped their execution (including his own) by requesting a short period of time so that he might be able to declare the matter to the king. Then Daniel went back to his living quarters and, along with his close friends, prayed and asked God to reveal this secret to him. God revealed the dream and the interpretation to Daniel in a vision in the night, and Daniel went to Nebuchadnezzar with the answer.

Babylon the Great

Daniel told the king not only what the dream was, but also what it meant:

> *"You, O king, were looking and behold, there was a single great statue; that statue, which was large and of extraordinary splendor, was standing in front of you, and its appearance was awesome. The head of that statue was made of fine gold, its breast and its arms of silver, its belly and its thighs of bronze, its legs of iron, its feet partly of iron and partly of clay.*
>
> *"You continued looking until a stone was cut out without hands, and it struck the statue on its feet of iron and clay, and crushed them. Then the iron, the clay, the bronze, the silver and the gold were crushed all at the same time, and became like chaff from the summer threshing floors; and the wind carried them away so that not a trace of them was found. But the stone that struck the statue became a great mountain and filled the whole earth.*
>
> *"This was the dream; now we shall tell its interpretation before the king.*
>
> *You, O king, are the king of kings, to whom the God of heaven has given the kingdom, the power, the strength, and the glory; and wherever the sons of men dwell, or the beasts of the field, or the birds of the sky, He has given them into your hand and has caused you to rule over them all. You are the head of gold.*
>
> *And after you there will arise another kingdom inferior to you, then another third kingdom of bronze, which will rule over all the earth.*
>
> *Then there will be a fourth kingdom as strong as iron; inasmuch as iron crushes and shatters all things, so, like iron that breaks in pieces, it will crush and break all these in pieces. And in that you saw the feet and toes, partly of potter's clay and partly of iron, it will be a divided kingdom; but it will have in it the toughness of iron, inasmuch as you saw the iron mixed with common clay. And as the toes of the feet were partly of iron and partly of pottery, so some of the kingdom will be strong and part of it will be brittle. And in that you saw the iron mixed with common clay, they will combine with one another in the seed of men; but they will not adhere to one another, even as iron does not combine with pottery.*

The Living Tapestry

And in the days of those kings the God of heaven will set up a kingdom which will never be destroyed, and that kingdom will not be left for another people; it will crush and put an end to all these kingdoms, but it will itself endure forever. Inasmuch as you saw that a stone was cut out of the mountain without hands and that it crushed the iron, the bronze, the clay, the silver, and the gold, the great God has made known to the king what will take place in the future; so the dream is true, and its interpretation is trustworthy."   Daniel 2:31-45

Since Nebuchadnezzar was the great king of Babylon, and Babylon was symbolic of the idolatrous world system, the prophetic dream was given to him as *"the head of gold."* After him would arise other kingdoms, but they would all ultimately be destroyed by the *"stone cut out without hands,"* an obvious reference to Christ in His second coming in glory to rule over the nations. His is the Kingdom that will never be destroyed, but will endure forever.

It is generally believed that the four kingdoms described by Daniel in this passage were the Babylonian, the Medo-Persian, the Greek and the Roman empire. It was during the old Roman empire that the everlasting Kingdom of the Lord Jesus Christ was set up, and it will be during a new or "resurrected" version of the Roman empire (in the form of a one-world government) that Jesus will return in glory and take over as the King of kings on the earth. Just as the Caesars of the old Roman empire set themselves up as gods, the Antichrist will declare himself to be god and demand to be worshiped as such (see Daniel 11:36 and 2 Thessalonians 2:4). He will be brought to an end by the coming of the Lord Jesus Christ, and at that time His everlasting Kingdom will be confirmed on the earth.

NINE PROPHETS AROUND THE TIME OF THE BABYLONIAN CAPTIVITY

Not only did the prophets of ancient Israel give forth a message in words (and sometimes actions as well), but also their names often contained a portion of what was being conveyed by God to the people. This was particularly true of those prophets who lived around the time of the Jewish exile to Babylon.

Babylon the Great

In order to illustrate this concept, it is helpful to divide these prophets into three groups: pre-exilic, during the exile and post-exilic. There were three prophets during the exile, and three afterwards. There were, of course, many before the exile, going back for hundreds of years. However, in order to properly limit the discussion to those nearest to the time of the Babylonian captivity, only the three pre-exilic prophets who lived nearest to that time period will be included. This gives us three time periods with three prophets in each group.

As the prophets are listed, along with the meanings of their names, it will become apparent that they relate, in a very definite way, to the changing relationship between the people and God during each of the three time periods. At times, the prophet's name also relates closely to the message that he was given to preach.

THREE PRE-EXILIC PROPHETS:

Habakkuk "to embrace"
Zephaniah "the Lord will hide" (or protect)
Jeremiah "appointed by Jehovah"

THREE PROPHETS OF THE EXILE PERIOD:

Daniel "God is my judge"
Ezekiel "God will strengthen"
Obadiah "servant or worshiper of Jehovah"

THREE POST-EXILIC PROPHETS:

Haggai "festive"
Zechariah "the Lord remembers"
Malachi "my messenger"

Each of the pre-exilic prophets saw a vision of the coming destruction and preached a message of warning to the people.

Habakkuk was the earliest of the three, and he foretold a coming judgment by the Chaldeans, a fierce and destructive people. God had

The Living Tapestry

tried for generations to embrace His people, while they had continually strayed and embraced false gods. The result was to be one of strict and severe judgment and a future restoration in which the earth would *"be filled with the knowledge of the glory of the* Lord, *as the waters cover the sea"* (Habakkuk 2:14). Habakkuk complained that he could not understand how God, being righteous and holy, could look favorably upon the wicked nation of Babylon that would prosper while it was inflicting judgment upon Israel. However, he was reassured that the Babylonians would be judged, and that their violence would return to destroy them (see Habakkuk 2:10-17).

The next prophet, Zephaniah, brought forth a message with a rather curious tendency to switch back and forth between prophecies of destruction and ones of hope. One of the key verses in his prophecy that offers hope for those who would seek the Lord speaks of the possibility of being "hidden" (the meaning of *Zephaniah*) in the day of God's wrath:

> *Seek the* Lord,
> *All you humble of the earth*
> *Who have carried out His ordinances;*
> *Seek righteousness, seek humility.*
> *Perhaps you will be hidden*
> *In the day of the* Lord's *anger.*   Zephaniah 2:3

There was, as always, a chance for repentance and avoidance of judgment along the way, before the condition of the people became so bad that the result was inevitable.

Jeremiah was the prophet who was sent by God to declare repeatedly, during the space of many years, that the appointed time of judgment was rapidly approaching. He was appointed to the unpleasant task of continually reminding the people about the impending judgment that was to be brought upon them through the Babylonians. His ministry continued right up to the destruction of Jerusalem and the Temple, and then ceased at about that time. Then came the three prophets whom God raised up during the exile in Babylon.

The names of the three exilic prophets, Daniel, Ezekiel and Obadiah,

Babylon the Great

had meanings which exactly corresponded to the situation of the people at that time in their relationship to God. God was their judge (*Daniel*), which brought about their condition. It was He who would be their strength (*Ezekiel*) and get them through the experience. In the process, they were to continue as servants and worshipers of Jehovah (*Obadiah*). There was also much, in the content of their prophecies, that pointed to the relationship of God's people to the nations and also a great deal about the coming restoration of the Temple of God.

The Lord remembered His people after the appointed amount of time was fulfilled for their captivity in Babylon. The book of Zechariah ("the Lord remembers") contains some of the most wonderful prophecies of redemption, the building of the Church and the final restoration of Israel to be found in the entire Old Testament. The overall tone for the message was set in chapter 1, where it says:

> 'Therefore, thus says the LORD, "I will return to Jerusalem with compassion; My house will be built in it," declares the Lord of hosts, "and a measuring line will be stretched over Jerusalem. Again, proclaim, saying, 'Thus says the LORD of hosts, "My cities will again overflow with prosperity, and the LORD will again comfort Zion and again choose Jerusalem." ' "   Zechariah 1:16-17

The jubilation of the Jewish people at the time of their restoration from captivity resulted in a mood which could well be described by the word "festive," as Haggai's name would indicate. This is accurately portrayed in the first three verses of Psalm 126:

> (A Song of Ascents)
> *When the LORD brought back the captive ones of Zion,*
> *We were like those who dream.*
> *Then our mouth was filled with laughter,*
> *And our tongue with joyful shouting;*
> *Then they said among the nations,*
> *"The LORD has done great things for them."*
> *The LORD has done great things for us;*
> *We are glad.*   Psalm 126:1-3

The Living Tapestry

The main theme in the book of Haggai was the rebuilding of the Temple. Because of that, Haggai has been referred to as "the prophet of the Temple."

The Temple also played a key role in the celebration of all the Jewish feasts or festivals. The Hebrew word for *festival* bears a close relationship to the prophet's name. The names of both Zechariah and Haggai describe aspects of the relationship between the Lord and His people at the time of the restoration of the Jewish people from captivity. Malachi, however, marks a transition from that period to the future. He brings God's message of a greater and more permanent restoration yet to come.

Malachi was the last of the three post-exilic prophets, and he was also the last prophet of the entire Old Testament period. His name means "my messenger," and signifies the fact that God was sending His final message to His people for that period.

The message of Malachi began with a review of the fact that God had chosen the Israelites above their brothers around them: *"I have loved Jacob; but I have hated Esau"* (Malachi 1:2-3). Then He reminded the people that their priests were to be messengers of God (see Malachi 2:7). In Hebrew, *Malak* means "messenger." But, Malachi warned, since the Israelites had corrupted the office of the priests, God would send His own messenger before Him to clear the way:

> *"Behold, I am going to send My messenger, and he will clear the way before Me. And the Lord, whom you seek, will suddenly come to His temple; and the messenger of the covenant, in whom you delight, behold, He is coming,"* says the LORD *of hosts. "But who can endure the day of His coming? And who can stand when He appears? For He is like a refiner's fire and like fullers' soap. And He will sit as a smelter and purifier of silver, and He will purify the sons of Levi and refine them like gold and silver, so that they may present to the* LORD *offerings in righteousness."* Malachi 3:1-3

The next visitation from God would be in person, following the appearance of His messenger, and the work of God would result in purification from all the evil present in His people. As He said in the

Babylon the Great

final chapter of Malachi, *"For you who fear My name, the sun of righteousness will rise with healing in its wings"* (Malachi 4:2). God Himself was going to personally intervene in order to bring about purification and healing in the lives of His people.

GOD'S PEOPLE ARE CALLED OUT OF BABYLON

After examining the origins, the idolatry, the rebellion and all of the evil symbolism surrounding Babylon, it is easy to see why God consistently calls His people out of her. Abraham was called out of Ur, and the wives of Isaac and Jacob were taken out of the same region. The Jewish people were brought back from there, and the Church (*ecclesia*, "the called out ones") is spiritually being brought out of Babylon. Without mentioning Babylon by name, the New Testament calls the believer in Christ out from among those who would practice idolatry:

> *Do not be bound together with unbelievers; for what partnership have righteousness and lawlessness, or what fellowship has light with darkness? Or what harmony has Christ with Belial, or what has a believer in common with an unbeliever? Or what agreement has the temple of God with idols? For we are the temple of the living God; just as God said,*
>
> *"I will dwell in them and walk among them;*
> *And I will be their God, and they shall be My people.*
> *Therefore, come out from their midst and be separate," says the Lord.*
> *"And do not touch what is unclean;*
> *And I will welcome you.*
> *And I will be a father to you,*
> *And you shall be sons and daughters to Me,"*
> *Says the Lord Almighty.*
>
> *Therefore, having these promises, beloved, let us cleanse ourselves from all defilement of flesh and spirit, perfecting holiness in the fear of God.*
> 2 Corinthians 6:14-7:1

The Living Tapestry

Near the end of the book of Revelation, God again gives a final call to His people to come out of Babylon, as judgment is being pronounced against the evil empire. A voice from Heaven will say, *"Come out of her, my people, that you may not participate in her sins and that you may not receive of her plagues"* (Revelation 18:4). This is one of the most consistent themes in the Bible, stretching from early in Genesis to the end of Revelation, and covering thousands of years in time. It was (and will be) spoken to people all around the world, of all races and nations.

This is a call that is being spoken today and is becoming more clearly heard as the world slips into increasing godlessness and chaos. God's ways are indeed higher than our ways. They are more purposeful, more far-reaching. They are complex and eternal. They involve concepts and numbers on an incomprehensible scale and truths that never change. As society changes, along with its ideas and morals, the truth that Christ is the Rock of Ages becomes increasingly evident. One day He will be openly manifested in His glory, and then all doubt and dispute will evaporate like a thin morning mist.

RESTORATION AND THE REBUILDING OF THE TEMPLE

The Jews were delivered from their captivity in Babylon late in the sixth century B.C., and this took place in stages over quite a number of years. The people of God, in the larger sense, are even now being delivered from their captivity to Babylon the Great, and God will complete that process.

The Balfour Declaration of 1917 helped to pave the way for Israel to become a state again in 1948, after nearly nineteen hundred years of exile among the nations. Jerusalem, as well as the Golan Heights, came under Jewish control in 1967, and after the near-disaster of the Yom Kippur War of 1973, the Israelis made various changes to improve the security of their borders.

The Church has undergone several major movements in parallel with God's work in Israel. The Pentecostal Movement began in the early twentieth century. The great healing revivals of the 1940s and the 1950s were followed by the Charismatic Movement of the late 1960s and the 1970s. The Church has further been refined and purified since

Babylon the Great

then with judgments upon sin, and now some people believe that a "third wave" of the Spirit is in progress.

With the Jews, restoration from captivity in Babylon was accompanied by the rebuilding of the Temple of God in Jerusalem. The physical Temple in Jerusalem has not yet been rebuilt in modern time, but the Jewish people have determined where it should be and have made many preparations for various articles that will be needed in the temple service. The Temple will indeed be rebuilt when the time is right, and God will bring it to pass.

The spiritual Temple, being built out of individual "living" stones, is not yet complete, but is in the process of being constructed. Both Temples will be completed simultaneously, at the culmination of God's work of *"bringing many sons to glory."* The Temple restoration in the sixth century B.C. was in many ways a type and figure with prophetic significance with regard to this final Temple restoration.

The names of the men involved in the rebuilding of the Temple in Jerusalem upon the return of the remnant of Israel were very significant. The high priest was named *Joshua*, "Jehovah-Savior" and has the same meaning as *Jesus*, the great High Priest of all of God's people. This Joshua was the son of *Jehozadak*, meaning "Jehovah justifies," just as the salvation of the believer in Christ is made possible by his being justified before God, his judge.

The governor's name was *Zerubbabel*, meaning "a shoot from Babylon," or "brought out of Babylon." His father's name was *Shealtiel*, which means "I prayed to God." In other words, in answer to prayers to God, the people who would be the builders of the Temple were brought out of Babylon.

Notice that Zerubbabel was not designated as a king, but rather as governor. Even though men who are brought out of Babylon may help in the work of restoration, and may even be involved in its oversight, they do not attain to the title of king. At the time of Zerubbabel, there was no king over Israel, and in the final restoration of God's people and His Temple, none of those who are brought out of Babylon will be king. Christ will be both King and High Priest. This was prophesied by Zechariah, who was a contemporary of these men:

The Living Tapestry

The word of the LORD also came to me saying, "Take an offering from the exiles, from Heldai, Tobijah, and Jedaiah; and you go the same day and enter the house of Josiah the son of Zephaniah, where they have arrived from Babylon. And take silver and gold, make an ornate crown, and set it on the head of Joshua the son of Jehozadak, the high priest. Then say to him, 'Thus says the LORD of hosts, "Behold, a man whose name is Branch, for He will branch out from where He is; and He will build the temple of the LORD. Yes, it is He who will build the temple of the LORD, and He who will bear the honor and sit and rule on His throne. Thus, He will be a priest on His throne, and the counsel of peace will be between the two offices." ' Now the crown will become a reminder in the temple of the LORD to Helem, Tobijah, Jedaiah, and Hen the son of Zephaniah. And those who are far off will come and build the temple of the LORD."   Zechariah 6:9-15

When the Bible says that *"the counsel of peace will be between the two offices,"* it is referring to the offices of king and priest. The Prince of Peace, called *"the Branch"* in this passage, will fill both the offices of King and High Priest and will reign forevermore.

BABYLON THE GREAT, THE MOTHER OF HARLOTS

After considering the origins and the pervasive nature of Babylon as described in the Bible, it is much easier to see why such sweeping statements are made in the book of Revelation regarding her influence in the earth and also her ultimate condemnation. The responsibility for all of the blood shed on the earth is laid at the feet of this idolatrous empire (see Revelation 18:24).

The things which are written in Revelation sound as though the kingdom of Babylon, in the end, is driven mainly by economics. Jesus Christ has said that one cannot serve both God and Mammon, and the choice is well-illustrated in a study of Babylon the Great. The world today is increasingly governed by financial considerations, and the great men of the earth are the wealthy businessmen rather than the politicians or the military leaders. Organized criminals are perhaps the

Babylon the Great

epitome of the image which Babylon evokes, serving money "at all cost." In the end, Babylon will receive a well-deserved condemnation.

It is interesting that many things which are accepted as normal, healthy commerce are included in the description of Babylon in Revelation. Even that which could otherwise be good, and a blessing to all involved, becomes a part of the evil empire when it is served and worshiped above (or even apart from) the Creator of it all. Excerpts from the book of Revelation will serve to illustrate some of these things:

> *And one of the seven angels who had the seven bowls came and spoke with me, saying, "Come here, I shall show you the judgment of the great harlot who sits on many waters, with whom the kings of the earth committed acts of immorality, and those who dwell on the earth were made drunk with the wine of her immorality." And he carried me away in the Spirit into a wilderness; and I saw a woman sitting on a scarlet beast, full of blasphemous names, having seven heads and ten horns. And the woman was clothed in purple and scarlet, and adorned with gold and precious stones and pearls, having in her hand a gold cup full of abominations and of the unclean things of her immorality, and upon her forehead a name was written, a mystery, "BABYLON THE GREAT, THE MOTHER OF HARLOTS AND OF THE ABOMINATIONS OF THE EARTH." And I saw the woman drunk with the blood of the saints, and with the blood of the witnesses of Jesus. And when I saw her, I wondered greatly.*
>
> Revelation 17:1-6

> *After these things I saw another angel coming down from heaven, having great authority, and the earth was illumined with his glory. And he cried out with a mighty voice, saying, "Fallen, fallen is Babylon the great! And she has become a dwelling place of demons and a prison of every unclean spirit, and a prison of every unclean and hateful bird. For all the nations have drunk of the wine of the passion of her immorality, and the kings of the earth have committed acts of immorality with her, and the merchants of the earth have become rich by the wealth of her sensuality."*
>
> Revelation 18:1-3

The Living Tapestry

"And the merchants of the earth weep and mourn over her, because no one buys their cargoes any more; cargoes of gold and silver and precious stones and pearls and fine linen and purple and silk and scarlet, and every kind of citron wood and every article of ivory and every article made from very costly wood and bronze and iron and marble, and cinnamon and spice and incense and perfume and frankincense and wine and olive oil and fine flour and wheat and cattle and sheep, and cargoes of horses and chariots and slaves and human lives."
Revelation 18:11-13

"And in her was found the blood of prophets and of saints and of all who have been slain on the earth."   Revelation 18:24

Notice that most of the commerce described (with the exception of the slave trade) is not evil in itself, but rather is incorporated into an evil system with evil motives. The day-to-day "business as usual" appearance of things might be one of a prosperous culture, with many people enjoying themselves (although it frequently is at someone else's expense).

It is instructive to note that the slave trade is not the only traffic in human lives, since Revelation 18:13 ends by saying *"slaves and human lives."* There are a multitude of potential examples of traffic in human lives in modern society, all quite legal and acceptable. The list might include insurance companies, HMOs (health maintenance organizations), lotteries or any method of making a profit based on a statistical rate of return due to the involvement of large numbers of people. Some of these organizations even refer to their business volume as the number of "covered lives," rather than any reference to people as individuals. Compassion could not be an integral part of such a volume-driven business even if its leaders so desired, and dedication to the "bottom line" precludes any such desire on their part.

This type of commercialism is difficult to avoid, and is everywhere evident in American society today, including the Church. This is, in fact, one of the greatest forces keeping the Church in captivity in Babylon. The love of money easily taints the motives even of those who

Babylon the Great

begin an endeavor with good intentions. The issue is generally not so much the type of commercial endeavor involved, unless it is frankly illegal, but rather who or what is being served by the one involved in it. Is there a consistent attempt to serve the Lord and obey His laws, or is the profit motive the overriding consideration? If the latter is the case, then the way is open for all sorts of problems and abuses.

This emphasis on money and trade is not new to the modern age, although the current scale is unprecedented in the recorded history of the world. Archaeology has uncovered striking evidence of many thriving commercial centers from several different time periods throughout history. For instance, some recent discoveries in Israel from the time of Christ reveal a lifestyle that was much more cosmopolitan than had been previously thought. A good deal of this was brought in and imposed by the Romans, who brought along with them not only commerce but a very debauched lifestyle.

There is also a suggestion in the Bible of a similar situation developing before the creation of man, having to do with the fall of Lucifer. This was mentioned in Chapter Three in the discussion of the change of Lucifer's name to *Satan*. It is impossible for us to know what type of trade was being conducted at that time, or how it led to violence and contributed to Satan's fall, but the Bible is quite explicit in its description:

> *"You were blameless in your ways from the day you were created, until unrighteousness was found in you. By the abundance of your trade you were internally filled with violence, and you sinned; therefore I have cast you as profane from the mountain of God. And I have destroyed you, O covering cherub, from the midst of the stones of fire. Your heart was lifted up because of your beauty; you corrupted your wisdom by reason of your splendor. I cast you to the ground; I put you before kings, that they may see you. By the multitude of your iniquities, in the unrighteousness of your trade, you profaned your sanctuaries. Therefore I have brought fire from the midst of you; it has consumed you, and I have turned you to ashes on the earth in the eyes of all who see you."*   Ezekiel 28:15-18

The Living Tapestry

Now that Satan has fallen and dragged a large portion of creation down with him, he has brought his methods along with him. As the king of Babylon the Great, the mother of harlots, he oversees this abundant trade that has been referred to in the book of Revelation, and also the violence and corruption that often accompanies it. It is out of such a place and out of such a way of living that God has continually called His people throughout the ages. It is out of Babylon that the Lord delivered His people hundreds of years ago, and it is out of Babylon the Great that He will deliver His people as this present age comes to a close.

A Prayer for the People of God

O great and mighty God, Ruler of Heaven and earth,
Look upon the oppressed condition of Your people, we pray, and have mercy upon us! We do not present this prayer because of any merit of our own, but rather we confess our sin and unworthiness, and that we have all gone into captivity in one way or another.
Dear Lord, call Your people out of Babylon, both the Church and the Jewish people. Deliver us from our captivity and restore Your Temple, that Your name may be worshipped and glorified! Deliver us from the world system which worships the moon, the stars, the creation and Mammon. Cause us to be a people separated unto You and made holy by the blood of Your Son Jesus Christ. And may we reign with You in righteousness forever, for You are worthy, Lord God Almighty!

Amen!

Endnotes:

1. *Unger's Bible Dictionary,* by Merrill F. Unger, Moody Press, Chicago, IL., 1981.
2. See Chapter 3, page 64.
3. See Chapter 3, page 88.

Chapter Seven

Mahlon

We had higher hopes than this. Ah, such high hopes! But, we must come down to earth, mustn't we?

When we were first married, Elimelech (I called him Eli) and I were so happy, and we couldn't wait to have a child. And now, we have waited nearly seven long years. We thought it would happen right away, like it did for all of our friends, but it didn't. After two years of waiting and hoping, we talked with the priest about it. He said we would have to ask God for a child. We presented the right sacrifices, but still it took this long!

Finally, thank the Lord, I conceived, and now we have a son! I had wanted to name him Perez, a noble name from our tribe, but now I guess that will have to wait. Last night, Eli and I agreed to name the baby Mahlon.

He somehow doesn't look as well as other newborn babies. His color is not quite right. I was afraid there would be something wrong with him, and it seems that my fears have been realized!

This fits the type of luck we have been having these past few years. First Eli hurt himself at work and had to stop for a while. Then, about the time he was getting completely well again, the work slowed down, and they didn't need him as much. Money has been pretty tight most of the time. We have a little land, but not much, and the crops haven't been very good lately.

Well, at least little Mahlon is hungry! Maybe he can grow and look better in a year or two. Right now, I guess I need a little rest. I feel pretty tired.

I wish Eli were home already. He said he wouldn't be gone long. Tomorrow is the Sabbath, so we must get ready, and next week the child has to be circumcised. I hope God gives us another son and that he looks stronger than his brother. The way things have been going for us, though, I'm afraid I can't be overly optimistic.

Maybe the crops will get better, and we could save some money. Oh, I can't think about those things right now, I must get some sleep. Mahlon is quiet now, so I had better take advantage of this. I may not get another chance right away.

— The Friendship of Ruth —

The story of Ruth and Naomi is a beautiful and well-known account of a relationship that endured through very hard times. The words of Ruth have become legendary, making her an icon of faithfulness, and they have caused her to be quoted in songs and poems throughout the centuries.

Ruth's famous speech to Naomi was spoken after all the men of their family had died, and there appeared to be very little hope of anything good in the lives of the two women. The family was living in a foreign land (Ruth's homeland) in order to escape famine in Israel, and the deaths they had experienced in the family only made the hard times that much worse. It was in this context that Ruth vowed to stay with Naomi no matter what transpired. In answer to Naomi's advice to Ruth, telling her to go back to her previous home and try to build a new life for herself, Ruth replied:

> *"Do not urge me to leave you or turn back from following you; for where you go, I will go, and where you lodge, I will lodge. Your people shall be my people, and your God, my God. Where you die, I will die, and there I will be buried. Thus may the* Lord *do to me, and worse, if anything but death parts you and me."*　　　　Ruth 1:16-17

Several features of this account serve to enhance its impact, but one of the most striking is what might be called the "paradox of the person." Ruth was a woman, a foreigner, a nobody. Her role was, on the surface, a small one. She was not involved in delivering the nation of Israel from an enemy, nor did she become a ruler or a great national figure.

The trappings of greatness were conspicuously absent from Ruth's life. Her claim to fame was nothing more than that of being a faithful friend to an unfortunate woman. However, in spite of such limitations (or maybe because of them, since God is in the business of exalting the humble), Ruth's story came to have a decided importance in the Word of God.

Most of the reasons for Ruth's importance to the Kingdom were not at all apparent, either to her or to others around her, during her lifetime. Nevertheless, her life was woven into the history of God's people and the coming of the Christ in a unique and timeless fashion. She should serve as an encouragement to every person who strives to live a faithful life, but feels as though most of it is mundane and insignificant. God can take the "ordinary" life and make of it something extraordinary.

FRIENDSHIP

Not only is this a beautiful and inspiring tale, but it is wonderfully integrated into several of the larger themes of the Bible in a way that could only be done by a sovereign God. Once again, the meanings of the names involved lend a great deal to an understanding of the message and help in weaving this book into the greater tapestry of the Scriptures as a whole.

Not surprisingly, the best place to begin is with Abraham, whom God declared to be the father of faith. It was said of Abraham that he was *"the friend of God"* (James 2:23), and the book of Ruth is first and foremost a story about friendship. The name *Ruth* means "friendship," and all of the rest of the names involved are significant as well. [1]

In the New Testament, Jesus reaffirmed this concept of divine friendship with His disciples:

> *"Greater love has no one than this, that one lay down his life for his friends. You are My friends, if you do what I command you. No longer do I call you slaves, for the slave does not know what his master is doing; but I have called you friends, for all things that I have heard from My Father I have made known to you."*   John 15:13-15

This type of friendship demands commitment, which Jesus demonstrated by giving His life for His friends. Ruth displayed a similar type

The Friendship of Ruth

of commitment when she promised Naomi that only death would separate them. Because of her faithfulness, this common woman of lowly circumstance found her place in the Scriptures and in the lineage of Christ.

FAITH

Not only is the book of Ruth about friendship, but it is also about faith. It seemed that something had gone awry with regard to this family's faith (although there were probably some very good reasons from their perspective). The story began with what should have been a very good start for a new family of believers in God.

There was a man named "My God Is King" (*Elimelech*), and he married a fine woman named "My Delight" (*Naomi*). That should have been an excellent beginning for a good and blessed marriage, but hardship soon changed the perspective. Precisely how the dreams of Elimelech and Naomi died cannot be known in detail, but time and circumstances soured their outlook on life.

Two sons were born to this union, and at that time, this was considered a great blessing from God. But instead of viewing their sons as a blessing and naming them appropriately, Elimelech and Naomi named their sons "Sickly" (*Mahlon*) and "Pining" (*Chilion*).

Unfortunately, things went from bad to worse, serving only to exacerbate this couple's dim outlook on life. Eventually, there was a famine in Israel of sufficient severity to force this family to move to another country in order to find sustenance. As if that was not bad enough, the father of the family soon died, and both of the sons married foreign women.

The family member who died first was "My God Is King" (*Elimelech*). However, the conviction that God was indeed king over the circumstances in their lives had already died years before. It was the death of that firm belief that gave rise to the problems in their faith, and the fact that Elimelech died first was symbolic of what was happening in their attitudes toward life.

The two sons, "Sickly" and "Pining," were not strong in their faith either, and they eventually died as well. At that point the women were left with very little, and they had to do something if they were to survive.

By this time, Naomi was beset by depression and despair. She was convinced that God Himself had turned against her. She told her daughters-in-law to return to their homeland and their own people. She intended to return alone to Israel. She had heard that there was food again in the land of Judah, so she decided to travel to *Bethlehem* ("the house of bread") and leave the two younger women behind.

As for the two daughters-in-law, "Stubbornness" (*Orpah*) did leave and return to her people to find another husband, but "Friendship" (*Ruth*) clung tenaciously to Naomi and would not forsake her. So it was that Ruth and Naomi travelled together to the land of Judah.

After reaching Bethlehem, Naomi told the women of that place to call her "Bitterness" (*Mara*) rather than "Sweetness" (another possible meaning of *Naomi*), because her life had become bitter. At such a low point in her life, Naomi certainly needed a friend to help her along the way. By being such a faithful friend, Ruth became a source of new hope for her mother-in-law. Thus, true friendship helped to renew faith in one whose faith had been exhausted.

HOPE

The pathway of renewed hope began when Naomi realized her hopeless estate and decided to turn to the "house of bread" for help. This same process applies to everyone who turns to Jesus Christ for salvation, since He is the Bread of Life. This is undoubtedly one of the reasons God caused Jesus to be born in *Bethlehem*, the "house of bread." Naomi was not yet aware of it, but both she and Ruth were going there to find their "kinsman redeemer."

Soon after the women had settled in Bethlehem, Ruth asked Naomi if she could go into the fields and glean some of the grain which was left over after the harvest. It was a Jewish law that a portion of the grain dropped in the field should be left for the poor, and Ruth and Naomi fit that description well.

While Ruth was busy gathering food for survival, she was noticed by a rich man, Boaz, who owned one of the fields, and he inquired as

The Friendship of Ruth

to who she was. When he found out her name, he instructed his servants to allow her to drink from their water and to glean among the sheaves, because he had heard about all that she had done for her mother-in-law, Naomi. Ruth went home and told Naomi about the kindness the man had shown toward her and that his name was *Boaz* (which means "quickness" or "fleetness").

In the culture of the time, it was customary for the nearest relative of a widow to marry her and raise up children by her in order to keep the family line alive. This was a means of providing support and security to widows. Naomi informed Ruth that Boaz was a close relative and told her about the proper way to display her interest in him.

It was at that point that the meaning of Boaz's name began to be shown in his actions. He wasted no time in going to the gates of the city and settling the issue with another man who was actually more closely related to Elimelech than he was. The other man declined the opportunity to redeem Elimelech's property (and so receive Ruth as his wife), so Boaz became the "kinsman redeemer" of Ruth and of her mother-in-law as well. This transaction was symbolic of what Christ does for the one who places his trust in Him.

After the marriage of Boaz and Ruth, they had a son named *Obed* ("servant" or "worshiper"), who was the grandfather of King David. All of these people were in the direct lineage of Christ, and so this foreigner named "Friendship" found her place into a type of "hall of fame," or "hall of faith," which ultimately led to the Messiah.

JACHIN

The name of Boaz was also important for another reason, connecting the messianic themes in the book of Ruth with the Temple in Jerusalem and the worship that took place there. It is in the association of the name *Boaz* with the name *Jachin* that these things become apparent.

Jachin does not appear in the book of Ruth, but *Boaz* and *Jachin* were the names Solomon gave to the two huge pillars in front of the Temple he built in Jerusalem (see 1 Kings 7:21). During the time of Ruth, the Temple had not yet been constructed. It would be her great-great-

The Living Tapestry

grandson Solomon who would build it, making it even more amazing that Boaz and Ruth chose the name *Obed* for their son.

Obed is the primary Hebrew word for worship which, of course, is the main reason the Temple was built. Obed was the grandfather of King David, whose conquests paved the way for his son Solomon to be able to build the Temple in Jerusalem.

Just as everything in the Temple had specific meaning, so also did the names of the pillars at the entrance. *Boaz*, as we have seen, means "quickness," and *Jachin* means "he will establish." The significance of Boaz's name was seen when he redeemed Ruth and Naomi, along with Elimelech's property, so quickly. When considered in connection with the Temple, the names of Boaz and Jachin taken together suggest that God will establish His work of redemption and His eternal Temple, and that He will do it quickly.

Since the Lord's work of redemption has been in progress for thousands of years already and is still not complete, this may seem like a rather far-fetched interpretation of these names. However, considering the scope and magnitude of the work and the people involved in building this great Temple, the time involved seems much more reasonable.

When it is also realized that these things are bringing about an eternal result that will never fade away, then the name "quickness" takes on an entirely different significance. The Bible addresses this concept in several New Testament passages:

> *But do not let this one fact escape your notice, beloved, that with the Lord one day is as a thousand years, and a thousand years as one day. The Lord is not slow about His promise, as some count slowness, but is patient toward you, not wishing for any to perish but for all to come to repentance. But the day of the Lord will come like a thief, in which the heavens will pass away with a roar and the elements will be destroyed with intense heat, and the earth and its works will be burned up. Since all these things are to be destroyed in this way, what sort of people ought you to be in holy conduct and godliness, looking for and hastening the coming of the day of God, on account of which the heavens will be destroyed by burning, and the elements will melt with in-*

The Friendship of Ruth

tense heat! But according to His promise we are looking for new heavens and a new earth, in which righteousness dwells.   2 Peter 3:8-13

For yet in a very little while, He who is coming will come, and will not delay. But My righteous one shall live by faith.
Hebrews 10:37-38

... for the Lord will execute His word upon the earth, thoroughly and quickly.   Romans 9:28

It will, one day, become readily apparent that, considering the scope and the magnitude of the project, the work of God in redeeming mankind was a "speedy" work.

Zion

Of the various people named in the book of Ruth, the story of Naomi, in particular, contains several types of allegory that relate closely to the lives of every Christian. The most obvious was already referred to above in the discussion of hope, and that is the need for everyone to recognize his or her hopeless estate and turn toward the "house of bread" in order to find the "kinsman redeemer."

Naomi's name also contains another allegory which involves the people of God as represented by the concept of Zion. In Chapter Three, Zion was discussed with regard to the idea that it refers to the people of God as well as a geographic location. Also in that chapter, reference was made to a very meaningful name change which was prophesied to occur in the lives of "the people of Zion."

For a quick review, *Zion* means "desert" or "wilderness," and it was foretold that the name would be changed to *Hephzibah* ("my delight is in her"). The name *Naomi* also means "my delight," although her life reached such a point of hopelessness that she advised others to call her *Mara* ("bitterness") instead.

Naomi was certainly undergoing a type of "wilderness" experience during those times of despair, just as Zion began as a wilderness and only later would become fruitful and delightful. She and Ruth were redeemed by Boaz, who was their "kinsman redeemer." The people of Zion were also redeemed by their own kinsman, Christ.

Redemption always involves the payment of a price, and for Boaz, this price involved the payment of money. In the case of Jesus Christ the required price was much greater, since He had to pay with His own blood.

Finally, when Christ is united with His people through this type of true friendship, the "offspring" is worship and service (the meaning of *Obed*), both gladly and freely given.

When Boaz and Ruth had a son, Naomi became his nurse, so that the neighbor women said, *"A son has been born to Naomi!"* (Ruth 4:17). So the picture was completed, and the desert made way again for the bearing of fruit.

Just as Isaiah repeatedly talked about rivers in the desert or the desert blooming and bearing fruit, the same theme shows up repeatedly throughout history in the lives of the people of God. Indeed, the real meanings of those passages in the book of Isaiah are not restricted to their geographic and horticultural possibilities, but instead are continually played out in the lives of people throughout the ages. God is in the business of bringing life to the desert and blessing to the lives of men.

Endnote:

1. For a list of these names and their meanings, refer to Appendix E.

Chapter Eight

The Key to Living Is Giving
by Helen Steiner Rice [1]

*A very favorite story of mine
Is about two seas in Palestine.*

*One is a sparkling sapphire jewel,
Its waters are clean and clear and cool,
Along its shores the children play
And travelers seek it on their way,
And Nature gives so lavishly
Her choicest gems to the Galilee:*

*But on to the south the Jordan flows
Into a sea where nothing grows,
No splash of fish, no singing bird,
No children's laughter is ever heard,
The air hangs heavy all around
And Nature shuns this barren ground:*

*Both seas receive the Jordan's flow,
The water is just the same, we know,
But one of the seas, like liquid sun,
Can warm the hearts of everyone,
While farther south another sea
Is dead and dark and miserly —
It takes each drop the Jordan brings
And to each drop it fiercely clings,
It hoards and holds the Jordan's waves
Until like shackled, captured slaves
The fresh, clear Jordan turns to salt
And dies within the Dead Sea's vault:*

*But the Jordan flows on rapturously
As it enters and leaves the Galilee,
For every drop that the Jordan gives
Becomes a laughing wave that lives —
For the Galilee gives back each drop,
Its waters flow and never stop,
And in this laughing, living sea
That takes and gives so generously
We find the way to life and living
Is not in keeping, but in giving!*

*Yes, there are two Palestinian seas
And mankind is fashioned after these!*

— The Jordan River: From Life to Death —

The Jordan River is the main water source and primary river system in the land of Israel. There are many features of the river which are symbolically very significant. Some of these are actually quite amazing when scriptural revelation, the meanings of various names and certain geographic features are studied in combination.

The meaning of *Jordan* is "descending" or "descender." The river flows from north to south, descending rather rapidly until it reaches the Dead Sea. Its course is continually winding, except where it widens to form two lakes, the Huleh and the Galilee (usually called the Sea of Galilee).

The tribe of Dan, one of the twelve tribes of Israel, settled near the source of the Jordan River. Remember that *Daniel* means "God is my judge," and *Dan* means "judge" or "judgment." Therefore, *Jordan* may also mean "descending from judgment." The symbolic importance of this river begins to take on new significance when considering that it descends from judgment to death (the Dead Sea). What a picture of life in this fallen world! It seems that God was careful to emphasize His message by making this the only river in the Holy Land.

Before proceeding with a discussion of the Jordan, however, several aspects of water's symbolism must first be considered.

The Water Paradox

All over the world and throughout history, water has been a crucial natural resource. The oceans cover approximately three-fourths of the surface of the earth with salt water and contain approximately ninety-seven percent of all the water on the planet. The world's fresh water supply is much more limited. Only one half of one percent of the water on the earth is fresh and readily usable. This comes, of course, in the form of precipitation, springs, rivers, lakes and aquifers.

The Living Tapestry

Fresh water is crucial for growing plants or livestock for food as well as for drinking and other purposes. The human body itself is over fifty percent water by weight, depending upon the individual (generally higher in males than females). In a newborn infant, water may constitute as much as eighty percent of body weight. This proportion gradually decreases as the baby grows.

For all of these reasons and more, water has long been a symbol of life. Nowhere is this more evident than in the Middle East, where water has been *the* crucial natural resource for every civilization which has ever existed there.

Water has also been a symbol of cleansing, which is apparent in both the Old and New Testaments. Jewish ceremonial washing and Christian baptism are both examples that are still practiced. The brass laver in the Outer Court of the Tabernacle was also used for ritual cleansing before entering the Tabernacle in the time of Moses. In the New Testament, the cleansing of the Church by Christ is said to occur *"by the washing of water with the word, that He might present to Himself the church in all her glory, having no spot or wrinkle or any such thing; but that she should be holy and blameless"* (Ephesians 5:26-27).

In addition, however, water can also represent judgment or sadness. The entire world was destroyed in the time of Noah with water, so that the symbol of life itself brought death. Also, the water of tears reveals sadness and suffering.

There were instances in the Old Testament of water as a source of disease or death, such as the "bitter waters" of Mara which were encountered soon after the exodus from Egypt. There was also a spring that was tainted at Jericho, and it was miraculously cured by Elisha the prophet. So, the symbolism of water is not universally good, but may depend upon its use or its purity.

THE SEA VERSUS THE RIVER

Although water is generally a symbol of life, as noted, its significance may vary depending upon its purity and the particular situation. This is nowhere more apparent than in the symbolic differ-

The Jordan River: From Life to Death

ences to be found in the Bible between the sea and the river. Of course, similar ideas can be found in other writings, and are not entirely unique to the Scriptures. "The Rime of the Ancient Mariner," for instance, speaks of a man dying of thirst in spite of the fact that he is surrounded by plenty of water.:

Water, water everywhere, and all the boards did shrink;
Water, water everywhere, nor any drop to drink. [2]

Other writings refer to the destructive power of the sea and its waves, whereas rivers are frequently revered because of their life-giving power. The Nile River was actually worshiped in ancient Egypt as the "Nile god," bringing productivity to the land. Many other rivers around the world have also been worshiped, at one time or another, by the people whose lives depended upon their waters.

The Bible may be unique in its consistent portrayal of the contrast between the sea and the river, and in applying these concepts so often to humanity. The Hebrew word for sea is *yam*, which means "roaring," and it is often used to describe the concept of the "sea of humanity" in its unsettled condition. The basic idea is one of human wickedness, as clearly stated by the prophet Isaiah: *"But the wicked are like the tossing sea, for it cannot be quiet, and its waters toss up refuse and mud"* (Isaiah 57:20). This concept is echoed in other passages as well, such as the psalm that speaks of the God *"who dost still the roaring of the seas ... and the tumult of the peoples"* (Psalm 65:7). The river, on the other hand, contains the idea of a flowing, life-giving source of blessing and goodness.

The sea is the confused, angry populace, whereas the river paints a picture of the people of God as a large, flowing conduit for the blessings of the Almighty. In Psalm 98, the two differing responses to the coming of the Lord are described:

Let the sea roar and all it contains,
The world and those who dwell in it.
Let the rivers clap their hands;
Let the mountains sing together for joy

The Living Tapestry

Before the LORD; *for He is coming to judge the earth;*
He will judge the world with righteousness,
And the peoples with equity. Psalm 98:7-9

The rivers clap their hands with joy because of God's coming, whereas the sea continues to roar in discontent and confusion.

There are also several other ways that this evil symbolism of the sea is reinforced in the Scriptures. Isaiah tells of the judgment of God upon the devil, who he referred to as *"the dragon who lives in the sea"* (Isaiah 27:1). In Revelation 13, the huge evil beast who is empowered by the dragon (the devil) also comes up out of the sea.

The deliverance of the people of God from Egypt was done through the sea. [3] In that instance, the sea was divided in order to make a way for God's people, but the same sea became the element of destruction for their enemies.

In the future glorious creation of *"a new heaven and a new earth,"* there will no longer be any sea (Revelation 21:1), in keeping with the fact that the sea symbolizes evil in this present age.

Another way to see this striking difference (and the way it relates to God's work) is to think about how water from the sea gets into the river. Both are, after all, made up of water. The salty water of the oceans is changed into the fresh water that becomes a river by a process that has several features. This involves the application of heat energy in order to extract the water from the ocean by evaporation, changing both its character and its purity, and the process of condensation, causing it to become a part of the river. It may happen by severe storm, steady rain, snow or even a trickling dew, but the end result is the same. Just so, God takes His chosen people out of the sea of humanity, applies heat in the form of the *"refiner's fire"* and puts them in the river as fresh water to give life and blessing wherever it flows.

Not everyone gets there the same way. For some the journey seems more stormy than for others, although all must make the same basic trip and undergo a conversion that is identical in its essential nature.

As always, the actions of Jesus were in complete harmony with all of the concepts of Holy Scripture. When He stilled the storm and calmed

The Jordan River: From Life to Death

the sea, He was demonstrating His authority over the teeming masses of humanity. The Bible clearly teaches that He will one day exercise that authority and take His rightful throne as the undisputed King of all the earth (see Revelation 11:15-17 and Daniel 7:13-14).

In similar fashion, the time when Jesus walked on the water was not simply a magic act, but showed His ability to remain above and separate from the waves of the sea. The fact that this same "sea" ultimately took His life (when He was murdered by human agency) only underscores the fact that He gave up His life willingly, and was not just a victim of circumstances. He had the ability to rise above His human captors and remain aloof, but chose not to do so — because of His love for mankind.

One of the most poignant pictures of Jesus' sacrifice is displayed in the prophet Jonah. That Jonah's experience was intended as a prophetic sign was clearly stated by Jesus in the New Testament:

> *But He answered and said to them, "An evil and adulterous generation craves for a sign; and yet no sign shall be given to it but the sign of Jonah the prophet; for just as Jonah was three days and three nights in the belly of the sea monster, so shall the Son of Man be three days and three nights in the heart of the earth."*   Matthew 12:39-40

Remember that *Jonah* means "dove," and that the Holy Spirit descended upon Jesus in the form of a dove at the beginning of His ministry (see John 1:32-34). Although the reasons were different, both Jesus and Jonah were "cast into the sea," experienced "death" for three days and nights and were miraculously delivered from that place of destruction by God Himself. Both were "swallowed by the sea monster," which was then forced to spew them back out.

In Jesus' case, the sea that destroyed Him was the sea of humanity. The sea monster was Satan, who has been called *"the dragon who lives in the sea"* (Isaiah 27:1). Jesus was raised from actual death, whereas Jonah was delivered from a deathlike state to make him a prophetic example of something much greater.

Jonah was delivered miraculously as a figure of Christ's resurrec-

The Living Tapestry

tion. Christ was raised from the dead to bring the hope of resurrection to all those who would believe in Him (see 1 Corinthians 6:14 and Romans 8:29). These symbols add significance to the deliverance of the Israelites from Egypt, since they were miraculously taken through the Red Sea.

This imagery helps to impart an understanding of what God is doing in the life of every believer throughout history. In a spiritual sense, every child of God is called out of Egypt, the land of idolatry and slavery to sin. Even Jesus Himself was called out of Egypt, although He had to travel to get there — since He had no sin. His parents were forced to flee to Egypt in order to escape from Herod (see Matthew 2:13).

All are brought through the "sea of humanity" as they are delivered from "Egypt." That same sea is the agent of destruction for God's enemies, just as it was for Pharaoh and his army (see Exodus 14:28).

After looking at the sea and what it represents in the Word of God, the river presents a contrast in every way (except that both are composed of water). It is this very contrast that will serve to make both the sea and the river appear even more definite in their meanings.

The Hebrew word for river is *nahar*, derived from a root word meaning "to flow." There are various rivers in the Bible, and they invariably bring life, cleansing and healing. However, these rivers have some unique and instructive differences. The Jordan River stands in stark contrast with several other rivers that might be called the River of Life.

THE RIVER OF LIFE

There are several references in the Bible to a river that flows from a supernatural source and takes fresh, life-giving water to everyone along its course. This is sometimes called "the River of God," and although it is never specifically called that in the Scriptures, it is nevertheless an apt term since the source always seems to be God Himself. There are three primary references to such a river: one in the original creation, one apparently when Christ returns to rule on this earth from Jerusalem and one when God creates the new heaven and

The Jordan River: From Life to Death

the new earth, where there is a "new Jerusalem" that comes down out of Heaven from God Himself.

With regard to the first river, the one flowing from the Garden of Eden, the Bible says very little. The Word of God never says that it flowed outward from God, but only that it flowed from Eden to water the earth:

> *Now a river flowed out of Eden to water the garden; and from there it divided and became four rivers. The name of the first is Pishon; it flows around the whole land of Havilah, where there is gold. And the gold of that land is good; the bdellium and the onyx stone are there. And the name of the second river is Gihon; it flows around the whole land of Cush. And the name of the third river is Tigris; it flows east of Assyria. And the fourth river is the Euphrates.*   Genesis 2:10-14

Eden probably means "pleasure," and the Garden of Eden was called *"the garden of God"* in the book of Ezekiel (Ezekiel 28:13). Even though this particular river's origin is not revealed, the implication is clear that the river flowed outward from the presence of God. Its source appears to have been supernatural, with a sufficient volume of water to divide into several rivers heading in varying directions and watering the earth.

Whether these rivers continued to flow after the fall of man in the garden, or whether part of the curse upon the land was a cessation of that flow of water is not revealed. Nevertheless, the first river that flowed out of the "Garden of God" might properly be called the first "River of God" in the Bible.

The second river that might be called the River of God is the one described by the prophet Ezekiel, in chapter forty-seven. What is revealed about that river comes on the tail end of several chapters describing the restored Temple in Jerusalem at the time of the restoration of Israel. When all of these things are to take place is not known, but the Bible says they will happen.

After describing the Temple in detail, the prophet Ezekiel then described the origin of a river flowing toward the east. It is important to

The Living Tapestry

note that the river begins rather small but quickly grows in size. In fact, the Hebrew word for *river* that is used in this instance is *nachar* rather than *nahar,* conveying the idea of a torrent instead of just a gentle flow of water. Even though it begins as a trickle, it quickly becomes too powerful to be forded.

> *Then he brought me back to the door of the house; and behold, water was flowing from under the threshold of the house toward the east, for the house faced east. And the water was flowing down from under, from the right side of the house, from south of the altar.*
> *When the man went out toward the east with a line in his hand, he measured a thousand cubits, and he led me through the water, water reaching the ankles. Again he measured a thousand and led me through the water, water reaching the knees. Again he measured a thousand and led me through the water, water reaching the loins. Again he measured a thousand; and it was a river that I could not ford, for the water had risen, enough water to swim in, a river that could not be forded. And he said to me, "Son of man, have you seen this?" Then he brought me back to the bank of the river.*
> *Now when I had returned, behold, on the bank of the river there were very many trees on the one side and on the other. Then he said to me, "These waters go out toward the eastern region and go down into the Arabah; then they go toward the sea, being made to flow into the sea, and the waters of the sea become fresh. And it will come about that every living creature which swarms in every place where the river goes, will live. And there will be very many fish, for these waters go there, and the others become fresh; so everything will live where the river goes."*
> *"And by the river on its bank, on one side and on the other, will grow all kinds of trees for food. Their leaves will not wither, and their fruit will not fail. They will bear every month because their water flows from the sanctuary, and their fruit will be for food and their leaves for healing."*   Ezekiel 47:1, 3-9 and 12

This river flows from under the altar in the House of the Lord, and

The Jordan River: From Life to Death

wherever it flows, it brings life. It even changes the waters of the sea from salt to fresh. Even the Dead Sea becomes alive — an exciting symbol of the resurrection.

It is also quite significant that the river flows toward the east. The Jordan River, by contrast, flows from north to south. The fact that this river flows in an easterly direction is important because, if followed to its source, it leads to God.

In fact, "the way back to God" is symbolically always toward the west in the Scriptures. This concept becomes evident when several different portions of the biblical account are examined together to find a common thread. For instance, the first man and woman were cast out of Eden, *"the garden of God,"* (Ezekiel 28:13), toward the east. Their way back (which would be westward) was blocked by the cherubim with the flaming sword (Genesis 3:24). Abraham, whose life was so important as the father of all who would be justified by faith,[4] was called by God to travel west to the Promised Land.

The children of Israel, after wandering in the desert, had to cross the Jordan from east to west in order to get back into the Promised Land. The Tabernacle, and later the Jewish Temple, always faced toward the east, so that the way into God's presence for the priest was toward the west, first to the Holy Place, and then into the Holy of Holies. The entire symbolic significance of the kingdom of Babylon being east of the Promised Land is part of this picture: God's people have to go westward in order to depart from Babylon and go back to the land of Israel.

At this point, one might rightly ask, "then what about Egypt?" It is not east of Israel. The key to understanding that piece of the puzzle is that a person is totally unable to go back to God from Egypt. Remember, the symbolism of Egypt involves the concept of slavery to sin, and a person must first be delivered from that condition before getting into a position from which he (or she) can then go "back to God." That deliverance from Egypt involves passing through the sea, with all of the symbolic significance of water baptism. Then, after a short trip (which God never intended to last for forty years), the Promised Land must be entered from east to west. All of this symbolism is important in understanding the difference between the River of Life and the Jordan River.

The Living Tapestry

The third and final river flowing from a supernatural source comes from the throne of God Himself in a future, glorified world where all of the evil of this world will have become nothing more than a shadowy memory:

> *And I saw a new heaven and a new earth; for the first heaven and the first earth passed away, and there is no longer any sea. And I saw the holy city, new Jerusalem, coming down out of heaven from God, made ready as a bride adorned for her husband. And I heard a loud voice from the throne, saying, "Behold, the tabernacle of God is among men, and He shall dwell among them, and they shall be His people, and God Himself shall be among them, and He shall wipe away every tear from their eyes; and there shall no longer be any death; there shall no longer be any mourning, or crying, or pain; the first things have passed away."* Revelation 21:1-4

At the time this takes place, God's dwelling with man will be such that no sun or moon will be needed for light, since His light alone will suffice. There will not even be any temple in that city, for God Himself will be the Temple. It is in this context that the true and eternal River of Life is found, flowing from the throne of God:

> *And he showed me a river of the water of life, clear as crystal, coming from the throne of God and of the Lamb, in the middle of its street. And on either side of the river was the tree of life, bearing twelve kinds of fruit, yielding its fruit every month; and the leaves of the tree were for the healing of the nations. And there shall no longer be any curse; and the throne of God and of the Lamb shall be in it, and His bondservants shall serve Him; and they shall see His face, and His name shall be on their foreheads.* Revelation 22:1-4

In this future blessed realm, the direction of the flow of the river is not mentioned. This may be because there is no longer the need for people to find the "way back to God," since His dwelling place will be with mankind permanently. Unfortunately, there will be those who continue to rebel against God and miss out on such a wonderful place.

The Jordan River: From Life to Death

The River of Life, the tree of life and the very presence of God Almighty will be out of their reach:

> *"But for the cowardly and unbelieving and abominable and murderers and immoral persons and sorcerers and idolaters and all liars, their part will be in the lake that burns with fire and brimstone, which is the second death."*   Revelation 21:8

JORDAN: THE RIVER OF THIS PRESENT LIFE

This brings us again to the Jordan River, the chief river of the land of Israel. The name *Jordan* means "descending," or possibly "descending from Dan." The river begins from three main sources at the base of Mount *Hermon*, which means "sacred mountain." These three rivers are (from west to east) the Hasbani, the Dan and the Banyas. The river then descends rather abruptly, so that by the time it flows into the Lake (or Sea) of Galilee, it is already six hundred and eighty feet below sea level. The river then flows out of the southern end of the Galilee and winds its way to the south, continuing to descend to the Dead Sea, about one thousand three hundred feet below sea level.

The Jordan River brings water and life to an otherwise very dry land, and at various times in the Bible it gives both cleansing and healing. Nevertheless, this river does not have the same purely life-giving quality as the River of Life, because it descends rather rapidly downward to the lowest place on the earth's surface (not including the ocean bottom), and ends in death.

Even at the river's origin, impending trouble is apparent. Both the Hasbani and the Banyas spring forth from the base of Mount Hermon, the "sacred mountain," as water out of the solid rock. [5] It is reminiscent of the water that flowed out of the rock supernaturally in the wilderness as the children of Israel wandered about in the desert for forty years. In spite of such a wonderful beginning, both of these rivers have idolatrous shrines right at their origins. In fact, the name of the Banyas is derived from the name *Paneas*, so called because of a shrine to the Greek god Pan located at its origin.

The Living Tapestry

The very name of the Dan River means "judgment," so the Jordan River brings not only the expected good things, but also judgment for sin and idolatry. It winds its way steadily downward on an inexorable course toward death. The Jordan is the river of *this* life rather than *the* River of Life.

In comparing the Jordan River with the River of Life, or the River of God, several contrasting points are immediately apparent. The source of the one is natural, the other is supernatural. One flows from Hermon, the other from God. The River of Life leads the traveler back to God, whereas the Jordan River actually blocks the way. The Jordan must be crossed in order to get back to God, just as this life must be lived for the same purpose. The Jordan ends in death, but the River of Life, on the other hand, ends up giving life to the dead.

With these things in mind, the symbolism of the Jordan can be viewed from an entirely new perspective. It supplied water for crops and abundant fish from its fresh waters. There was healing for Naaman the Syrian, and cleansing, when John the Baptist was administering his baptism for the remission of sins. Nevertheless, the storms on the Lake of Galilee could be dangerous, the river's flood stage could be destructive and the final destination was a dead sea of brine.

The life of Jesus in relation to this river was particularly instructive. He spent most of His ministry around Galilee, and a disproportionate number of His disciples were called while making their living as fishermen there. He asked His most piercing question, *"Who do you say that I am?"* at Caesarea Philippi, right at the idolatrous source of the Jordan River's biggest tributary. [6]

Jesus demonstrated His ability to cross "the river of this life" at its widest point without getting wet when He walked across the Lake [Sea] of Galilee. Nevertheless, He immersed Himself in this life, including death at the end, as symbolized when He submitted Himself to baptism in "the river of this life" by John the Baptist.

Jesus Christ identified Himself fully with the people of God, including being baptized by John, although He Himself had no sin in His life. He allowed Himself to be immersed in the Jordan when He could have simply walked over it on the surface and not gotten the least bit wet in the process.

The Jordan River: From Life to Death

The crossing of the Jordan River (at flood stage) by Joshua, when the water was miraculously divided, was a very significant sign upon the entry of the Israelites into the Promised Land (see Joshua 3:13). Joshua was told by God:

> *"Every place on which the sole of your foot treads, I have given it to you, just as I spoke to Moses."*
> *"Only be strong and very courageous; be careful to do according to all the law which Moses My servant commanded you; do not turn from it to the right or to the left, so that you may have success wherever you go."*   Joshua 1:3 and 7

The Israelites had been given miraculous passage through the river which symbolizes this present life, but there was a warning attached. They had to *"be careful"* to obey the law God had given them. As long as they did that, success was theirs. Unfortunately, they sinned in various ways, and victory was incomplete.

In fact, the children of Israel continued to struggle over the years, having alternately more or less success in overcoming their enemies, depending upon their level of obedience to God. When idolatry would creep into their lives, their enemies would gradually gain the upper hand. The Israelites would then experience times of repentance, renewal and deliverance. This sequence of events happened over and over again, until the land was finally subdued by David, and the people enjoyed peace under his son Solomon (see Chapter Nine).

After the time of David and Solomon, idolatry and division continued in Israel, with their attendant struggles, until the people were finally carried off into captivity in Babylon, with all of the spiritual significance discussed in Chapter Six.

All of these events in the lives of the Israelites apply symbolically to the believer in Christ today. *Joshua* is the Old Testament name with the same meaning as *Jesus* in the New Testament. Jesus Christ is the "captain of our salvation," just as Joshua was at the time of the conquest of the Promised Land.

The believer today is given the possibility of a miraculous crossing of the Jordan River, the river of this life. There is a promise of victory over the enemies of God in the earth, but there is still the same warning attached: *"Only be careful"* to obey the Lord, avoiding idolatry and *"the sin which so easily entangles us"* (Hebrews 12:1).

Looking at the Church, one might be tempted to doubt the veracity of these things. However, just as the children of Israel were often defeated and oppressed by their enemies because of their disobedience and idolatry, the Church has also suffered a similar fate. Just as the Israelites eventually were carried off into captivity in *Babylon* (the idolatrous world system, the word meaning "confusion"), so the Church has been taken captive as well.

In both cases, however, God is able to bring about restoration, and the final result will be *"a people for God's own possession"* (1 Peter 2:9) who will be holy and wholly dedicated to Him. It will be obvious at that time that He alone is worthy of praise and worship, and anything that might become an idol will pale in comparison. At that point in time, the Jordan River will be gone, and the life-giving River of God will again be the chief river of the Holy Land.

Endnotes:

1. "Just For You," Helen Steiner Rice, Doubleday & Company, Inc., Garden City, NY, 1967.
2. "The Rime of the Ancient Mariner" by Samuel Taylor Coleridge
3. See Chapter 6, page 117.
4. See Chapter 3, page 63.
5. See Chapter 3, page 71.
6. See Chapter 3, page 70.

Chapter Nine

Miriam

Jochebed was just sitting there, watching the sun set over the Nile. It was very beautiful, but not nearly so much as it used to be. She and Amram had not been married long, but they had hoped for a better life than this. These were the thoughts going through her mind as she sat there, but she was afraid to give voice to any of them.

"My father Levi told me about the way things used to be. I know the whole story of our people ... about the sons of Israel coming to Egypt during the famine and settling here, and about Joseph being the prime minister of all of Egypt. Because of Joseph, the children of Israel had enjoyed the favor of Pharaoh. Since then, however, things have changed a great deal. Many of the changes were gradual, but lately things are getting worse quickly.

"When my older brother Kohath grew up, and even during most of my childhood as well, life has been good for my people. Each family has a plot of land and some livestock, and the Egyptians have pretty much left us alone to tend to our own affairs. Over the past few years, however, they have begun to exact taxes and then to impress some of our men into forced labor. The men are beginning to talk of slavery! How bad can things get? The whole attitude of the Egyptians toward us seems to have changed.

"Now I am pregnant with our first child, and what I just heard sends a chill through my body all the way to my toes. I hope the baby will be a girl! (I never thought I would want that!) Apparently the Egyptians have developed the opinion that our people are becoming too numerous, and the new pharaoh has just sent out an edict. I am trying not to form the thought of it in my mind. What if the child is a boy? I have heard that they are going to start killing our newborn babies if they are boys in order to keep our people from becoming too numerous and powerful.

"Would they really do such a thing? I had thought that the Egyptians were our friends! My head starts spinning whenever I begin to think about it all.

"Our fathers had such high hopes for us when we were born. They named my husband **Amram** — 'high people'! And me then named **Jochebed**, 'Jehovah her glory'!

"We are looking like low people with no glory in sight! If I have a son, I don't know what I'll do, but we cannot go on living under such oppression forever. I believe this is a daughter. We will name her **Miriam**, 'rebellion,' because it must come some day before we are utterly destroyed!"

— Miriam and the Family Rebellion —

Having already taken a brief look at rebellion in the form of Lucifer and Nimrod and the entire kingdom of Babylon, which exists in a state of rebellion against God, it might seem as though such rebellion must always result in a permanent state of enmity with God. Such a condition would indeed be hopeless, if He is, as His name suggests, Almighty. Hopelessness appears to be the case for Lucifer, who became Satan, since the Bible tells us clearly of his ultimate destruction. Complete destruction also awaits the kingdom of Babylon as well, with no hope of reconciliation with God along the way.

In spite of these examples, there exists the hope of reconciliation and peace with God for those who have rebelled against Him. Jesus Christ paid for such hope with His own lifeblood, reversing the condition of hopelessness for the rebel who desires to change (or rather, to be changed by Christ). Nevertheless, this type of thing is never treated lightly in the Scriptures, frequently resulting in the death of the rebel, and sometimes even his family or others nearby. In spite of this physical death, there is still the hope of redemption for his spirit:

> *I have decided to deliver such a one to Satan for the destruction of his flesh, that his spirit may be saved in the day of the Lord Jesus.*
> 1 Corinthians 5:5

This hope of redemption is also shown in the fact that the family line is usually (although not always) spared. The blessing of the Lord upon that family can continue after the act of rebellion and the immediate retribution have passed.

There seems to be a difference between those who exist in a perpetual state of rebellion, having therefore no personal relationship with God, and those who belong to God but find themselves temporarily in rebellion against Him.

The former group is personified by Satan and symbolized by Babylon. Unfortunately, even the people of God can find themselves in rebellion against the Lord, although in their case the condition is not permanent. Such a state generally occurs due to either ignorance or presumption and can have some very harsh consequences. However, even though God's judgment may be harsh toward His own, the outcome for those who do not belong to Him at all is much worse:

> *For it is time for judgment to begin with the household of God; and if it begins with us first, what will be the outcome for those who do not obey the gospel of God? And if it is with difficulty that the righteous is saved, what will become of the godless man and the sinner?*
> 1 Peter 4:17-18

Therefore rebellion against God, and the resulting judgments upon the agents of sedition is a very serious subject, one the Church needs to hear in this late hour.

The rebellious state of the world at large, symbolized by Babylon and ruled over by Satan, will not be dealt with in this chapter, since it has already been discussed. Here, the focus will be upon rebellion within the "household of God," or among the people of God.

There were several instances of such rebellion occurring among God's people actually involving close family members of the ones whom God placed in positions of authority over the children of Israel. There were, of course, examples of rebellious acts in every generation from Adam onward throughout history. That, in itself, is nothing new. Here, however, the discussion will be limited to several instances of rebellion against God-appointed leadership among the people of Israel, and the significance of some of the names involved in those episodes.

MIRIAM AND A "SMALL" REBELLION

Early in the wanderings of the children of Israel, not long after they left Egypt, they remained for a time in a place called *Hazeroth* (meaning "villages"). There is no indication in the narrative of the length of their stay there, but the scene is reminiscent of the "settling" of people in villages. In all probability, they did not actually settle in

Miriam and the Family Rebellion

villages as we know them, but the meaning of the place nevertheless suggests that idea.

Invariably, when people live together in close communities, there arise disputes and interpersonal conflicts. Frequently the first disputes occur where the relationships are the closest, and that is within the family. Numbers recorded such a family dispute, but in this case, it was much more than just a family squabble. Miriam and Aaron, who were sister and brother to Moses, spoke against him. They objected to his wife, who was a foreigner, and they also questioned his authority (see Numbers 12:1-2).

Moses had been appointed as the leader by direct action of God Himself, and that fact had been confirmed by many powerful signs over an extended period of time. Therefore, what would otherwise have been a family dispute became a rebellion, not only against the authority of Moses, but against God Himself. God spoke directly against them, and punishment was meted out to Miriam in the form of leprosy, so that immediately she *"was leprous, as white as snow"* (Numbers 12:10).

One might very easily wonder why Miriam was struck with leprosy, while Aaron apparently remained untouched, since the Bible clearly states that both of them were involved. It could be that Miriam instigated the sedition, since her name was mentioned first, when saying that they spoke against Moses. However, in that culture, the man was generally held to be in authority and, therefore, more responsible, than the woman, making it that much more difficult to explain why all of the judgment should go to Miriam and none to Aaron. This seeming incongruity actually serves to draw attention to the episode and show that the real judgment was upon rebellion against authority rather than upon the individuals in question.

The name *Miriam* [Hebrew, *Mir-yam*] actually means "rebellion" or "obstinacy," and it is this rebellion within the family of God that is the real problem. This short episode serves as a pattern and type of rebellion in the household of God.

"Rebellion" (Miriam) was actually called a prophetess and had been active in worshiping the Lord. She had been the author of praise songs upon the deliverance of the people from Egypt and had led the people

The Living Tapestry

in dancing and praising God for His mighty deliverance. She was the sister of the God-appointed leader and the high priest. She had many reasons to feel that her opinion was weighty and deserved attention, but those very factors deceived her into acting presumptuously.

Such a course of events frequently occurs when people get a taste of success and position and then act on their impulses, rather than continually submitting to God's authority and sovereignty. David understood this human tendency when he wrote Psalm 19. Even though he was king of the whole land, he knew that he was, therefore, even more susceptible to sins caused by his own suppositions:

> *Who can discern his errors? Acquit me of hidden faults.*
> *Also keep back Thy servant from presumptuous sins;*
> *Let them not rule over me;*
> *Then I shall be blameless,*
> *And I shall be acquitted of great transgression.*   Psalm 19:12-13

This type of presumption generally involves the thought that when a person achieves some success in the church or in serving God in some capacity, God therefore has a special obligation to that one because of it. On the other hand, the person may assume that he now has unusual insight into God's way of thinking, that his or her own opinion must somehow be very close to God's and is, therefore, deserving of similar weight or authority.

The extreme example of presumption would be the person who lives in total disregard for God's words and His laws, but nevertheless supposes that God will forgive and bless him just because He is gracious and loving. This type of person somehow believes that God will be on his side regardless of the way he or she lives.

These thought patterns are delusional, but unfortunately the more subtle and religious ones do not always seem that way at the time. The conclusions of some people about what God would want or what He would do in a certain situation might seem entirely logical at the time ... that is, within the limits of their human understanding. God, however, is not laboring under the same limitations. As the Word of God says, *"His understanding is inscrutable"* (Isaiah 40:28), and *"His greatness is unsearchable"* (Psalm 145:3).

Miriam and the Family Rebellion

The only acceptable position for a believer is one of complete submission and obedience to God's will. The psalmist, as an introduction to this concept, wrote about the excellence of God's laws and His Word and the importance of obeying what He had already written for mankind. Here are the verses immediately preceding those above:

> *The law of the LORD is perfect, restoring the soul;*
> *The testimony of the LORD is sure, making wise the simple.*
> *The precepts of the LORD are right, rejoicing the heart;*
> *The commandment of the LORD is pure, enlightening the eyes.*
> *The fear of the LORD is clean, enduring forever;*
> *The judgments of the LORD are true; they are righteous altogether.*
> *They are more desirable than gold, yes, than much fine gold;*
> *Sweeter also than honey and the drippings of the honeycomb.*
> *Moreover, by them Thy servant is warned;*
> *In keeping them there is great reward.*   Psalm 19:7-11

After this came the prayer for God Himself to keep His servant back from presumptuous sins, as though this type of presumption was still a possible pitfall — in spite of honoring God's commandments to the best of one's ability. As is so often the case, pride can come in masquerading as something else and deceive its owner. The only solution is a humble reliance on God's own personal protection and deliverance from such subtle snares, while at the same time striving to listen to Him and obey.

A Subtle Rebellion

After the Israelites had wandered around in the desert for some time, there occurred something that was very instructive with regard to rebellion within the family of God. This involved two of the sons of Aaron, the high priest in charge of the service to God in the Tabernacle.

The two sons were Nadab and Abihu (see Leviticus 10:1-5). They were working as priests in presenting the various offerings to the Lord and decided to add a little variety to the routine. Rather than putting the burning coals on the altar of incense and then offering the incense upon it, as was the prescribed method, they decided to offer incense to

The Living Tapestry

the Lord from their firepans. When they did that, *"fire came out from the presence of the LORD and consumed them, and they died"* (Leviticus 10:2).

Not only did Aaron's two sons perish, but they had had no offspring, and so their family line was also blotted out as well. This passage may seem harsh, but it must be remembered that God is putting forth examples that are eternal in their meaning and their impact. Hopefully, it will become more apparent when the meanings of the names of the people involved are included, and the resultant picture is examined in the light of its eternal significance.

Before examining the names of those involved in this incident, it is first necessary to look back into Aaron's family connections and something that crept in unnoticed. The Scriptures say that the serpent was very *"subtle"* (*"subtle and crafty,"* Genesis 3:1, AMP), and Aaron's wife was the sister of a man named *Nahshon* ("serpent"). Nahshon was the captain of the tribe of Judah, and is named in several places in the lineage of David and, therefore, of Christ. It is very crafty on the part of the serpent to "creep in" to such a place, from where he could do his subtle work. This is not to say that Nahshon was himself a "child of the devil," but rather that these names bring a symbolism into the picture that was orchestrated by God for a purpose.

This illustrates the way the serpent infiltrates into "the family of God" and then brings about destruction. What a key position, right in the middle of the lineage of the Messiah and connected to the high priest by marriage!

The other names in Aaron's marriage are quite good, not only in his generation but also in the subsequent ones. His wife's name was *Elisheba* ("God is an oath"), and her father's was *Amminadab* ("my kinsman is noble"). Amminadab's great-grandson (and Nahshon's grandson) was Boaz, and the names surrounding Ruth and Boaz were discussed in Chapter 7. From them came *Obed* ("servant" or "worshiper"), *Jesse* ("wealthy"), *David* ("beloved") and *Solomon* ("peaceful one").

Aaron had four sons, two of whom were involved in this, and two who were not. Nadab and Abihu offered *"strange fire"* and were destroyed. *Nadab* means "liberal" or "spontaneous," and *Abihu* means "he is my father." Neither one of these names appears very remarkable

Miriam and the Family Rebellion

on the surface, but when considered in the context of what occurred in Leviticus 10, they take on new significance.

Nadab was using a rather liberal interpretation of the prescribed method when he offered incense on his own firepan, and was being, in a sense, spontaneous in his actions. He probably felt that he had the privilege to "add a little spice" to the proceedings, since he had been doing it the same way for some time. After all, he was the high priest's son and was well experienced in his job, and his brother agreed to it.

What they did wasn't much of a change, but what Nadab didn't know was that it had great spiritual and eternal significance. The altar of incense was just in front of the veil between the Holy Place and the Holy of Holies. It was the final stop on the way into the very presence of God and, especially at that point, the holiness of God had to be remembered and appreciated.

Remember that holy means "other," and it must be kept in mind that God is not identical with man, differing only in size and strength. God created man in His *image*, and according to His *likeness*. The holy Son of God became man so that men could become sons of God. An entire book could be written (and there are several) about the wonder of being made in the image of the Almighty God. Nevertheless, He is still God and men are not. He is working to make men who will be *like* God, but they will not *be* God. He is holy and must be approached according to His instructions.

After looking at Nadab, what can be said about the name *Abihu*? What can be the problem with the name "he is my father?" First, consider that this rebellion was subtle and, although the punishment was swift and severe because God was fully aware of the true implications of the act, the infraction would seem rather minor in the eyes of most men. The problem with the name *Abihu* was also rather subtle and can best be appreciated by looking at a conversation Jesus had with some Jews in the Temple in Jerusalem.

In that exchange, the issue of fatherhood was addressed. The key question to be answered was: "Who is your father?" This is well-illustrated in this discussion with Jesus in the Temple:

> *"I know that you are Abraham's offspring; yet you seek to kill Me, because My word has no place in you. I speak the things which I have*

The Living Tapestry

seen with My Father; therefore you also do the things which you heard from your father."
They answered and said to Him, "Abraham is our father."
Jesus said to them, "If you are Abraham's children, do the deeds of Abraham. But as it is, you are seeking to kill Me, a man who has told you the truth, which I heard from God; this Abraham did not do. You are doing the deeds of your father."
They said to Him, "We were not born of fornication; we have one Father, even God."
Jesus said to them, "If God were your Father, you would love Me; for I proceeded forth and have come from God, for I have not even come on My own initiative, but He sent Me. Why do you not understand what I am saying? It is because you cannot hear My word. You are of your father the devil, and you want to do the desires of your father. He was a murderer from the beginning, and does not stand in the truth, because there is no truth in him. Whenever he speaks a lie, he speaks from his own nature; for he is a liar, and the father of lies."
John 8:37-44

Therefore the problem in the name *Abihu*, "he is my father," is in knowing who "he" is. The "father" of both the motivation and action of Abihu and his brother Nadab was not God, but rather the serpent. This distinction in Abihu's name is rather subtle, but involves the crucial issue of fatherhood. In similar fashion, it was a subtle temptation, but it occurred at a very strategic point, right at the threshold of the very presence of God. As the psalmist said:

Righteousness and justice are the foundation of His throne.
Fire goes before Him,
And burns up His adversaries round about.   Psalm 97:2-3

The presence of God can be a very dangerous place if a person is in an adversarial position in his relationship with the Almighty, and God always sees the true motivation of the heart very clearly.

After the deaths of Nadab and Abihu, two of their cousins were called upon to carry their bodies away (see Leviticus 10:4). They were

Miriam and the Family Rebellion

sons of *Uzziel*, which means "my strength is God," and their names were *Mishael* ("who is what God is?") and *Elzaphan* ("whom God protects"). These names demonstrate some of the important lessons to be derived from this tragedy. In order to be able to survive and carry away those who were destroyed, their strength had to come from God. The names of the two who did the carrying demonstrated both God's holiness ("who is what God is?") and the fact that their survival in such a situation depended upon protection from Him ("whom God protects").

Even the names of the two surviving sons are important. They were *Eleazar* ("help of God") and *Ithamar* ("land of palms"). The one typifies the fact that survival takes place only with God's help, and the other represents a well-watered place in the midst of the desert. Those who are often described in the Bible as *"the remnant"* (for instance, see Isaiah 37:31-32), those who are not destroyed in judgment, are those who are watered by God, who is *"the fountain of living water"* (Jeremiah 17:13). They will bear fruit in the midst of what would otherwise be considered a desert waste (refer to the discussion of Zion, Chapter Three). In the Holy Land, that would likely appear as a "land of palms," and so Ithamar portrays the "remnant" which remains and bears fruit after the judgment of God has destroyed the others.

An Organized and Open Rebellion

Not long after these things, there occurred a more organized rebellion against Moses and Aaron. Two hundred and fifty leaders of the congregation, *"men of renown,"* came forward and challenged their leaders' authority (see Numbers 16:2). This respected and powerful group claimed that Moses and Aaron had usurped various privileges and offices that should rightfully have been shared with others. In particular, the office of the priesthood was solely in the hands of the family of Aaron, even though some of these leaders were themselves of the tribe of Levi. They wanted to claim the right to share in the priestly duties, rather than being confined to the service of the Tabernacle, which they perceived as being an inferior position.

When this challenge was issued, Moses immediately responded by falling on His face and placing the settlement of the matter squarely in the hands of God (see Numbers 16:4). He then told the conspirators to appear before the door of the Tabernacle the next day, assuring them that God would clearly show His choice of leaders to everyone.

When the next day arrived, and all of the leaders were gathered together, the Lord spoke to Moses, telling him to get out of the way. He was about to destroy the entire congregation. Moses then interceded for the others, and only the leaders of the insurrection were destroyed.

The manner in which these men were destroyed was quite unusual and frightening, in order to make it quite clear that God Himself was making the judgment. The earth opened up and swallowed the ringleaders of the revolt, along with their families and livestock, taking them *"down alive to Sheol [the nether world]"* (Numbers 16:33). In addition, *"fire came forth from the LORD"* and destroyed the two hundred and fifty leaders who were gathered together before the Tent of Meeting (Numbers 16:35).

All of these incidents of rebellion were very tragic. The larger the rebellion, the greater the tragedy. In this particular example, hundreds of people perished. In spite of that, the people of the congregation began to grumble the next day, laying the blame for the disaster at the feet of Moses and Aaron, and further judgment ensued. Thousands perished before the plague was halted by the intercession of the servants of God.

Knowing of His grace and mercy, all of these responses may seem very harsh on the part of God, but such "family" rebellions have a way of growing ever larger and more disastrous if not dealt with quickly and decisively. In the rebellion to be discussed in the next section, that is exactly what happened, when Absalom's subtle rebellion was allowed to grow into a national civil war.

In order to more fully appreciate some of the reasons for this insurrection against Moses (and ultimately against God), a study of the names of those involved again helps to shed a great deal of light on the subject. The rebellion was led by a man named *Korah*, which means "baldness."

This whole episode in Israel's history was later referred to as "Korah's rebellion." The significance of this name lies in the concept,

Miriam and the Family Rebellion

discussed in the New Testament (1 Corinthians 11), of head covering being in some sense symbolic of being under authority. It is in that context that we see the possible meaning of the man named "baldness" as the leader of this rebellion.

Korah would not remain under authority as God intended, but rather attempted to grasp a higher position, because of his own qualifications. He was a cousin to Moses, and a very prominent leader already. His father's name was *Izhar* ("oil" or "anointing") and his grandfather's name was *Kohath* ("assembly"), indicating both an ecclesiastical and a social prominence. Korah undoubtedly believed that the things he was demanding were simply his due.

The men who joined with Korah were also men of impeccable credentials, being leaders among the people and of good background in their society. The two most prominent were *Dathan* ("from a spring" or "belonging to a fountain") and *Abiram* ("my father is exalted"). They were sons of *Eliab* ("God is my father"). As is often the case, however, those who are born into families of greatness begin to think more highly of themselves than they ought (see Romans 12:3).

These men were joining in the rebellion against Moses because of pride in their own positions and jealousy of someone else's position. There was nothing wrong with their names or with the names of their fathers. In fact, the names are in total agreement with the rather exalted positions they already enjoyed. They simply lusted for a higher place and fell because of it.

This scene is very reminiscent of what happened to Lucifer who, although he enjoyed a very exalted position in God's creation, decided to exalt himself yet higher. In the process, he fell to the very bottom.

In spite of the terrible nature of Korah's rebellion and the ensuing consequences, the mercy of God shows through wonderfully. Apparently some of Korah's children were spared, either because they were living in a separate place at some distance away, or because they fled when Moses spoke words of warning before the earth swallowed up Korah and the portion of his family that was with him.

Years later, some of the descendants of Korah became quite prominent in the Levitical service, and several of the psalms in the Bible were written by *"the sons of Korah."* A look at the psalms attributed to these men (see Psalms 42, 44-49, 84, 85, 87 and 88) reveals some wonderful verses about God's protection in times of trouble, His greatness and His ability to satisfy the thirsty soul.

When considering these psalms in the context of the history of the sons of Korah, they become even more precious and the impact is magnified. The mercy of God shines through the judgment like a ray of the sun after a severe and destructive thunderstorm.

A Small, Subtle Rebellion Becomes a Large Organized One

So far, this chapter has examined progressively larger and more obvious instances of rebellion in the family of God and, more particularly, in the family of Moses, whom God placed in charge of His people. After the time of Moses, Joshua led the people in the conquest of the Promised Land, and there ensued a period of rule by various judges.

Several hundred years later, the people began to cry out for a king, and Saul was chosen to be the first king of Israel. He was succeeded by David, and it is the story of David and his son Absalom that is central to this discussion. However, it is first necessary to take a look at the origins and some of the symbolism surrounding David's kingdom in the Scriptures in order to better appreciate the importance of Absalom's rebellion.

The best place to begin is with a woman named *Hannah* ("grace"), her husband *Elkanah* ("God has taken possession") and their son *Samuel* ("the name of God") (see 1 Samuel 1:1-20). Elkanah had two wives, one of whom had several children and was named *Peninnah* ("coral" or "pearl"); the other was Hannah, who was barren. The man loved Hannah and was good to her, but the other wife was in the habit of provoking her and irritating her, since she had children and Hannah did not.

In the course of time, Hannah became very depressed because of this and sought the Lord earnestly for help. She asked God for a son and promised to dedicate him to serve the Lord all his life. God an-

Miriam and the Family Rebellion

swered her, and thus Samuel was born. He grew up to be one of the greatest prophets in all of Israel's history. It was through the prophet Samuel that God would "take possession" of the kingdom of Israel, according to the name of his father Elkanah.

As Samuel grew, it became apparent that God was with him and that He spoke through him regularly. Samuel became the ruler of Israel and governed as a "judge" over the nation.

As Samuel became older, the people began to see that he would not be around forever and that his sons did not seem to be growing up to be great leaders. Because of this, and because of their desire for protection from a particularly noxious leader of the nearby Ammonites named *Nahash* ("serpent"), they demanded a king to rule over them. This was yet another example of the people's rejection of God's authority, since He was ruling over them through His prophet.

Samuel warned the people of the dangers to them of having a king like the surrounding nations, but they were adamant in their demand. So, God chose the tallest and most handsome man in all of Israel and set him over them to be their king.

This entire episode in the history of God's people, the children of Israel, occurred at a very crucial juncture. Samuel, whose name means "the name of God," was the last of the judges of Israel. It was to him that the people's rejection of God's authority was expressed, and it was through him that the kingdom was established in Israel.

The first king, named *Saul* ("asked for" or "desired"), was a king who was granted according to the people's desire. *David* ("well-beloved") was chosen by God to replace him. His kingdom came to be symbolic of the Kingdom of God. The issue of rebellion against God-ordained authority became a key issue in each of these men's lives, albeit in very different ways.

In the life of Saul, his refusal to obey the word of the Lord given to him through Samuel was the reason that the kingdom was taken away from him (see 1 Samuel 15:10-35). His infractions may have seemed small at the time, but Saul's persistent pride, lack of true repentance and attempted excuses only served to confirm the defects of heart underlying his disobedience.

The Living Tapestry

In the midst of that dialogue between Samuel and Saul is to be found the most direct and well-known statement about rebellion against God's authority in the entire Bible:

> *And Samuel said,*
> *"Has the* LORD *as much delight in burnt offerings and sacrifices*
> *As in obeying the voice of the* LORD*?*
> *Behold, to obey is better than sacrifice,*
> *And to heed than the fat of rams.*
> *For rebellion is as the sin of divination,*
> *And insubordination is as iniquity and idolatry.*
> *Because you have rejected the word of the* LORD*,*
> *He has also rejected you from being king."*   1 Samuel 15:22-23

God then chose David, the son of Jesse, to replace Saul and promised to establish David's kingdom.

After David was anointed to be king, Saul remained king for many years, relentlessly pursuing David and trying to kill him. During that time, David steadfastly refused to rebel against God-ordained authority. On at least two occasions he could easily have killed Saul, but would not do so since God Himself had placed Saul in his position as king (see 1 Samuel 24:10-11 and 26:8-9). In fact, when a young man told David of Saul's death in battle, in the process claiming to be the agent of Saul's euthanasia (since the king was not yet dead, or so the man asserted), David had him executed because he said he had destroyed the Lord's anointed (see 2 Samuel 1:10-16). The issue of authority as delegated by the Almighty was thus demonstrated by God through these examples, and the kingdom was established in the line of David, the man who refused to usurp that authority.

The words spoken by the prophets regarding David's kingdom clearly show that his kingdom was not only one that was blessed by God, but rather it was meant to typify the greater and enduring Kingdom of God Almighty. That concept was made even more apparent by the greatness of the kingdom under David's son *Solomon* ("peaceful one"), since Jesus Christ will rule on earth over the greatest kingdom ever as the Son of God. Solomon ruled over the greatest kingdom Is-

Miriam and the Family Rebellion

rael ever had and also built the Temple, the very thing which Jesus Christ is doing spiritually.

Look at what Nathan the prophet said to David regarding these things:

> *"When your days are complete and you lie down with your fathers, I will raise up your descendant after you, who will come forth from you, and I will establish his kingdom. He shall build a house for My name, and I will establish the throne of his kingdom forever. I will be a father to him and he will be a son to Me; when he commits iniquity, I will correct him with the rod of men and the strokes of the sons of men, but My lovingkindness shall not depart from him, as I took it away from Saul, whom I removed from before you. And your house and your kingdom shall endure before Me forever; your throne shall be established forever."* 2 Samuel 7:12-16

It was through Solomon that the prophecy obtained a fulfillment in one of David's sons. However, it is through Jesus Christ that the throne will be established forever, an everlasting house being built for the name of the Lord. Even now, these things are still in the process of being accomplished by Him.

In order to properly appreciate the true significance of Absalom's rebellion, it is essential to remember the historical setting. Samuel the prophet was the last of the Israelite rulers called "judges," and the one who established the first kingdom in Israel. He presided as God's spokesman over this crucial time of transition, a time of great prophetic and symbolic significance.

Samuel's birth was miraculous, his mother's name was "grace" (*Hannah*), and his very name meant "the name of God." In all of this, God was in the process of "making a name for Himself," as the name of His prophet suggested. He had redeemed the Israelites in order to make a name for Himself (see 2 Samuel 7:23), and the Temple that would soon be built would be called a house for His name. The man whom God chose as king was David, whose name ("well-beloved") was reminiscent of the voice from Heaven that said of Jesus Christ: *"this is my beloved Son, in whom I am well-pleased"* (Matthew 3:17).

The Living Tapestry

The son of David who would build the Temple of God, who was renowned for his wisdom and who became the greatest of the kings of Israel, was *Solomon* ("peaceful one"). In the life of Solomon, Christ is portrayed, since He is the Builder of the Temple, the Wisdom of God, the King of Kings and the Prince of Peace. However, it was not Solomon, but Absalom, who was first favored as David's successor to the throne of Israel.

David's son Absalom stood poised to inherit this kingdom — the kingdom God was establishing in Israel with such extensive prophetic significance. Absalom was actually situated at the very center of the fulfillment of God's plan in the earth. He was favored with great charm and good looks. He had the favor of his father, the king, and the people of the nation loved him.

The name *Absalom*, "the father's peace," only serves to illustrate the potential destiny of this son. Absalom could have been the one to establish the everlasting kingdom foretold by the prophet. He had every opportunity to be the agent of the peace for which his father had fought long and hard. Even his hair, the length and thickness of which were legendary, added to the picture. Such long hair was a symbol of strength in Israel because of the historic example of Samson, the man of great physical strength who delivered Israel from her enemies.

Nevertheless, instead of peace, Absalom brought civil war. Rather than establishing David's kingdom, he almost brought about its demise. Instead of his hair becoming a symbol of Israel's strength, it became the agent of his personal destruction. He was killed after his hair became entangled in a tree and left him hanging there defenseless.

This tragedy took place because Absalom refused to wait for his succession to the throne to occur at the proper time. His rebellion had rather small, subtle beginnings, but eventually grew into a very destructive and costly civil war. He began by undermining the king in his relationship with the people, presenting himself as a better alternative:

> *And Absalom used to rise early and stand beside the way to the gate; and it happened that when any man had a suit to come to the king for judgment, Absalom would call to him and say, "From what city are*

Miriam and the Family Rebellion

you?" And he would say, "Your servant is from one of the tribes of Israel."

Then Absalom would say to him, "See, your claims are good and right, but no man listens to you on the part of the king." Moreover, Absalom would say, "Oh that one would appoint me judge in the land, then every man who has any suit or cause could come to me, and I would give him justice."

And it happened that when a man came near to prostrate himself before him, he would put out his hand and take hold of him and kiss him. And in this manner Absalom dealt with all Israel who came to the king for judgment; so Absalom stole away the hearts of the men of Israel. 2 Samuel 15:2-6

After some years, when Absalom felt that he had adequate support among the people, he led a revolt and declared himself king in *Hebron* ("alliance"). He then proceeded to march against Jerusalem.

Because of the obvious strength of this opposition, David and his followers fled. He left behind a few trusted people as spies and informants, one of whom was named Hushai. Hushai was instructed to remain in Jerusalem for the specific purpose of attempting to thwart the advice of one named *Ahithophel*. In this role, he became instrumental in saving David from destruction at the hands of Absalom.

It seems that Ahithophel was highly regarded as a very wise counselor in David's kingdom, in spite of the fact that his name meant "brother of foolishness." Absalom had enlisted him into his service as a valuable asset to his budding kingdom. The fact that Ahithophel was Bathsheba's grandfather probably made Absalom's job of recruiting him that much easier.

Hushai, whose name means "hasty," had been a good and faithful friend to David, who had told him to remain behind because he feared the counsel of Ahithophel. In order to fulfill his mission, Hushai told Absalom, *"As I have served in your father's presence, so I will be in your presence"* (2 Samuel 16:19). It then came about that, when David had fled, Absalom asked for advice as to what should be done. Ahithophel gave what turned out to be the wise counsel, to pursue David immediately and destroy him before he had time to organize a resistance.

The Living Tapestry

Hushai countered this advice with the proposal that David was too smart to be in the open, but was hiding somewhere. He advised Absalom to wait and take the time to gather all Israel together in great numbers in order to attack David and his men, so that victory would be assured. That gave David enough time to get away and prepare for battle, and to choose the proper place in which to fight. Ironically, the "brother of foolishness" (*Ahithophel*) had given the wise counsel, which was ignored, while "hasty" (*Hushai*) had advised them not to act in haste, thereby bringing about their ultimate defeat.

When David learned of Ahithophel's counsel, he crossed over to the other side of the Jordan River. There he received help from several people he had come to know during his earlier wanderings in the wilderness. They provided food and drink to help revive David's men for the battle.

David went to a place called Mahanaim, which has a very significant meaning. That was where Jacob received help from God when *"the angels of God met him"* as he was on his way to meet his estranged brother Esau (Genesis 32:1-2). Therefore he named that place *Mahanaim*, which means "two companies," or "double host."

Before the battle against Absalom began, David and his men received help from God, and with the resultant "two companies" (his own men, plus the angels of God to help) was able to defeat Absalom and his huge army. Absalom himself was found hanging from a tree by his long hair, having become entangled while riding beneath it on a donkey. He was then slain by Joab, who was the leader of one third of David's forces. This ended Absalom's rebellion.

A consideration of the events leading up to David's reign, the prophecy about the everlasting nature of his kingdom and the meanings of some of the names involved help to illustrate the profound significance of Absalom's rebellion. It is important to remember that Absalom seemed destined for what Solomon finally achieved. However, he was unwilling to wait for God's timing, and not only ruined his own future in the process but also brought about great death, destruction and misery in all of Israel.

Even the names of the two men's mothers add something to the

Miriam and the Family Rebellion

overall picture. Absalom was the son of *Maacah*, which means "oppression." Solomon was the son of *Bathsheba*, or "daughter of the oath." It was through Bathsheba that God's oath to David about establishing his kingdom through his son would be fulfilled. It was also a sign of great grace on the part of the Lord and hope for everyone, that king Solomon should be born of such an adulterous union. This doesn't mean that God simply excused the sin of David and Bathsheba. Their first child died, and the sword never left David's household afterwards.

Both the kingdom of David and the rebellion of Absalom have enduring significance, as they portray truths that still apply today, pointing to the everlasting Kingdom of the Son of God. The reign of Solomon, in its greatness, seems to suggest the coming reign of the Messiah:

> *So King Solomon became greater than all the kings of the earth in riches and in wisdom. And all the earth was seeking the presence of Solomon, to hear his wisdom which God had put in his heart.*
> 1 Kings 10:23-24

As David was growing old and about to die, his eldest surviving son, Adonijah, made a play for the throne. David, however, had promised the kingdom to his son Solomon; Adonijah was acting on his own, without the king's blessing. Upon hearing about this son's actions, David immediately made Solomon king over Israel.

Solomon was able to quickly secure his kingdom, and he ruled with great success for forty years. His one weakness was the influence his many foreign wives exercised over him toward the end of his life. In spite of his failures later in life, the reign of Solomon in many ways typifies the reign of Christ over the people of God. Solomon's wisdom and greatness have already been mentioned, as was his role as the builder of the Temple of God. The extent of his kingdom encompassed most of the known world at that time.

The name *Solomon* also means "peaceful one," just as Christ is the Prince of Peace. Nathan gave Solomon another name from God,

The Living Tapestry

Jedidiah ("beloved of Jehovah"), just as God the Father said of Jesus, *"This is My beloved Son."* The prophecy about David's future kingdom, referred to previously, made reference to both David's natural son and the Messiah, who was to come and usher in the everlasting Kingdom referred to by the prophet Daniel:

> *"I kept looking in the night visions,*
> *And behold, with the clouds of heaven*
> *One like a Son of Man was coming,*
> *And He came up to the Ancient of Days*
> *And was presented before Him.*
> *And to Him was given dominion,*
> *Glory and a kingdom,*
> *That all the peoples, nations, and men of every language*
> *Might serve Him.*
> *His dominion is an everlasting dominion*
> *Which will not pass away;*
> *And His kingdom is one*
> *Which will not be destroyed."*   Daniel 7:13-14

Even Solomon's great proliferation of wives may have some prophetic significance as it relates to the reign of Christ. The Bride of Christ is to be composed of many people from many nations, just as Solomon had many wives from foreign countries. Of course, Solomon was unable to make this a pure type of union and maintain his loyalty to God, because his wives brought their idolatrous practices with them. Christ, on the other hand, will have a pure and spotless Bride, with no remnant of idolatry. Though many in the Bride of Christ may have idolatry in their backgrounds, they will be purged and purified before uniting with Him. Besides, Jesus Christ is not subject to the influence of idolatry drawing Him away from His devotion to God the Father, as Solomon apparently was.

All of these elements of comparison and contrast between the reign of Solomon and that of Jesus Christ serve as examples and types of what is to come. However, the events surrounding the kingdoms of David and Solomon, as well as the rebellions of Absalom and others

Miriam and the Family Rebellion

before him, are available to us now as examples of both proper and improper attitudes in living and growing under the authority of the King of Kings. The consequences of rebellion against God cannot be ignored, and the events of today are being built into the Lord's everlasting Kingdom, just as surely as were those of the past.

MARY AND THE FAMILY REBELLION

All of these examples of rebellion against the authority of the Almighty lead inexorably to a consideration of the same tendency that is resident within every child of God. It began with Adam and Eve, and will not be finished until the last of God's children is perfected. The seed of sedition lurks insidiously beneath the surface in the hearts of the saints. It is this unseemly fact that might explain why the very mother of the Lord Jesus was named Mary.

If one were to discover that *Mary* the mother of Jesus had a name meaning "rebellion," the first impulse would undoubtedly be to dismiss it as a coincidence. After all, it was a popular name in that time and place. Certainly Jesus' mother was not of the rebellious sort! There were many women named Mary, possibly because of Miriam the sister of Moses. Nevertheless, the meaning of the name of the mother of Jesus was no accident.

How can this apparent contradiction be explained? The text very clearly describes Mary as a cooperative and faithful woman. When the angel told the virgin that she was to have a child by the Holy Spirit of God, her reply was simple and obedient. She said, *"Behold, the bondslave of the Lord; be it done to me according to your word"* (Luke 1:38).

After seeing to it that so many names were so significant throughout the history of the Israelites, could it be that God paid no attention to the name of the mother of Jesus? On the contrary, the fact is that no better name could have been chosen in all of creation for the woman who would bring Jesus into the world. It was the "family rebellion" that created the need for Jesus to come to the earth as Redeemer.

The seed that would grow into the child named Jesus was planted in *Mary* ("rebellion") in the same way the Holy Spirit plants a seed in the heart of each believer in Christ. Just as Mary, during childbirth, forced

The Living Tapestry

Jesus into the world, it was the rebellion of the very children of God that "pushed" Him into His own creation in the form of one of His creatures.

There is probably no greater analogy in the entire Bible than this one. Christ was formed within the one named "rebellion." In similar fashion, He is to be formed on the inside of each one of God's rebellious children, within their hearts. The best response to the work of God within is identical to that of Mary: *"Behold, the bondslave of the Lord; be it done to me according to your word."*

Mary's expression of gratitude is also a pattern to be emulated by each rebellious child of the King who experiences His gracious gift of redemption:

> *And Mary said:*
> *"My soul exalts the Lord,*
> *And my spirit has rejoiced in God my Savior.*
> *For He has had regard for the humble state of His bondslave;*
> *For behold, from this time on all generations will count me blessed.*
> *For the Mighty One has done great things for me;*
> *And holy is His name."*   Luke 1:46-49

Indeed, the consequences of rebellion against God cannot be ignored. However, as the Lord Jesus Christ has demonstrated, those consequences are not limited to the rebels alone. Not only do such consequences spill over to affect other rebellious children, but even the innocent one is touched.

God has identified Himself with the innocent by sharing in that suffering which is the inevitable result. Jesus Christ was born out of the people's rebellion, and He also paid their resultant debt. Greater love has no one than this.

Chapter Ten

Mephibosheth

I can hardly believe that we are about to have our first child! I am so excited that I can hardly wait. Jonathan tells me that he feels sure that it will be a son. He says that God has spoken to him and told him so. I do not know how he can be so sure, but I hope that he is right. I am so afraid, though, with all the war and fighting, and Jonathan has to be right in the middle of it all. He is a prince, and I love him so much, but even a prince can be killed in battle! Dear God, protect him and our son who is soon to be born.

We were talking about a name for the baby last night. Jonathan said that perhaps we could name him Kish *after his grandfather. I would rather name him something with real meaning, perhaps something noble or full of wisdom.*

Oh, Kish is not bad, I don't mean that. But there are a few really bad names, like Ish-bosheth, *for instance. What a perfectly awful name! "Man of shame!" Indeed! Kish is a wonderful name compared to that one.*

Last night, after our discussion about names, I had a dream. In the dream, our son's name was supposed to be somehow related to that horrible name of Jonathan's brother. It wasn't clear how it would be related and not be equally terrible, but the dream itself was very vivid. We were being told by a wise old prophet that our son's name was to be similar but somehow not objectionable. I wish the name itself would have been spelled out in the dream if it was really supposed to be.

Oh, I wish Jonathan were here! He's not supposed to be home from his battle camp for several days, and he left so early that I didn't have time to ask him what he thought about all this. He will know what to do. If God speaks to him, then perhaps He will tell him what the name is to be.

I wonder what ever possessed his father to name his brother "man of shame." I have heard that King Saul is sometimes troubled by evil spirits and gets in a very foul mood, which might last for days. Maybe he named his son in the midst of one of those episodes.

I have thought and thought and can't seem to get this out of my mind. The only name that I can think of is Mephibosheth, *"dispeller of shame" — to get rid of the shame altogether. But, I have never heard of such a name before. Perhaps Jonathan will know what name will be best. I will have to somehow rest my mind until he gets here.*

— Mephibosheth and the Shame of Rebellion —

The previous chapter examined some of the consequences of rebellion against God, beginning with small and subtle examples and moving onward to progressively greater ones. The next chapter will take a look at the cumulative effects of ongoing rebellion upon an entire society. In this one, the goal is more narrowly focused. The idea here is that personal rebellion results in varying degrees of deep-seated shame, that will inevitably affect not only the life of the one involved, but also spill over into the lives of others. The consequences of this can be profound, depending upon the magnitude of the rebellion and the position of authority of the individual involved.

The Two Kings

The first king of Israel was *Saul* ("asked for" or "desired"), son of Kish, of the tribe of Benjamin. The Israelites were unhappy about their leadership. Specifically, they desired to have a king to rule over them instead of God's prophet. This was displeasing to God. The people were actually saying that they didn't want God to govern them through a prophet, but wanted to be more like the other nations around them. The Lord warned the people of Israel that they would regret their decision, but nevertheless He granted their request.

Saul was tall, athletic and good looking. He was made king according to the desire of the people (the meaning of his name).

Several aspects of comparison between Saul and David have already been reviewed, especially their attitudes toward God-ordained authority. When David was anointed by Samuel the prophet to be the next king of Israel, he was a young man, probably still in his teens. Soon after that anointing, he was enlisted into the service of King Saul as his armor bearer (see 1 Samuel 16:21).

David was known to be a skillful musician, and therefore his duties included providing soothing music for King Saul whenever an "evil spirit" would come upon him. It was while fulfilling his duties as Saul's armor bearer that David happened to hear the challenges of Goliath, the champion of the Philistines, whereupon he decided to fight the champion himself. Also, during this time of service to Saul, a close friendship developed between David and Saul's son Jonathan.

With all of David's talents and successes, however, it wasn't long before jealousy arose in Saul, and he became intensely suspicious of the lad. He decided to kill David, and almost succeeded on more than one occasion.

In spite of all of his father's animosity, however, the love Jonathan had for David never died. It was Jonathan who warned David of the king's intention and of his need to flee to safety. David then spent quite a number of years running from Saul. During all this time, he steadfastly refused to kill Saul, even when he had the opportunity. He would not raise his hand against the Lord's anointed.

When Saul, along with three of his four sons, was killed in the battle against the Philistines on Mount Gilboa, David was grieved — in spite of the fact that he could finally become king of Israel. During his period of mourning, he composed this lament:

> *"Your beauty, O Israel, is slain on your high places!*
> *How have the mighty fallen!*
> *Tell it not in Gath,*
> *Proclaim it not in the streets of Ashkelon;*
> *Lest the daughters of the Philistines rejoice,*
> *Lest the daughters of the uncircumcised exult.*
> *O mountains of Gilboa,*
> *Let not dew or rain be on you, nor fields of offerings;*
> *For there the shield of the mighty was defiled,*
> *The shield of Saul, not anointed with oil.*
> *From the blood of the slain, from the fat of the mighty,*
> *The bow of Jonathan did not turn back,*
> *And the sword of Saul did not return empty.*
> *Saul and Jonathan, beloved and pleasant in their life,*
> *And in their death they were not parted;*
> *They were swifter than eagles,*

Mephibosheth and the Shame of Rebellion

They were stronger than lions.
O daughters of Israel, weep over Saul,
Who clothed you luxuriously in scarlet,
Who put ornaments of gold on your apparel.
How have the mighty fallen in the midst of the battle!
Jonathan is slain on your high places."   2 Samuel 1:19-25

THE SONS OF SAUL

Saul had at least four sons, and possibly five. In 1 Chronicles 8:33, four of his sons are listed: Jonathan, Malchi-shua, Abinadab and Eshbaal. There is one other son listed in 1 Samuel 14:49; his name was Ishui. It is unclear whether Ishui died young, preventing the inclusion of his name in the other references, or if Ishui might be another name for Abinadab or Eshbaal. Either way, at the time of Saul's death, there were four sons, three of whom were killed along with him on Mount Gilboa. The one remaining son was Eshbaal. At times, his name was given as *Eshbaal* ("man of Baal"), while at other times, he was referred to as *Ish-bosheth* ("man of shame").

Upon the death of Saul, David and his men went to Hebron, and there David ruled as King of Judah. The rest of Israel, however, was not yet part of his kingdom, but was ruled over by this one surviving son of Saul, *Ish-bosheth* ("man of shame"). There followed several years of war between Judah and the other tribes of Israel. During that time, the kingdom of David grew steadily stronger, while the house of Saul progressively weakened. Finally, both Ish-bosheth and the commanding general of his army (Abner, his uncle) were murdered, and the elders of all of the tribes of Israel came to David at *Hebron* (which means "alliance"). There they made a covenant with him and made him king over the entire nation. As soon as he was king over all Israel, David mounted a military campaign against Jerusalem and conquered it, and from there he reigned for the next thirty-three years.

Soon after his conquest of Jerusalem, David made inquiry as to whether there were any survivors of the house of Saul to whom he might *"show the kindness of God"* (2 Samuel 9:3). This he desired to do, in spite of the fact that Saul had pursued him for years, and even after becoming king, he had remained at war with the house of Saul for several more years.

In response to David's request, there was found a wealthy servant from the house of Saul, by the name of *Ziba*. He informed David of a son of Jonathan whose name was *Mephibosheth* ("dispeller of shame"). Mephibosheth had been living on the other side of the Jordan in a place called *Lo-debar* ("no pasture"). Mephibosheth was crippled in both feet, and was living as the guest of a man named *Machir* ("sold"), the son of *Ammiel* ("my kinsman is God"). King David invited Mephibosheth to come and live as his guest and to eat at his table. Thus, the man who wrote Psalm 23, about God the King making His people to lie down in green pastures, took this grandson of Saul away from the place of "no pasture" and made him his personal guest.

There is a similarity between the names of two of these descendants of Saul, Ish-bosheth and Mephibosheth. The latter half of each name is *bosheth*, the Hebrew word for "shame." *Ish-bosheth* therefore means "man of shame," and *Mephibosheth* can be rendered as "dispeller of shame" or "exterminator of shame." Both of these men are called in other places by names that end in "Baal" rather than "bosheth," clearly indicating the abhorrence for idolatrous gods in the minds of the Israelites. Ish-bosheth is also called *Eshbaal* ("man of Baal"), and Mephibosheth is referred to in other places as *Merib-Baal* ("contender with Baal"). Why Saul would name one of his sons "man of Baal" is difficult to say, but the names of both of these men became quite significant as the events of their lives unfolded.

Ish-bosheth ("man of shame") was the one surviving son of Saul, and he tried to be king in place of David, the man anointed to that office by the prophet of God. Ish-bosheth attempted a shameful thing and met a shameful end.

Mephibosheth ("dispeller of shame"), on the other hand, was chosen to survive and cause the family of Saul and Jonathan to continue. It was through him that the shame upon the house of Saul could, in a sense, be done away with. He was invited to dine in a place of honor at the table of King David, thus restoring honor to the family that had been defeated and destroyed.

Mephibosheth and the Shame of Rebellion

THE SHAME OF DAVID

The symbolism surrounding the names of Mephibosheth and Ishbosheth, however, is much more far-reaching than just the house of Saul, and it involves the concept of shame in the lives of God's people. In the previous chapter, several aspects of the rebellion of Absalom were examined. Of special interest, at this point, is the fact that Absalom's rebellion was characteristic of the great disasters that result from rebellions within the Kingdom of God. It occurred at a very critical point in the history of Israel, at the beginning of kingdom rule, and at a time when God was establishing some very important precedents.

In addition to that, there were amazing prophecies of messianic proportions spoken regarding the kingdoms of David and whomever his heir to the throne might be. It was in that context that Absalom's rebellion took place, putting a special emphasis upon associated events.

During David's flight from Absalom, he encountered a report concerning Mephibosheth. At first glance, the story does not seem very important. It is almost as though it is mentioned only in passing, not as an integral part of the narrative. However, upon closer inspection, while at the same time considering the meanings of the names involved, a somewhat different picture takes shape.

The most crucial point is that David was not simply fleeing from Absalom and his army. He was, in a very real sense, fleeing from his own shame and from the fruit that it had borne in his family. Certainly, David was not directly responsible for the rebellion of Absalom and his followers, but indirectly he had a great deal to do with it.

David's sin with Bathsheba involved both adultery and murder, and his persistent feelings of guilt for those crimes rendered him unable to effectively make judgments against such things in the lives of the members of his own household. He failed to deal with the rape of Absalom's sister, Tamar, which later resulted in the murder of the rapist by Absalom (see 2 Samuel 13).

David continued in this same type of avoidance of his responsibility to bring judgment for such crimes by refusing to mete out the proper punishment for Absalom's crime of revenge. By the time Absalom was exalting himself openly, king David was in an established pattern of

The Living Tapestry

avoiding confrontation with his son and failed to do so again. The final result was open rebellion, with devastating results, both personally, for David, and also nationally. The whole affair almost cost David his life and his kingdom, not to mention the disastrous effects upon the nation as a whole. The resultant battle was no small skirmish; it destroyed the lives of twenty thousand men in Israel in a single day.

Part of the judgment God pronounced against David for his adulterous affair with Bathsheba and the murder of Uriah (as well as of the soldiers who happened to be with him) was that the sword would never leave his household (see 2 Samuel 12:10-11). God could foresee the inevitable consequences of David's sin, and how the unfolding of events in David's family would lead to this judgment. The Lord had only to withhold His gracious hand and not intervene on David's behalf, thereby ensuring that he would reap what he had sown. David, along with his family, was stuck with the unsavory fruit of his own devices.

Unfortunately, this tragedy was also greatly magnified by the fact that he was king. Therefore, not only did David and his family suffer from the consequences of his shame, but the entire nation was made to suffer along with them.

THE DISPELLER OF SHAME

Into the midst of this seemingly hopeless and disastrous situation stepped a man whose name meant "the dispeller of shame." He played very little active part in the rebellion of Absalom or in the civil war that resulted. Nevertheless, his name, along with the contrast between *Mephibosheth* ("dispeller of shame") and *Ish-bosheth* ("man of shame"), and the circumstances surrounding his relationship with king David, all served to illustrate certain concepts that can then be generally applied to all of the people within the Kingdom of God.

Mephibosheth was the man from the shamed and defeated family of Saul who was chosen by King David to be honored. He was the son of Jonathan, whom David loved, emphasizing the role of love in the process of getting rid of shame in our lives.

Mephibosheth was displayed in stark contrast with the other surviv-

Mephibosheth and the Shame of Rebellion

ing descendant of Saul, *Ish-bosheth* ("man of shame"), who chose to resist and fight against the rightful king. The "man of shame" fought against the king, whereas the "dispeller of shame" was honored in the king's presence.

Mephibosheth was even privileged, during a time of crisis in David's life, to bring a blessing to the king. These things take on new and greater meaning when applied to a person's relationship with the King of Kings. There is a choice available — whether to choose the way of love and obedience, becoming a dispeller of shame in the lives of others, or to fight against the King and truly be a man of shame.

As David was fleeing from Jerusalem and from Absalom, with a rather small band of followers, he was met by a man named *Ziba*, who was a servant of Mephibosheth. *Ziba* is apparently not a name of Hebrew derivation, but is thought to probably mean a "branch" or "twig." Ziba met David and his company with provisions in order to sustain them. He brought them a blessing from *Mephibosheth* ("the dispeller of shame"). However, as a comparison of these two passages will show, he came not only with sustenance, but also with a lie.

> *Now when David had passed a little beyond the summit, behold, Ziba the servant of Mephibosheth met him with a couple of saddled donkeys, and on them were two hundred loaves of bread, a hundred clusters of raisins, a hundred summer fruits, and a jug of wine. And the king said to Ziba, "Why do you have these?"*
> *And Ziba said, "The donkeys are for the king's household to ride, and the bread and summer fruit for the young men to eat, and the wine, for whoever is faint in the wilderness to drink."*
> *Then the king said, "And where is your master's son?"*
> *And Ziba said to the king, "Behold, he is staying in Jerusalem, for he said, 'Today the house of Israel will restore the kingdom of my father to me.'"*
> *So the king said to Ziba, "Behold, all that belongs to Mephibosheth is yours."*
> *And Ziba said, "I prostrate myself; let me find favor in your sight, O my lord, the king!"*   2 Samuel 16:1-4

The Living Tapestry

> *Then Mephibosheth the son of Saul came down to meet the king; and he had neither cared for his feet, nor trimmed his mustache, nor washed his clothes, from the day the king departed until the day he came home in peace.*
>
> *And it was when he came from Jerusalem to meet the king, that the king said to him, "Why did you not go with me, Mephibosheth?"*
>
> *So he answered, "O my lord, the king, my servant deceived me; for your servant said, 'I will saddle a donkey for myself that I may ride on it and go with the king,' because your servant is lame. Moreover, he has slandered your servant to my lord the king; but my lord the king is like the angel of God, therefore do what is good in your sight. For all my father's household was nothing but dead men before my lord the king; yet you set your servant among those who ate at your own table. What right do I have yet that I should complain anymore to the king?"*
>
> *So the king said to him, "Why do you still speak of your affairs? I have decided, 'You and Ziba shall divide the land.'"*
>
> *And Mephibosheth said to the king, "Let him even take it all, since my lord the king has come safely to his own house."* 2 Samuel 19:24-30

Ziba obviously hoped to use this distressful situation for his own dishonest gain. When he arrived with help for David, David was running for his life and was so distressed that he was inclined to believe the lie. Because of the circumstances, he rewarded the deceiver.

When David later learned the truth, he apparently had so much on his mind already, and was so relieved that the conflict was finished, that he simply wanted the whole situation to "go away." He therefore told them to divide the land, giving half to each, thereby avoiding the trouble of making the correct judgment.

The more just decision would probably have reversed anything given to Ziba, punishing him as well, but evidently David was too exhausted from everything that he had endured to press the issue.

The Lie

All of this has a very important general application in the life of every believer who finds him- or herself in the midst of a struggle. That

Mephibosheth and the Shame of Rebellion

which happened to David is repeated in the life of most, and probably all, of God's children at one time or another. As the person is fleeing from the consequences of his or her own rebellion and that of those around them, the "dispeller of shame" meets them with both sustenance and a lie. The gifts are in the form of hope and a boost in faith, helping to sustain them in the midst of it all. The lie, on the other hand, is a little more subtle.

God has a procedure in place for doing away with the shame which is due to the consequences of whatever sort of rebellion a person has allowed to be manifested in his life. Our Father has paid the precious price of redemption with the blood of His own Son, Jesus Christ. The lie is that "the process" has defected and is on the side of the enemy. In other words, while the person is in the midst of the trial, the actual process that is working on his behalf to exterminate the shame seems to have turned against him. It seems to be adding to the burden of shame instead of relieving it.

Ziba told David that the "dispeller of shame" had turned against him, which seemed reasonable in the heat of the moment. The results of his own shame were so real that David concluded, "Why not? Everyone else is against me, and everything else has gone wrong." An identical thing occurs in the mind of each one who is undergoing the work that God uses to bring about the undoing of shame. Some plausible "twig" comes along with a little disparaging word, and immediately it looks as though the entire process is working for the enemy.

At this point, even though knowledge of God's work of redemption helps to sustain the weary one, it may easily appear that the process itself is at odds with the desired end. Weariness and the "heat of the moment" often alter a person's perspective, rendering accurate perception difficult or impossible. That is one reason why faith is important in the midst of trial, since God is at work in His people, and He is able to do a work that is good and lasting. In the end, the person who has embraced Mephibosheth will find him still on his side. The gifts are real and will help to sustain, and the lie is just that — a lie.

Chapter Eleven

Lo-Ammi

Here I am, with child again. Already I have two, and what strange names they have! Hosea insisted on naming the first one Jezreel, *possibly after the valley nearby. Of course, as always, he had a more involved explanation as to why he wanted to name the boy this. And, as usual, he said that God had told him to use that name.*

Then I had a beautiful little girl, and he wanted to name her Lo-Ruhamah, *of all things! No compassion! I really fought that one, but his mind was made up. I wonder what he will come up with for this one. I hope it is something a little more reasonable, like "Joseph" or maybe "Hezekiah." If it is a girl, perhaps he'll settle for "Mary" or "Ruth." I'm really getting tired of these weird names.*

There's no reasoning with him when it comes to such things, but still it's hard to understand. There has never been anyone in his family with a name that has even a vague similarity. It's no wonder that I don't feel like spending much time at home, considering these and other differences between Hosea and myself.

The other day, one of the women said to me, "Gomer, he is a good man, and you should appreciate him and stay true to him." What does she know about my life? She is the type (one of those self-righteous ones) who should keep her opinions to herself! I am the kind of woman who enjoys a good time. I have a lot of friends. What's wrong with that? There is nothing very unusual about that in today's society.

Oh, those religious folks never go along with anything that has any fun in it. What do they do for a good time anyway? I have personal needs that those people can never understand, and that is the way I was born. Surely God would not give me such needs and then turn around and judge me harshly for indulging them!

Come to think of it, I'm only doing what comes naturally to me. These children will start to tie me down a little if I'm not careful, but that's all the more reason to get away and "cut loose" a little. We won't live forever, so we have to make the most of the time we have.

Oh, yes, I care for the children, but they can't control my life completely, and my mother and sisters don't mind helping with them part of the time. Hosea will be home pretty soon. I wonder what sort of strange things he will have to say to me today. Well, at least he never gets real angry and violent like some men. That's one good thing about his religion!

— Hosea on America —

The previous two chapters dealt with the subject of rebellion and some of its consequences. Chapter Nine discussed the progressive nature of rebellion, showing its tendency to grow in severity if left unchecked. Chapter Ten considered the effects of personal shame arising out of rebellion against God's laws. There occurs also a widespread, pervasive degradation of an entire society's morality as the general populace increasingly lives in defiance of God. The prophet Hosea, the first of the minor prophets in the Old Testament, described a nation in exactly that condition — the very state in which America finds herself today.

Hosea addressed Israel's departure from God head-on, with some very remarkable and unusual methods. Early in his ministry, for example, God instructed Hosea to take *"a wife of harlotry"* as a sort of object lesson for the people. The marriage of Hosea to Gomer became an analogy, comparing her unfaithfulness toward Hosea with that of the people of Israel toward God. God was like a loving, faithful husband to His people, but they had gone after other gods like a harlot after strange lovers. The resulting state of affairs in the morality and godliness of the general populace was disastrous and eventually led to their demise as a nation.

A point-by-point comparison with specific events in the history of the United States of America will not be made, but rather it will be left to the reader to perceive those connections. America may not have been directly founded upon God's Word in quite the same way as the nation of Israel was, but even the historical revisionists cannot deny the importance of this country's Judeo-Christian heritage. The recent decline in the national morality of America is a matter of record, although many seem to have lost the concept of moral absolutes in this modern, "enlightened" age.

Modern scientific achievement and American ingenuity notwithstanding, the results of such decline remain unchanged, regardless of the opinions of the general public or the media. Neither natural laws nor spiritual ones are likely to change by democratic vote. The fact that people agree on things which are not true only makes matters worse. The moral decline of a society leads inexorably toward a time of judgment.

Hosea's Place in History

Hosea ("salvation") the son of *Beeri* ("my well" or "my pit") was called by God to be a prophet in Israel during the reign of Jeroboam the son of Joash (about 787-747 B.C.), also known as Jeroboam II. At that time, Israel was composed of two kingdoms; the northern one was called Israel, and the southern, Judah.

The kingdom had been divided after the reign of Solomon, about 926 B.C. The northern kingdom was originally established by the revolt of Jeroboam I, also known as Jeroboam the son of Nebat. In order to establish his reign and to ensure that the division of Israel into two kingdoms would be a lasting one, Jeroboam sought a way to make the separation a religious as well as a political one, so that the general populace would not feel any connection to the southern kingdom of Judah. This is what the Bible says of his solution:

> *And Jeroboam said in his heart, "Now the kingdom will return to the house of David. If this people go up to offer sacrifices in the house of the* LORD *at Jerusalem, then the heart of this people will return to their lord, even to Rehoboam king of Judah; and they will kill me and return to Rehoboam king of Judah." So the king consulted, and made two golden calves, and he said to them, "It is too much for you to go up to Jerusalem; behold your gods, O Israel, that brought you up from the land of Egypt." And he set one in Bethel, and the other he put in Dan.*
> *Now this thing became a sin, for the people went to worship before the one as far as Dan. And he made houses on high places, and made priests from among all the people who were not of the sons of Levi. And Jeroboam instituted a feast in the eighth month on the fifteenth day of the month, like the feast which is in Judah, and he went up to the altar; thus he did in Bethel, sacrificing to the calves which he had made.*

Hosea on America

And he stationed in Bethel the priests of the high places which he had made.   1 Kings 12:26-32

This was the legacy inherited by Jeroboam II about a hundred and fifty years later. With this unholy foundation, the society had progressively deteriorated in a moral sense. However, the people felt that everything was going well because the reign of Jeroboam II was quite prosperous.

The name *Jeroboam* means "the people increase," which heightens the impact of the story, since it was the people's increasing prosperity that helped to dull their sensitivity to the nation's moral decline. All of the "economic indices," including the "Samaritan Stock Exchange," gave the impression that all was well. They were having great success against their enemies, with deliverance from the oppressive influence of Syria, and the extension of their borders in several directions.

The kingdom now almost reached as far as it had during the reign of Solomon, but what appeared to be a great restoration was only political and economic. The prevailing morality was indicative of their spiritual bankruptcy, and the prophets of the day foretold the coming disaster. The debauched and idolatrous lifestyle of the people of Israel was so well-known that the Jews of the southern kingdom continued to hold them in contempt hundreds of years later in the time of Christ. Amos, who was a contemporary of Hosea's, described the mood of the day very well:

> *This is what the LORD says:*
> *"For three sins of Israel, even for four, I will not turn back my wrath.*
> *They sell the righteous for silver, and the needy for a pair of sandals.*
> *They trample on the heads of the poor as upon the dust of the ground and deny justice to the oppressed.*
> *Father and son use the same girl and so profane my holy name.*
> *They lie down beside every altar on garments taken in pledge.*
> *In the house of their god they drink wine taken as fines."*
>
> *Hear this, you who trample the needy and do away with the poor of the land, saying,*

The Living Tapestry

"When will the New Moon be over that we may sell grain, and the Sabbath be ended that we may market wheat?" — skimping the measure, boosting the price and cheating with dishonest scales, buying the poor with silver and the needy for a pair of sandals, selling even the sweepings with the wheat. Amos 2:6-8 and 8:4-6, NIV

There was a profane mixture of religion with their *real* gods of profit and pleasure. Is there any need for a detailed comparison with America, with its proliferation of churches? There is lying and debauchery in the highest places in the land, and all of it is excused as though it is unimportant.

The divorce rate today among couples in the church is practically identical to that in the general populace. Homosexuality is allowed in many churches as an "alternative lifestyle." Legalized abortion now kills more Americans than all of the wars in the nation's history, and the most dangerous place in the entire country is not the inner city, but the mother's womb.

All of this says nothing of the prevalence of violence, drunkenness and the love of money. *Newsweek* magazine can have a cover boasting a picture of a feminine-looking bull with an almost demonic appearance and a title that says "Like it or Not, You're Married to the Market" (April 27, 1998), and no one even comments on such a horrible image. No wonder many refer to this as a "post-Christian" America!

There were evidently many similarities between the northern kingdom of Israel in the eighth century B.C. and the U.S.A. of the early twenty-first century A.D.

Hosea's Family

With the first words that Hosea heard from God, he was told to take a wife who was a harlot and have children with her. This unlikely command was given because of the spiritual harlotry of the people of Israel. Hosea therefore married a woman named *Gomer* ("complete"), the daughter of one named *Diblaim* ("double cake").

The first child of this union was a son, and the Lord told Hosea to name him *Jezreel* ("God sows"). Gomer then had two more children (which were probably not Hosea's children). Only regarding the first child does the Bible say *"she bore* him *a son"* (Hosea 1:3). The others are called *"children of harlotry"* in chapter two. The second and third children were then named *Lo-Ruhamah* ("not given compassion") and *Lo-Ammi* ("not my people").

With the naming of these two children, God was saying that He would no longer have compassion on the people of the northern kingdom of Israel, and that they were not His people. However, immediately after that declaration, a passage of great hope was spoken by the Lord:

> *Yet the number of the sons of Israel*
> *Will be like the sand of the sea,*
> *Which cannot be measured or numbered;*
> *And it will come about that, in the place*
> *Where it is said to them,*
> *"You are not My people,"*
> *It will be said to them,*
> *"You are the sons of the living God."*   Hosea 1:10

Such was the pattern throughout the book of Hosea, with statements of the deplorable state of affairs and the resulting inevitable judgments interspersed with hopeful passages promising restoration from God.

The names of the various members of Hosea's family have profound implications when considered in the historical context. In certain passages of scripture, the importance of the meanings of the people's names may be rather hidden, but not so in the book of Hosea. The instructions that were given to the prophet Hosea made it quite clear that the names of his children were to be an integral part of the message God wanted to convey. He was told directly that he was to give them certain names for certain reasons.

Jezreel ("God sows") was to indicate that there would be judgment upon the house of Jehu for the bloodshed that occurred at Jezreel, and also that the northern kingdom of Israel would be defeated in the Valley of Jezreel. The name was also meant to indicate much more, as the end of chapter two suggests:

The Living Tapestry

*"For I will remove the names of the Baals from her mouth,
So that they will be mentioned by their names no more.*

*And I will betroth you to Me forever;
Yes, I will betroth you to Me in righteousness and in justice,
In lovingkindness and in compassion,
And I will betroth you to Me in faithfulness.
Then you will know the* LORD.
"And it will come about in that day that I will respond," declares the LORD.
*"I will respond to the heavens, and they will respond to the earth,
And the earth will respond to the grain, to the new wine, and to the oil,
And they will respond to Jezreel.
And I will sow her for Myself in the land.
I will also have compassion on her who had not obtained compassion,
And I will say to those who were not My people,
'You are My people!'
And they will say, 'Thou art my God!' "*   Hosea 2:17 and 19-23

Hidden within the name of the firstborn son (and probably the only child of Hosea) was a promise of restoration, as God said, *"I will sow her for Myself in the land"* (Hosea 2:23). That rather cryptic message is actually a very momentous statement of purpose on the part of the Almighty. When He sows something, He knows how to make it grow to fruitful maturity.

The obvious message, that God would forsake the people because of their sin and that judgment was impending, was contained in the meanings of the names of a son (Lo-Ammi) and a daughter (Lo-Ruhamah) of harlotry. Even such harsh judgments upon those two children of immorality, however, were quickly followed by promises of restoration, as the passage above demonstrates.

Not only were the children's names significant, but those of the other family members were as well. They were especially so because of the society in which all of this occurred. *Gomer* meant "complete," even though she was utterly unfaithful, just as the people thought they had everything they needed, in spite of their spiritual poverty. Gomer was the daughter of *Diblaim* ("double cake"), a statement suggesting prosperity. They were rich enough to enjoy not just bread, but cake, and even a two-layer cake.

Hosea was the son of *Beeri*, which means either "my well" or "my pit." Each meaning brings forth a different aspect of the process involved in God's salvation and deliverance. It comes as a *"well of water springing up to eternal life,"* as Jesus said in John 4:14.

God's salvation also may come out of difficult circumstances, as illustrated by the story of Joseph, whose troubles began when he was thrown into a pit by his own brothers and then sold into slavery. There is also the example, described in chapter 2, of Moses' hands being held up by Aaron (the high priest) and *Hur* ("hole" or "pit"). The trying circumstance can itself cause the child of God to seek Him and thereby find His presence and His blessing.

The possibility of the salvation coming "out of" an experience that would be a type of "pit" fits very well into the themes preached by Hosea, since he foretold the occurrence of a great deal of judgment and hardship before restoration would take place. However, it is very important to remember throughout the entire book that the name *Hosea* means "salvation" or "deliverance." After all, the book was named after Hosea, and the real central message was ultimately one of God's intervention on behalf of the people for their good.

The Decay of a Godly Society

After describing his family life, with the symbolism of his wife and children, Hosea went on to describe the trends that godlessness had caused in the society of his day. The beginning of it all seemed to be the fact that a spirit of harlotry was rampant in the land, preventing the people from properly seeking God (see Hosea 4:12 and 5:4). Of course, this was the point of the prophet's marriage.

The whole land suffered because of all of the evil (see Hosea 4:1-3), and the people perished because of a lack of knowledge of God (see Hosea 4:6). When problems were recognized, and solutions were sought because of the effects of the pervasive evil, people no longer

The Living Tapestry

knew how to look to God for help, turning instead to man-made solutions (see Hosea 7:10-11). They turned in every direction except the right one, as the narrative said, *"they turned, but not upward"* (Hosea 7:14-16).

These people were not stupid. They knew that their institutions were permeated with problems and that something needed to be done. Undoubtedly, there was educated and thoughtful debate, and perhaps laws and programs were implemented to address some of the most pressing issues. Nevertheless, no one thought to seek help from the one source capable of causing real change. It is also unlikely that these people would have willingly submitted to the type of change that would have been necessary, considering the depth of their depravity.

Eventually, things were in such a sorry state that the enemies of the people, both physical and spiritual, were able to come in for the kill. The prophet foretold what was about to occur:

> *Put the trumpet to your lips!*
> *Like an eagle the enemy comes against the house of the* LORD,
> *Because they have transgressed My covenant,*
> *And rebelled against My law.*
> *They cry out to Me,*
> *"My God, we of Israel know Thee!"*
> *Israel has rejected the good;*
> *The enemy will pursue him.* Hosea 8:1-3

The backslidden Israelites still thought they knew God, in spite of the overwhelming evidence to the contrary! The very next verse says that they had set up their entire structure of government without God, and they were dedicated to idol worship rather than to the worship of the true God. The entire disaster was summed up in just a few words, when it was said: *"They sow the wind, and they reap the whirlwind"* (Hosea 8:7).

What followed next was a very telling commentary. God said of them, *"Though I wrote for him ten thousand precepts of My law, they are regarded as a strange thing"* (Hosea 8:12). The very writings that were foundational in their society had become strange to the people and now appeared, to them, to be foreign, incomprehensible and even irrelevant! What were in reality words of life from the Almighty now fell on deaf ears. Things had gotten so bad that the true prophet was thought to be a fool, and the inspired man demented. There was no other choice but judgment and destruction (see Hosea 9:7).

Certainly God would have preferred honest repentance and the reception of truth over disaster. He would always prefer it that way, but unfortunately what would appear to be a small rebellion tends to build and grow into an ever-expanding mess, rendering that preferable way an impossibility.

BETH-AVEN

Beth-aven was a place that was mentioned in the Old Testament only seven times, and three of those were in the book of Hosea. It was located east of *Bethel* ("house of God"), and literally means "house of nothingness." The fact that this "house of nothingness" was located east of the "house of God" was symbolically very important. Remember (Chapter Eight) that "the way back to God" was always toward the west. Therefore, the fact that Beth-aven was east of the place where God was to be found, and was called a place of "nothingness," indicated that there was to be no small significance to that place — in a figurative sense.

In order to properly understand these things, it is necessary to look at the first mention of Beth-aven by name in the Scriptures (see Joshua 7:2). Beth-aven was near a small Caananite town called *Ai* (possibly meaning "place of ruins"), the place of the first defeat of the Israelites after crossing the Jordan River into the Promised Land. The importance of those events was heightened by the symbolism surrounding Joshua (whose name means "Jehovah is Savior," identical to Jesus) as the leader of the people of God. He was leading them in astonishing and miraculous victory by the power of God ... until they came upon Ai. The "easy" victories they had been experiencing came to a screeching halt when they attacked that town.

Ai itself was nothing much, and looked so harmless that Joshua and

The Living Tapestry

his men decided not to send all their men against the place, but only sent three thousand. Unfortunately, they suffered a humiliating defeat, causing them to fear that the rest of the inhabitants of the land would see their vulnerability and mount an overwhelming attack against them.

As they sought the Lord about what had happened at Ai, God spoke plainly to Joshua, telling him that they had been beaten because someone in the camp had sinned and broken the covenant with God. They had been banned from taking certain types of spoil from their enemies, and one of the men had kept something forbidden and hidden it. As long as that type of evil was concealed in the congregation, they would not be able to stand before their enemies.

The following day, a search was conducted for the guilty party, and a man named *Achan* ("troublesome") was chosen by lot. He then confessed to what he had done, led the searchers back to his tent and revealed the contraband buried inside. Besides silver and gold, he had kept a beautiful robe or "mantle" from Shinar (Babylon).

Certainly, Achan could not have known all of the ways the land of Shinar, the future kingdom of Babylon, typifies the evil and idolatrous world system. He only knew that what he had done was wrong, but considered the beauty of the things he had stolen too enticing to resist.

The real impact of that one act was much more far-reaching than any of those men knew at the time. It takes a perspective that includes an understanding of Babylon, and the warfare of Jesus Christ against it, in order to come close to seeing what was at stake there.

It is also instructive to look at the names contained in Achan's family line. He was of the tribe of *Judah* ("praise"), from which the Lord Jesus Christ would later come. His father's name was *Carmi* ("my vinedresser"), bringing to mind images of God the Father as the Vinedresser caring for His people in the earth (see John 15). The father of Carmi was *Zabdi* ("my gift"), who was the son of one named *Zerah* ("rising, as of the sun"). What an astounding progression to have it end in one named "troublesome." In spite of such wonderful family connections, not to mention the great victories they had experienced, Achan ignored the warnings and succumbed to temptation.

That incident was a beginning, a first, in what would otherwise have been a glorious and victorious campaign of God's people against their enemies. They were led by Joshua, the type of the victorious Christ leading His people in triumph. They had crossed the Jordan, "the river of this life," enjoying the miraculous works of God on their behalf. This man named "troublesome" initiated a rebellion in the ranks, and that rebellion only mushroomed with the passing of time. Any reference to Ai or to Beth-aven takes these concepts into account and helps to bring forth an image of the way such rebellion interrupts the work of God.

In response to what Achan had done, Joshua and the people took the offending man, his family and all of their possessions into a nearby valley and destroyed them all. Then they covered everything with stones as a monument to what had occurred there. The place was named the Valley of *Achor* ("trouble"), and must be near Beth-aven. Afterwards, Joshua and the people of Israel defeated and destroyed Ai, turning it into a pile of rubble (*Ai* means "the ruin").

Beth-aven was mentioned only once more in the book of Joshua (see Joshua 18:12), where it was referred to as a wilderness. There were two other references to the place outside of the book of Hosea, both occurring in Samuel (see 1 Samuel 13:5 and 14:23). Samuel was writing about the great battle of Saul's army against the Philistines. After he defeated the Philistines, Saul disobeyed the Lord and was rejected as king of Israel. That was a pivotal point in the history of Israel, and the difference between Saul's rebellion and David's respect for God-ordained authority was discussed in Chapter Nine.

From that same episode also came the well-known rebuke spoken to Saul by Samuel: *"to obey is better than sacrifice"* (1 Samuel 15:22) and *"rebellion is as the sin of divination"* (1 Samuel 15:23). Therefore it is readily apparent that rebellion is at the origin, the very heart, of the symbolism of Beth-aven. These names are designed to reinforce the idea that rebellion indeed leads to a "house of nothingness."

In the book of Hosea, Beth-aven was mentioned three times. The first two mentions accompanied indirect references to Saul. The first (see Hosea 4:15) spoke of Gilgal (the place where Saul was anointed to be the first king of Israel) right alongside Beth-aven, as if to equate the two. The second (see Hosea 5:8) referred to sounding an alarm because of impending destruction in Gibea, which was Saul's hometown. A warning was given to Benjamin, the tribe from which King Saul was descended.

The third mention of Beth-aven by Hosea (Hosea 10:5) was in *"the calf of Beth-aven."* That was undoubtedly a reference to the idolatrous golden calf Jeroboam I had erected in Bethel. The prophet was thereby comparing the idolatry that had occurred in *Bethel* ("the house of God") with the actual place called "the house of nothingness," actually some distance east of there. He was saying, in effect, that their practices had changed the one into the other, and that they had indeed brought about their own destruction.

Promise of Restoration

Hosea certainly had a hard message, one of rebellion and destruction. His could have easily been a hopeless and depressing one, had it not been for the wonderful grace of the Lord. Such words of comfort and hope can be found scattered throughout the book of Hosea, so that about the time everything sounds like utter disaster, God promises a time of renewal and restoration.

The earliest hint of a word of hope came after the birth of *Lo-Ruhamah* ("no compassion"), but that one was limited to the house of Judah only. After saying that He would no longer have compassion on the house of Israel (the northern kingdom), the Lord promised to show compassion to the house of Judah (the southern kingdom). That was a very limited promise. However, after the birth of *Lo-Ammi* ("not my people"), the prophet foretold something much greater, a statement that can give hope to people everywhere:

> *Yet the number of the sons of Israel*
> *Will be like the sand of the sea,*
> *Which cannot be measured or numbered;*
> *And it will come about that, in the place*
> *Where it is said to them,*
> *"You are not My people,"*
> *It will be said to them,*
> *"You are the sons of the living God."*   Hosea 1:10

Hosea on America

The very next word of hope that Hosea prophesied was given in response to the "spiritual harlotry" of the people of Israel. In order to grasp the true greatness of that promise, it helps to understand the connection between Beth-aven, the Valley of Achor and the critical nature of Achan's sin. Remember that Achan committed the very first act of rebellion against God during the otherwise completely victorious campaign of God's people against their enemies. Not only that, but all of the symbolism that has already been reviewed added significance to that rebellious act.

The miraculous crossing of the Jordan River, the fact that they were led by Joshua, the Old Testament type of the victorious Christ, and the entire picture of being delivered from Egyptian bondage and wilderness wanderings all add to the impact of Achan's act. In spite of the magnitude of the problems and the spiritual meaning of it all, God promised to cause hope to spring forth from that seemingly hopeless situation, and to bring "marital" reconciliation between Himself and His unfaithful people:

> *"Therefore, behold, I will allure her,*
> *Bring her into the wilderness,*
> *And speak kindly to her.*
> *Then I will give her her vineyards from there,*
> *And the valley of Achor as a door of hope.*
> *And she will sing there as in the days of her youth,*
> *As in the day when she came up from the land of Egypt.*
> *And it will come about in that day,"* declares the LORD,
> *"That you will call Me* Ishi *['my husband']*
> *And will no longer call Me* Baali *['my Baal')."*   Hosea 2:14-16

God Himself would redeem the faithless harlot and be a husband to her, and the valley of Achor, the place where the beginning of rebellion and disobedience was punished by complete destruction of the rebel, would become a "door of hope."

Some of the most beautiful words of restoration and hope, especially after a consideration of the depths to which the society as a whole had fallen, can be found at the end of the book of Hosea. Israel can return to

The Living Tapestry

God, and He will restore her. In spite of all her rebellion, God is willing to heal her apostasy and to love her freely:

> *Return, O Israel, to the LORD your God,*
> *For you have stumbled because of your iniquity.*
> *Take words with you and return to the LORD.*
> *Say to Him, "Take away all iniquity,*
> *And receive us graciously,*
> *That we may present the fruit of our lips.*
> *Assyria will not save us,*
> *We will not ride on horses;*
> *Nor will we say again, 'Our god,' to the work of our hands;*
> *For in Thee the orphan finds mercy."*
>
> *I will heal their apostasy,*
> *I will love them freely,*
> *For My anger has turned away from them.*
> *I will be like the dew to Israel;*
> *He will blossom like the lily,*
> *And he will take root like the cedars of Lebanon.*
> *His shoots will sprout,*
> *And his beauty will be like the olive tree,*
> *And his fragrance like the cedars of Lebanon.*   Hosea 14:1-6

If America is suffering from moral decline, and if she has stumbled because of her iniquity, then God is issuing a clear call for repentance and offering a wonderful reconciliation. The sins of America are not too hard for God to deal with. He is able to make her blossom like the lily and bring forth beauty where there were only ashes.

Let everyone who sees this predicament pray that the Lord would *"take away all iniquity, and receive us graciously."* The world system will not save America, nor will her technology, nor her riches be able to do so. The works of her hands make very poor gods that cannot save anyone. Only in the Lord can the orphan (also translated "fatherless") find mercy.

That short phrase seems, at first glance, to speak of only a few, poor orphans who might otherwise end up in an orphanage. However, the destruction of the family has become the bane of America, bringing with it a curse on the land. There has been an astounding proliferation of the fatherless. It has actually reached the point that the majority of the households in many large cities are without a father. It has become commonplace for men to "father" children and then refuse to be real fathers to them.

After studying the Scriptures, portraying God as the heavenly Father, and then beginning to understand the pivotal role of Abraham, as the father of all who believe, the crucial importance of fatherhood begins to come to light. May God indeed intervene and have mercy on the fatherless, and on this country that has been called "one nation, under God."

Chapter Twelve

Reuben

I know I'm not pretty like Rachel, and Jacob never really wanted me in the first place. My father thought he needed to do what he did in order to get me "married off." I'm sure he was doing what he thought was best, but now I have to live as an unwanted piece of personal property. I'm not sure if I feel more like a camel with a limp or an actual disease of the body that Jacob is unable to get rid of.

I knew from the beginning that he didn't really want me as a wife, but I wish he didn't make it so plain all the time! If I were just an animal, at least I wouldn't have these emotions to deal with on top of it all. Surely there must have been a man somewhere who would have treasured me for who I am, rather than this unending predicament!

Maybe my father was right. Maybe such a man would never have come, and I wouldn't have married at all.

But now, I have a chance to become valuable in my husband's sight! I am with child, and if only this baby is a son!

Jacob has been with Rachel almost all the time, but God has given me the ability to bear him a son first. I know it is a boy, I can feel it. He will see that I am valuable in other ways, even if I am not very good to look at. Perhaps he will then notice all the other ways I have striven so hard to be an asset to him — all the work, the cooking, the constant attention to any detail that would be of help to him. When I give him a son, he will notice the other things as well.

I don't really hope for him to love me. No, I don't even think I need that. Rachel is beautiful, and I don't begrudge her his love. It is natural for him to be attracted to her and not to me. I can easily live with that — if only he will somehow come to want me for who I am or at least for what I can do for him. Please, God, let me be seen as desirable to him in some way, for some reason!

This will be a son, his first son. The fruit of his loins, the first fruit of his body. Then he will see. At least, he must begin to see these things and help bring some meaning into my life. After all, I'm not just one of his many animals.

If he will let me, I want to name the boy **Reuben**, *so that even his name will declare to Jacob that I have done something for him that he cannot ignore. "Look, Jacob, a son!"*

— The Children of Israel —

I'm sure you will agree, by now, how utterly amazing it is to see the seemingly endless proliferation of symbolism and eternal meaning portrayed in the names and situations in the Scriptures. Without a doubt, the surface has only been scratched, but regardless of the depth of the dig, the Bible yields wonderful rewards. No wonder the Word of God is referred to as hidden or buried treasure!

There remains one key group of names that must yet be considered, for they form an integral part of the picture the Lord is painting for all to see. The children of Israel, who were often referred to as God's chosen people, were descended from twelve men, the twelve sons of Jacob (whose name was changed to *Israel*), [1] and were also sometimes called the twelve tribes of Israel. In addition to the twelve boys, Jacob also had one daughter, but nothing is known of her offspring.

Jacob's thirteen children were born to four different mothers (see Genesis 29:32-35:18), and the family had grown to about seventy people by the time they had to travel to Egypt because of the severe famine. When the Israelites were delivered from slavery in Egypt about four hundred years later, their numbers had grown to more than a million (Exodus 12:37 speaks of six hundred thousand men, not including children).

The People of God

At times, it may seem a little difficult to understand why the descendants of one family were singled out to be called God's chosen people, especially considering their constant disobedience and idolatry. In order to understand why this group of people is so honored by God, it is necessary to first look at the faith of Abraham and God's promises to him.

The Bible refers to the Lord as *"the God of Abraham, Isaac, and Jacob"* (Exodus 3:16). The centrality of Abraham as the father of all believers

The Living Tapestry

has been described in an earlier chapter. God had clearly told him that he would be the father of many nations, and in many ways Abraham became symbolic of the heavenly Father Himself!

Isaac has been seen to portray Christ in many ways, as the father's only son who was offered up to death on Mount Moriah. Isaac then had twins by Rebekah, who was a type of the Church. The Lord said of the twins, *"Jacob I loved, but Esau I hated"* (Romans 9:13). Esau represented the man of the flesh, for whom spiritual things held no importance, whereas Jacob, although not without defects, sought and valued the things of God.

The struggles of Jacob as he was changed to Israel have been reviewed in Chapter Three, and he was seen to be a type of every believer who has to "wrestle with God" and be changed in the process.

All of those things were mentioned before, but they are necessary prerequisites to understanding why the children of Israel hold such a central position as "the people of God." They represent the offspring of all that God had portrayed in the lives of those three key men — Abraham, Isaac and Jacob (who became Israel).

In a sense, the children of Israel are symbolic of the entire group of God's children, although His children will, in reality, be from many nations and like the sand on the seashore or the stars of the sky for number.

The deliverance from Egypt, the wanderings in the wilderness, the conquest of the Promised Land and the subsequent captivity in Babylon were all very significant spiritually. All of God's people experience those same things — to one degree or another — and the lessons are written as examples for living as a child of God.

Before embarking upon a discussion of the names of the twelve sons of Israel, it will be helpful to have them listed for easy reference. Here are the sons in order of their birth, with the meanings of their names, and the mother who bore them. Jacob's daughter and the two sons of Joseph are then listed separately.

Name	Meaning	Mother
Reuben	"behold, a son"	*Leah* ("weary")
Simeon	"heard," or "hearing"	Leah

The Children of Israel

Levi	"attached"	Leah
Judah	"praise"	Leah
Dan	"judged"	Bilhah (Rachel's maid)
Naphtali	"wrestlings"	Bilhah
Gad	"fortunate"	Zilpah (Leah's maid)
Asher	"happy"	Zilpah
Issachar	"wages"	Leah
Zebulun	"will dwell"	Leah
Joseph	"add to me"	Rachel ("ewe")
Benjamin	"son of my right hand"	Rachel
Dinah	"justice"	Leah
Manasseh	"making to forget"	Asenath (Joseph's wife)
Ephraim	"double fruitfulness"	Asenath

If the names of the twelve sons of Israel are listed in sequence, substituting the meaning of the name in place of the name itself, the developmental story of a child of God emerges. A sequential listing of all twelve sons nicely reveals the plan outline, but certain other features are illustrated by subdividing them according to their respective mothers.

Alongside this entire thought process stands the only sister, whose name means "justice," just as the concept of justice is always present in all of God's dealings with His people. The Bible says: *"Righteousness and justice are the foundation of Thy throne"* (Psalm 89:14), and when speaking of the Messiah, it says that He will bring justice to the nations (Isaiah 42:1-4). Therefore, God's justice is never forgotten, and is ever present as the "only sister" as He deals with His sons.

THE SONS OF LEAH

The names of the sons of Leah contain within their meanings the outline of the process through which God takes each person on his or her journey of faith. Leah was the unloved wife, but the one who nevertheless bore most of Israel's sons, including the one from whom the Messiah would come. Her name fits the magnitude of the task that was hers. Upon her, fell the wearying job of bearing most of the children (three times as many sons as any of the other women, as well as the only daughter), and symbolically the main portion of the work of redemption fell squarely upon her shoulders. No wonder her name was "weary"!

A look at the names of her sons yields the central idea of the work of God in *"bringing many sons to glory"* (Hebrews 2:10). It begins with the declaration "behold, a son" as the introduction into the process. Some of what follows has been discussed in similar terms in Chapter Three, since Simon Peter and Matthew had names whose meanings were identical with those of the next two sons in the sequence.

Simon is equivalent to Simeon, and Matthew was called Levi before he became a disciple of Christ. *Simeon* has to do with "hearing," and faith comes by hearing the Word of God (see Romans 10:17). Just as Simon was changed to Peter when he heard the Gospel of God, Simeon represents the point at which the person hears from God's Word and is changed into one of God's children.

After hearing, there is a change in attachments (*Levi*), as the new believer becomes attached to God Himself rather than the world. After that, he begins to praise God (*Judah*), as he comes to comprehend the greatness of the transformation that has occurred and the greatness of the God who has called him to a new life.

After the first four sons of Leah, there was an interruption while several sons were born to the two maids, Bilhah and Zilpah. In similar fashion, the progress that was flowing along nicely in the life of the new "man of God" suffers interruption at the same point. It is more than simply a "bump in the road," and involves what may at times be some very difficult and troubling life experiences. Even though this part of the journey may be disruptive, it is nevertheless an integral part of the plan.

The next paragraph describes this trouble-filled portion of the process a little more fully, but first a look at Leah's last two sons. After a period of time that varies with the individual, there ultimately occurs a change in "wages" (*Issachar*), from those of death to those of life. The Bible says that *"the wages of sin is death"* (Romans 6:23), but it also says that the wages of the righteous is life (see Proverbs 10:16). This exchange is made possible because of the atoning sacrifice of Christ, who basically exchanged His wages for ours.

The Children of Israel

The final outcome is contained in the name of Leah's final son, *Zebulun* ("will dwell"). The hope of all believers, as stated at the end of Psalm 23, is to dwell in God's household forever, enjoying His goodness and His presence.

THE SONS OF THE MAIDSERVANTS

Placed conspicuously in the midst of Leah's sons are four sons who were born to the two maidservants of Israel's wives. The fact that they were sons of the maidservants is a pivotal point. This portion of the journey involves trouble and discipline, and could easily be viewed as an extraneous and unwanted sideshow. On the contrary, it is actually the servant of the believer, working on his behalf.

Because of the defects that are still resident in the budding child of the Almighty, judgments (*Dan*) of various types will occur and will inevitably result in wrestlings (*Naphtali*). Those wrestlings come in the form of struggles with the internal defects and also with the concept of who God is and what He is like. Has He abandoned the person because of those defects? Will the inborn, innate sins ultimately destroy him? Does the person really want God's way or would he prefer to yield to temptation?

All of these conflicts are interwoven with whatever consequences of sin the individual has to live with, invariably leading to what could be described as "mighty wrestlings." Those are the exact words spoken by Rachel in describing her struggle in the face of her barrenness and her sister's fecundity (see Genesis 30:8). As the child of God goes through these things, he too has feelings of barrenness because he is simply unable to bear the quantity and quality of fruit that he would like.

The next son of the maidservants was *Gad* ("fortunate"). That seems a little incongruous after considering all of the struggles and conflicts, but the Bible says, *"Blessed is the man whom Thou dost chasten, O LORD, and dost teach out of Thy law"* (Psalm 94:12). Since God is at work in the person, those things that seemed so terrible actually turn out to be a blessing in disguise. Then, as if to emphasize the fact that these things really are for the person's own good, the next son's name was

The Living Tapestry

"happy." The realization that the struggles are all for his own good serves as a basis for happiness and undying hope.

THE SONS OF RACHEL

The real numerical explosion of God's family is revealed by the names of the sons of Rachel. That fact is somewhat ironic, since she struggled so long with the inability to conceive, and then had only two sons, compared with Leah's six. The name *Rachel* means "ewe," reminiscent of the concept of the people of the Lord being like sheep, with Christ as the Good Shepherd.

Rachel's first son was Joseph, whose name meant "add to me." As God adds people to His ever-expanding family of millions, the fulfillment of the prophecy given to Abraham takes place in a veritable explosion, akin to the big bang theorized to have been involved in the creation of the physical universe. As Joseph's name ("add to me") suggests, the sheep in God's fold have been increasing for thousands of years, a process that continues to this day.

Not only did Joseph's name suggest such growth in God's family, but the life that he lived was in perfect harmony with this concept of an expansion which would include all nations. He was the prime minister of Egypt, the very nation which symbolizes slavery to sin. That nation which might be viewed symbolically as the worst of them all was the one where Joseph ruled and where the people of Israel flourished. Israel's family grew from seventy people to more than a million while they lived in Egypt, a growth of more than one and one half million percent!

Even the name of Joseph's wife, *Asenath* ("belonging to Neith"), added to the picture of an expansion that would come to encompass all the nations on earth. Neith was an Egyptian goddess equivalent to the Roman Minerva or the Greek Athena. These were goddesses of wisdom, technical skill and invention. The nations of the world, as history has so effectively shown in modern times, highly value the very attributes claimed by those ancient goddesses. In addition, those are the very things that have made possible worldwide exploration, settlement and population growth.

The Children of Israel

Joseph has become the father and Asenath the mother of the most rapidly expanding portion of the family of God, resulting in worldwide spread. This was also foretold by Moses in the blessing that he spoke concerning Joseph. This prophecy, spoken by Moses near the end of his life, suggested a phenomenal increase that would occur "all at once." It talked of *"pushing the peoples"* to the end of the earth. Here is the final portion of Moses' words concerning Joseph:

> *"And with the choice things of the earth and its fulness,*
> *And the favor of Him who dwelt in the bush.*
> *Let it come to the head of Joseph,*
> *And to the crown of the head of the one distinguished among his brothers.*
> *As the first-born of his ox, majesty is his,*
> *And his horns are the horns of the wild ox;*
> *With them he shall push the peoples,*
> *All at once, to the ends of the earth.*
> *And those are the ten thousands of Ephraim,*
> *And those are the thousands of Manasseh."* Deuteronomy 33:16-17

The very meaning of Joseph's name, toward the end of the list that describes the process involved in the formation of God's children, is simply a declaration of the Lord's intention for the Gospel to be spread to all nations. Joseph's two sons were *Manasseh* ("causing to forget") and *Ephraim* ("double fruitfulness"). In their names are contained the ideas of the great fruitfulness that would eventually fill all the earth with the children of God (*Ephraim*), and the fact that such a great result would cause those same people to forget (*Manasseh*) their troubles and oppression along the way.

In Revelation 7, there is a passage telling of the people of God standing before the Christ, shouting victoriously about His salvation. In that passage, the list of the twelve tribes of Israel begins with *Judah* ("praise"), the one from which Christ was descended. The tribe of *Dan* ("judged") is left out, and instead *Manasseh* ("causing to forget") is listed in its place, because the people have passed out of judgment into life (see John 5:24), and the time of hardship is finished. After the list of the various tribes, there is described an innumerable host before the throne of God:

> *After these things I looked, and behold, a great multitude, which no one could count, from every nation and all tribes and peoples and tongues, standing before the throne and before the Lamb, clothed in white robes, and palm branches were in their hands; and they cry out with a loud voice, saying, "Salvation to our God who sits on the throne, and to the Lamb."* Revelation 7:9-10

The Lamb of God, the Savior of the world, then receives worship from the great multitude from every nation that no one can count. The kind of growth in numbers that only God can cause and only He can properly manage, will have occurred. Amazingly, it will have happened one soul at a time, by addition, just as Joseph's name ("add to me") would indicate.

The second son of Rachel, and the last of the sons of Israel, was Benjamin. "The son of my right hand" was the end of the statement concerning God's children, and refers to the supremacy of the Messiah and His involvement in every aspect of the process. Christ is seated at the right hand of the Father in Heaven, but there was a time when He was suffering on this guilty sod.

Rachel, who died giving birth to Benjamin, said that the child should be named *Ben-oni* ("the son of my suffering"). However, Israel named him Benjamin instead (see Genesis 35:18). In similar fashion, the Christ was the Son of suffering in the eyes of the Father, but He became the Son of His right hand.

THE SONS OF ISHMAEL

There was a time in the life of Abraham when he grew discouraged, tired of waiting for the promise of God. At that time, his name was still Abram, and his wife was still called Sarai. The Lord had promised them a son, but Sarai was barren. In addition to that, they were both growing old. Sarai suggested to Abram that he take her servant woman named Hagar and have a child with her. He did so, and Ishmael was born (see Genesis 16:1-11).

The Children of Israel

Because of the conflict that developed between these two women, Hagar fled from Sarai. During her wandering in the desert, an angel of the Lord appeared to her:

> *Now the angel of the* Lord *found her by a spring of water in the wilderness, by the spring on the way to Shur. And he said, "Hagar, Sarai's maid, where have you come from and where are you going?"*
> *And she said, "I am fleeing from the presence of my mistress Sarai."*
> *Then the angel of the* Lord *said to her, "Return to your mistress, and submit yourself to her authority." Moreover, the angel of the* Lord *said to her, "I will greatly multiply your descendants so that they shall be too many to count." The angel of the* Lord *said to her further,*
> *"Behold, you are with child,*
> *And you shall bear a son;*
> *And you shall call his name Ishmael,*
> *Because the* Lord *has given heed to your affliction.*
> *And he will be a wild donkey of a man,*
> *His hand will be against everyone,*
> *And everyone's hand will be against him;*
> *And he will live to the east of all his brothers."*   Genesis 16:7-12

This passage describes the origin of the sons of Ishmael.

As the years passed, God visited Abraham again. By that time, Ishmael was already thirteen years old. During that visitation, several key things were established. God changed the names of Abram and Sarai to *Abraham* and *Sarah*. The rite of circumcision was instituted, so that Abraham was circumcised when he was ninety-nine years old. A son was promised to Abraham and Sarah, and Abraham was told that God would make His covenant with the descendants of Isaac rather than with those of Ishmael (see Genesis 17:1-21). Thus a difference was set forth in the way God would deal with the sons of Ishmael and the sons of Israel (Isaac was Israel's father).

There are several points of comparison and contrast that are worthy of consideration in this regard. By way of comparison, both Isaac and Ishmael were sons of Abraham. They would both be the father of twelve sons (Isaac would be the grandfather), their descendants eventually numbering in the millions. A promise was given to each of

The Living Tapestry

them by God Himself, so that the proliferation of their descendants was actually due to the blessing of God. There were also some similarities in meanings among the two sets of twelve sons' names. Here is the biblical account of the sons of Ishmael, followed by a list of their meanings:

> *Now these are the records of the generations of Ishmael, Abraham's son, whom Hagar the Egyptian, Sarah's maid, bore to Abraham; and these are the names of the sons of Ishmael, by their names, in the order of their birth: Nebaioth, the first-born of Ishmael, and Kedar and Adbeel and Mibsam and Mishma and Dumah and Massa, Hadad and Tema, Jetur, Naphish and Kedemah. These are the sons of Ishmael and these are their names, by their villages, and by their camps; twelve princes according to their tribes.*   Genesis 25:12-16

Name	Meaning	Name	Meaning
Nebaioth	"heights"	Massa	"burden"
Kedar	"dark-skinned"	Hadad	"sharp" or "keen"
Adbeel	"disciplined of God"	Tema	"desert"
Mibsam	"sweet odor" or "spice"	Jeturen	"closure"
Mishma	"hearing"	Naphish	"living being"
Dumah	"silence"	Kedemah	"east" or "eastward"

These are the sons of Ishmael. A comparison of these meanings with those of the sons of Israel reveals a few points of similarity. One pair that is obvious is *Mishma* ("hearing") and *Simeon* ("heard" or "hearing"). A couple of others could be viewed as related, even though they are not identical. *Adbeel* ("disciplined of God") has some similarity to *Dan* ("judged"). *Zebulun* ("will dwell") might show some relationship to *Tema* ("a desert") or *Kedemah* ("eastward"), since those were descriptive of their dwelling places.

What are more striking, and much more revealing, are the contrasts between the two groups. The differences speak volumes, since God made His covenant with the sons of Israel (through Isaac) and not with the sons of Ishmael. It is imperative to look first at the circumstances of the births of Ishmael versus Isaac, and the symbolic significance of

The Children of Israel

their mothers. The New Testament refers to this when discussing the Church:

> *For it is written that Abraham had two sons, one by the bondwoman and one by the free woman. But the son by the bondwoman was born according to the flesh, and the son by the free woman through the promise. This is allegorically speaking: for these women are two covenants, one proceeding from Mount Sinai bearing children who are to be slaves; she is Hagar. Now this Hagar is Mount Sinai in Arabia, and corresponds to the present Jerusalem, for she is in slavery with her children. But the Jerusalem above is free; she is our mother. For it is written,*
> *"Rejoice, barren woman who does not bear;*
> *Break forth and shout, you who are not in labor;*
> *For more are the children of the desolate than of the one who has a husband."*
> *And you brethren, like Isaac, are children of promise. But as at that time he who was born according to the flesh persecuted him who was born according to the Spirit, so it is now also. But what does the Scripture say? "Cast out the bondwoman and her son, for the son of the bondwoman shall not be an heir with the son of the free woman." So then, brethren, we are not children of a bondwoman, but of the free woman.* Galatians 4:22-31

Not only was Hagar a bondwoman, she was an *Egyptian* bondwoman. That is a key point because of Egypt's symbolism as the land of slavery to sin. In addition to that, in having a child by her, Abraham did not act out of faith in God but rather out of frustration (not to mention his wife's frustration). What he did was not necessarily immoral in that culture, but the motivation was not one of trust in God's promise.

Another important point is that Ishmael was born prior to Abraham's circumcision, whereas Isaac was conceived immediately afterwards. All of these symbols lend to the overall picture of two contrasting groups — as far as their relationship with God is concerned.

When studying the sons of Israel, the progression in their names' meanings was found to be very important. The same reasoning applies

The Living Tapestry

to those of Ishmael's sons. This group begins with "heights" (*Nebaioth*) and ends with "eastward" (*Kedemah*), quite different from the Israelites. "Heights" is suggestive of a place of exaltation or pride, and that is an unhealthy place to begin in dealing with the Almighty. The twelve names end with "eastward," symbolic of the direction which is away from God. [2]

Contained within the list are some names that might otherwise be good, such as *Mishma* ("hearing"), were it not for the origin and the progression involved. Even *Mishma* ("hearing") was followed immediately by *Dumah* ("silence"), suggesting the lack of an ongoing relationship with God. *Adbeel* ("disciplined of God") and *Massa* ("burden") convey the idea of a legalistic religious type of interaction with God, rather than a vibrant, loving one.

There is one more important thing to recognize when considering these two groups of twelve sons, and that involves another difference in the way they were descended from Abraham. In addition to the things noted above about their mothers and the motivation behind their conceptions, there is a difference regarding the "directness" of their descent from Abraham.

The twelve sons of Ishmael were his direct progeny and immediately became "princes" of their respective tribes. Through Isaac, however, God first made a division between the two twins, Jacob and Esau. The contrast between these two brothers has been addressed previously, [3] with Esau being the man of the flesh for whom spiritual things were not important. Jacob (who became Israel) was the one who, although flawed and needing to be changed, valued the things of the spirit.

Only after dividing the offspring between the flesh and the spirit did God proceed to bring forth the twelve sons of Israel and their offspring. These then became the "people of God," bringing with them all of the symbolism relevant to the process. The foundations, the motives, the process and the character development all continue to apply to the work of God in the earth throughout the ages.

God's Workmanship

The entire progression of the sons of Israel, from "behold, a son" to

The Children of Israel

"the son of my right hand," depicts God's work in the formation of His children in the earth. With this in mind, it is much easier to understand how God could refer to the children of Israel as His chosen people. Through this process, God is making Abraham into the father of many nations. His children will be like the sands of the seashore or the stars of the sky for number, and Christ is the Son of His right hand through the entire process. We must say, with Paul of old:

> *Oh, the depth of the riches both of the wisdom and knowledge of God! How unsearchable are His judgments and unfathomable His ways!*
> Romans 11:33

THE TAPESTRY

If a person were to sit and imagine, without preconceived theological notions, what sort of thing God would create if He were to form a work of art, how might such thoughts develop? What would be the size and scope of such a thing? What manner of form and beauty would reside in His sculpture or painting? What sort of tapestry would He make? What might some of its features be?

Perhaps some active imagination would begin to select a few likely features that would be apparent in a major work of art if it were created by God Himself. If that masterpiece were a tapestry, it would undoubtedly be extremely large and of great scope. The threads might be very long and span ages of time. The possible colors would be endless, and the images could be ... why, they could even be alive!

If the elements had life in themselves, then the entire scene could unfold while the varicolored threads wove themselves together! It might even appear as though the tapestry were weaving itself, rather than being woven.

As those living parts interacted among themselves, thoughts and actions that appeared to be disconnected could eventually be found to be different portions of the same thread. The whole thing could become so wondrous and complex that there would be no way to view it all at once.

The various images, as they developed, might have many levels of meaning, some of them incomprehensible without the help of the Art-

The Living Tapestry

ist. There would be no end of possibilities if the imagination were allowed to envision the specific images themselves.

This scenario is in fact what God is doing. The size and complexity of His project is staggering. The Bible gives an outline and provides a framework for understanding some things about God's creation, but His work is far too vast to be described in detail in any one volume. His tapestry involves millions upon millions of individual pictures, each strategically placed and very much alive. All of the threads are interconnected. Some of the threads have been mentioned in this book, and the meanings of the names involved have helped to identify them and tie them together.

In spite of the magnitude of this great work, there are a few common features uniting the entire project, displaying it as the undeniable work of one Artist. All of the symbolism invariably leads in the same direction — toward the Son of God, Jesus Christ. He is the pattern being used in fashioning all of God's children. Therefore His image constantly appears in one form or another.

The children of Israel are a type of the people of God, and through them came the Messiah and the Word of God. Though there may be many millions of individuals from many different nations in God's great family, they all take on the essential features of Christ as they are changed into His image. This is the legacy of the children of God.

The Lord has indeed created a work of art, the likes of which have never been seen before, and the implications of which are eternal. No wonder the psalmist declared:

> *Blessed be the LORD God, the God of Israel,*
> *Who alone works wonders.*
> *And blessed be His glorious name forever;*
> *And may the whole earth be filled with His glory.*
> *Amen, and Amen.*   Psalm 72:18-19

Endnotes:

1. For a brief history of Israel, please refer to Appendix B.
2. Please refer to Chapter 8 for a more complete discussion of this concept.
3. Please refer to Chapter 3 and the discussion of Abraham, Sarah and Jacob.

Appendices

A. The Order of the Contents

Yes, even the order of the chapters has symbolic significance. For instance, Chapter Five concerns the names in Genesis 5. Chapter Six is about Babylon, the evil empire, and this number is rather symbolic of evil. The number six is one short of seven, which is the number for perfection, and the number of the Antichrist in the book of Revelation is 666.

Chapter Seven is about Ruth and the kinsman redeemer and the perfection made available to mankind because of the friendship of Christ. Chapters Eight through Eleven discuss the water of life and several aspects of rebellion against God, but their chapter numbers have no particular significance. The significance of Chapter Twelve, the final chapter, is obvious, since it deals with the twelve sons of Israel.

The real reason for writing this explanation, however, does not lie in the order of these aforementioned chapters, but rather in the first two. The most important chapter in the book is the one about the names of God Himself. It was made Chapter Two, not because God is second, but because the things that were stated in Chapter One needed to be stated prior to dealing with the names of God.

Just as we view the universe from a perspective that is based on earth, each of us is trapped inside a particular physical body, from which we view the "universe" around us. First realizing our own smallness and grappling with the limited nature of our perspective serves as a necessary step in the process of allowing God to reveal Himself to us. It is helpful to remember who we are and what we are like as we then begin to find out about who God is and what *He* is like. Chapter One had to be Chapter One as a reminder of our smallness, so we could begin to see something of His greatness.

Immediately following the chapter about God is the one about name changes. That follows logically, since God, in His greatness and mercy,

The Living Tapestry

affects changes in the lives of those with whom He interacts. No one can be touched by God, even in a "small" way, without being changed.

Chapter Four is called "The Irony of Malchus," and follows close behind the one dealing with some of the changes God makes in our lives. That is because, as soon as God begins to change us, we then interact with others and have certain effects on them. That is what the chapter is about, and is especially ironic since all of God's changes in us are for the good, in contrast with some of the ways we then impact others.

B. A Brief Summary of the History of the Children of Israel

The entire story began about 2000 B.C. with a man named Abraham. He was descended from the son of Noah named Shem, as discussed in Chapter Six. Abraham received a promise from God to make of him a huge family, more numerous than the stars of the sky or the sand on the seashore.

Abraham's son by his wife Sarah was Isaac, who had the twins Jacob and Esau. God chose Jacob as the one through whom to fulfill the promise to Abraham and changed his name to Israel (discussed in Chapter Three). Israel had two wives and through them and his wives' maids had twelve sons and one daughter. The offspring of the twelve sons of Israel became the "children of Israel," and, eventually, the nation of Israel.

Joseph was Israel's eleventh son and his favorite, because the child was the first son of his favorite wife, Rachel. The older brothers hated Joseph and sold him into slavery in Egypt. Years later, during a severe famine, the remaining sons of Israel had to go to Egypt to get food in order to survive. By that time, Joseph had risen from slavery to being prime minister of the entire nation.

Because of Joseph's favored position, the entire family of Israel moved to Egypt and lived there. As time passed and new pharaohs came along, the Israelites no longer enjoyed the favor of the Egyptians, and were, instead, made to be slaves and put to forced labor.

When things had become intolerable for the Israelites, God raised up Moses to deliver His children from their bondage. Through various miracles and judgments, the last being the death of the firstborn in ev-

Appendices

ery household of the Egyptians, the pharaoh was finally convinced to let the Israelites go.

No sooner had Pharaoh released the Israelites, however, than he and his entire army pursued them and would have destroyed them at the Red Sea. It was then that God miraculously parted the waters so that the children of Israel could cross over on dry ground. When the Egyptians tried to follow, the waters closed in over them and drowned them all.

The children of Israel then headed for the land of Canaan, which they had left over four hundred years previously, upon moving to Egypt. God told them to go and take the land, but because of their fear and unbelief, they were made to wander around in the desert for forty years until Moses' generation passed away.

After those forty years had passed, the conquest of the Promised Land began under the leadership of Joshua, who had been Moses' servant. Joshua was an Old Testament type of Christ, and his name had a meaning identical to that of Jesus in the New Testament. Joshua led the children of Israel into the current land of Israel by crossing the Jordan River from east to west. At the time, the river was at flood stage, but was miraculously parted in a manner reminiscent of the parting of the Red Sea. Joshua and the people then conquered a large part of the country, but never succeeded in completely destroying the people who were dwelling there, as God had commanded them to do.

There then followed several hundred years of rule by various judges, the last of whom was Samuel the prophet. The people then cried out for a king, since all the nations around them had one. This displeased God, but he gave them Saul, the most handsome and tallest man among them, to be their first king. This period of rule by kings began about 1095 B.C.

Saul was not obedient to God and was eventually replaced by David, who consolidated his kingdom by warfare. His son, Solomon, ruled in peace over the greatest kingdom in the history of Israel. After Solomon, the kingdom was divided into two parts. There was a northern kingdom, consisting of ten tribes, and a southern one of two tribes. Over the next several hundred years, there were a series of kings, some of whom were good, but most of whom were very evil. The northern kingdom, especially, suffered from a consistent succession of evil rulers.

The Living Tapestry

Eventually, the children of Israel were in such a sorry state that God pronounced judgment upon them. Because of their persistent idolatry, they were defeated and carried off into captivity to be servants in a land of idolatry. This happened first to the northern kingdom at the hands of the Assyrians, but not long afterward, the southern kingdom was conquered by the Babylonians. The city of Jerusalem fell in 586 B.C.

After being in captivity in Babylon for about seventy years, there began a restoration of the people of Israel to their homeland. By that time, the Babylonian empire had been defeated by the Persians, and Artaxerxes the king allowed some of the Jews to return to their homeland and begin rebuilding the Temple.

The children of Israel continued to live in the land of modern-day Israel for the next several hundred years, but were ruled by various governors. No longer did they have a king, nor did they really have a kingdom. The nation of Israel was actually at a crossroad between Africa, Asia and Europe, and found itself under the rule of first one and then another foreign government.

By the time of Christ's birth, Israel was under the authority of Rome, with Herod the Great installed as a puppet king. Throughout the New Testament period, this remained unchanged, with Rome in control and various members of the Herodian family line acting as local rulers. Finally, the nation of Israel was completely destroyed when the Jews revolted against Rome, and the remnants of them were scattered around the ancient world, except for a few remaining villages.

Jerusalem fell and the Temple was completely destroyed in A.D. 70. A small handful of Jewish people resisted for about three more years at Masada, but the fortress was finally conquered by the Roman army, forcing the Jews inside to commit mass suicide in order to avoid capture.

C. THE MEANINGS OF THE NAMES *ABEL* AND *CAIN*, THE FIRST TWO SONS OF ADAM AND EVE

There is no indication of why Abel's name was chosen; Cain's name was derived from the Hebrew word for "getting," since Eve had gotten a child from the Lord (see Genesis 4:1). The names of these two sons became prophetic. Abel's life was like a breath. He was a shepherd, so grassy meadows would be to his liking. The word for spear in Hebrew is identical with Cain, who became the murderer.

Appendices

Abel — "breath" (Hebrew *Hebel*) "grassy field or meadow" (Hebrew *Àbel*).

Cain — "a spear"; "possession" (Hebrew *quanah*) "to get, to acquire."

D. Several Names Which Mean "the Gift of God" or "the Gift of Jehovah"

Nathanael — God, in this case, is *el* from *Elohim*. *Nathan* means "a giver" or "gift."

John — This is short for Jonathan, with Nathan as part of the name, therefore "Jehovah's gift."

Matthew — derived from *Mattathias*, the Greek form of *Mattathiah*. Another possible rendering of *Mattathiah* is *Mattaniah*, and here the similarity between *Mattan* and *Nathan* can be seen more easily. The ending, -ah, is derived from *yah* or *jah*, just as in Hallelujah. This is taken from *YHWH*.

E. The Names in the Book of Ruth

Ruth	"friendship"
Naomi	"my delight"
Elimelech	"my God is king"
Mahlon	"sickly"
Chilion	"pining"
Orpah	"stubbornness"
Boaz	"quickness" or "fleetness"
Obed	"servant or worshiper," grandfather of King David
Ephrathite	"same as Ephraimite" or "descendant of Ephraim"
Ephratha	"fruitful"
Ephraim	"double fruitfulness"
Bethlehem	"house of bread"

F. The Names in Chapter 9: "Miriam and the Family Rebellion"

Miriam	"rebellion" or "obstinacy"
Mary	same as Miriam
Nadab	"liberal" or "spontaneous"

The Living Tapestry

Abihu	"he is my father"
Mishael	"who is what God is?"
Elzaphan	"whom God protects"
Uzziel	"my strength is God"
Eleazar	"help of God"
Ithamar	"land of palms"
Elisheba	"God is an oath"
Amminadab	"my kinsman is noble"
Nahshon	"serpent"
Korah	"baldness"
Dathan	"belonging to a fountain"
Abiram	" my father is exalted"
Elkanah	"God has taken possession"
Hannah	"grace or gracious"
Peninnah	"coral" or "pearl"
Samuel	"name of God"
David	"well-beloved"
Saul	"asked for" or "desired one"
Absalom	"the father's peace"
Solomon	"peaceful one"
Jedidiah	"beloved of Yah," another name for Solomon